OLD-TIME
CROCHET
Made Easy™

Edited by Laura Scott

HOUSE of
WHITE
BIRCHES
PUBLISHERS
SINCE 1947

Old-Time Crochet Made Easy

Editor: Laura Scott
Technical Editor: Agnes Russell
Design Manager: Vicki Blizzard
Copy Editor: Mary Nowak
Publications Coordinator: Tanya Turner
Technical Artists: Chris Moorman, Allison Rothe, Jessica Rothe

Photography: Tammy Christian, Jeff Chilcote, Justin Wiard
Photography Stylist: Arlou Wittwer
Photography Assistant: Linda Quinlan

Production Coordinator: Brenda Gallmeyer
Book Design: Vicki's design studio
Cover Design: Jessi Butler
Graphic Artist: Vicki's design studio
Production Assistants: Janet Bowers, Marj Morgan
Traffic Coordinator: Sandra Beres

Publishers: Carl H. Muselman, Arthur K. Muselman
Chief Executive Officer: John Robinson
Marketing Director: Scott Moss
Book Marketing Manager: Craig Scott
Product Development Director: Vivian Rothe
Publishing Services Manager: Brenda R. Wendling

Printed in the United States of America
First Printing: 2000
Library of Congress Number: 00-132490
ISBN: 1-882138-65-1

Every effort has been made to ensure the accuracy and completeness of the instructions in this book. However, we cannot be responsible for human error or for the results when using materials other than those specified in the instructions, or for variations in individual work.

An Old-Time Welcome

In the not-too-distant past, much of a woman's worth was evaluated by the quality of her needlework. Though many of us (myself included) are relieved that women today have many opportunities to explore in addition to needlework, our admiration for the ladies who created such lovely needlework is not diminished.

At a recent family gathering, my mother brought out several boxes of her mother's and grandmother's linen to distribute to my sisters and myself. We spent several happy hours sorting through the pieces and admiring the handiwork. Most of the pieces were accented with crocheted edgings and lace of some sort. Although much of the history of these pieces has been lost, I still consider each one to be a treasure which I will someday pass on to my children.

The inspiration for this book comes from the fervent desire many of us have to not lose the ability to recreate some of those wonderful patterns from yesteryear. My staff and I dug through boxes of old needlework magazines searching for the prettiest and most inviting old-time patterns from before 1950. Many of these patterns date back to the early 1900s. What you hold in your hands is the finished product of many months of searching for patterns, rewriting patterns in today's terminology, and re-creating each pattern with materials readily available today.

My hope is that with this book, you'll be able to create your own crocheted keepsakes from the most beautiful of yesterday's patterns.

With warm regards,

Laura Scott

Laura Scott, Editor
Old-Time Crochet Made Easy

Contents

Chapter One

Classic Doilies

Silver Bells Doily. 8
1914 Oval Doily 10
Hairpin Doily. 13
Rickrack Doily. 14
Nanny's Zinnias 18
Star With Cluny Border 20
Pineapple Doily 25
Kaleidoscope 28
Plentiful Petals 30
Pansy Doily 32

Chapter Two

Keepsake Filet

Briar Roses 38
Pretty Flowers 40
ABC Floral Sampler 42
Square-a-Day Tablecloth. 46
Crochet Tidy. 48
Timeless Treasure Frame 53
Family Heritage 54
Roses in Bloom 56
"Sunday Best" Guest Towel & Washcloth. 58

Chapter Three

Grandmother's Kitchen

Fans Across the Border Hostess Set. 64
Granny's Bloomers Pot Holder 68
Ear of Corn Pot-Handle Cover 69
Open Mesh Shopping Bag 71
French Kitchen Dishcloth 72
Ruffled Pot Holder or Hot Mat. 74
Seashell Place Mat Set. 76
Floral Kitchen Set. 78

Chapter Four

Elegant Edgings

Fanciful Flowers 84
Delicate Edgings 86
Pretty Pastel Edgings 88
Dainty Scallops 91
Irish Lace Edging 92
Filet Edgings 94
Hairpin Lace Edged Hankies 96
Linens & Lace Edgings 98

Chapter Five

Vintage Toys & Dolls

Victorian Children Vintage Dolls 104
Lovable Puppy 108
Playful Lamb 110
Old-Style Teddy Bear 113
Humpty Dumpty 116
Dapper Frog 118

Chapter Six

Timeless Wearables

Twinkletoes Dress 124
Butterfly Mesh Blouse & Scarf 126
Wraparound Turban 128
Sparkling Scarf 130
Tam-o'-Shanter 133
Shoulderette 135
Cascade Collar 137
Filet Collar .139
Embroidered Booties 141
Envelope Purses 142
Raised Shell Bag 144
Women of France Shawl 145
Stylish Stole 148

Chapter Seven

Antique Gifts & Novelties

Glove Purse 152
Kewpie Hair Pin Holder 154
Little Lampshade 156
Pin Set Barrette 158
Irish Crochet Picture Frame 160
Wishbone Thimble Holder 162
Table Decorations 164
Powder Jar 166

Chapter Eight

Collectible Afghans

Victoriana Rose Wreath 172
Mosaic Tiles Afghan 174
Baby Afghan in Star & Afghan Stitch 176
Columbia Patchwork Afghan 178
Indian Stripe Afghan 180
Pompom Afghan 182
Hop O' My Thumb 184
Fan Afghan 186
Field of Flowers 188

Stitch Guide 191

Poems, Stories & Facts

The Song of the Hope Chest 17
Mayrain 23
Left-Handed Filet Crochet 27
Hairpin Crochet 35
A Trolley Conductor Who
Makes Filet Lace 51
Family Heirlooms Last for Decades 61
Mrs. Someone Else 67
A Look at Crochet Hooks 81
And She Did It all Herself 90
Irish Crochet 93

General Instructions 190

Chapter One

Classic Doilies

Many crocheters from around the early 1900s used pretty tidbits to accent their doilies. Rickrack, bells and other unique odds and ends made their doilies extra appealing and eye-catching. Create those masterpieces from days gone by with this collection of ten beautiful doilies!

Silver Bells Doily

This doily is worked from a pattern in a book by Flora Klickman, published in England in 1912. Use metallic yarn, add a few bells and you have a perfect Christmas centerpiece that can easily be made by a novice crocheter. With a vase of Christmas greenery and ornaments set on its center, it will make your holiday table look stunning.

Design revised by Maggie Petsch Chasalow

SKILL LEVEL: BEGINNER

SIZE
17½ inches in diameter

MATERIALS
➤ J&P Coats metallic Knit-Cro-Sheen crochet cotton size 10 (100 yds per ball): 2 balls white/silver #1S
➤ Size 7 steel crochet hook or size needed to obtain gauge
➤ 21 (9mm) silver jingle bells
➤ Sewing needle and thread

GAUGE
Rnds 1–4 = 3¼ inches in diameter
Check gauge to save time.

PATTERN NOTES
Weave in loose ends as work progresses.

Join rnds with a sl st unless otherwise stated.

DOILY CENTER
RND 1 (RS): Ch 24, sl st to join to form a ring, ch 3 (counts as first dc throughout), 41 dc in ring, join in 3rd ch of beg ch-3. (42 dc)

RND 2: Ch 3, dc in next st, ch 3, sk next st, [dc in each of next 2 sts, ch 3, sk next st] rep around, join in 3rd ch of beg ch-3. (14 ch-3 sps)

RND 3: Ch 3, dc in next dc, ch 4, [dc in each of next 2 dc, ch 4] rep around, join in 3rd ch of beg ch-3. (14 ch-4 sps)

RND 4: Ch 3, dc in next dc, ch 5, [dc in each of next 2 dc, ch 5] rep around, join in 3rd ch of beg ch-3. (14 ch-5 sps)

RND 5: Ch 3, dc in next dc, ch 7, [dc in each of next 2 dc, ch 7] rep around, join in 3rd ch of beg ch-3. (14 ch-7 sps)

RND 6: Ch 3, dc in next dc, ch 9, [dc in each of next 2 dc, ch 9] rep around, join in 3rd ch of beg ch-3. (14 ch-9 sps)

RND 7: Ch 1, sc in same st as joining, ch 9, sc in next dc, 9 sc in next sp, [sc in next dc, ch 9, dc in next dc, 9 sc in next sp] rep around, join in beg sc. (14 ch-9 lps)

INNER BELL BAND
First Bell
ROW 1: Sl st in first ch-9 lp, ch 3, 13 dc in same sp, turn. (14 dc)

ROW 2: Ch 3, dc in next dc, [ch 3, sk next dc, dc in each of next 2 dc] rep across, turn. (4 ch-3 sps)

ROW 3: Ch 3, dc in next dc, [ch 4, dc in each of next 2 dc] rep across, turn. (4 ch-4 sps)

ROWS 4–8: Rep Row 3, working 1 more ch between each pair of dc on each row; at end of Row 8, ch 5, fasten off. (4 ch-9 sps at end of Row 8)

Second Bell
ROW 1: With RS facing, sk next ch-9 lp on Rnd 7 of doily center, attach thread with sl st in next ch-9 lp, ch 3, 13 dc in same sp, turn. (14 dc)

ROWS 2–8: Rep Rows 2–8 of first bell; at end of Row 8, ch 5, join in top of first st of last row of previous bell, fasten off. (4 ch-9 sps at end of Row 8)

Next Four Bells
ROWS 1–8: Rep Rows 1–8 of 2nd bell.

Last Bell
ROWS 1–7: Rep Rows 1–7 of 2nd bell.

ROW 8: Ch 3, sl st in 5th ch of last ch-5 on last row of first bell, continue across as for Row 8 of 2nd bell, do not fasten off, turn.

RND 9: Sl st in ch-5 sp, ch 1, beg in same sp, *[3 sc, ch 9, 3 sc] in ch-5 sp, sc in each of next 2 dc, 9 sc in next ch-9 sp, [sc in next dc, ch 9, sc in next dc, 9 sc in next sp] 3 times, sc in each of next 2 dc, rep from * around, join in beg sc, fasten off.

OUTER BELL BAND
First Bell
ROW 1: With RS facing, sk first ch-9 lp after joining, attach thread with sl st in next ch-9 lp, ch 3, 13 dc in same sp, turn. (14 dc)

ROWS 2–8: Rep Rows 2–8 of 2nd bell for inner bell band; at end of Row 8, do not ch 5, fasten off. (4 ch-9 sps at end of Row 8)

Second Bell
ROW 1: With RS facing, sk next ch-9 lp on last rnd of inner band, attach thread with sl st in next ch-9 lp, ch 3, 13 dc in same sp, turn. (14 dc)

Continued on page 16

1914 Oval Doily

This charming little doily with the unusual shape first appeared in August 1914. Work it all in one color as shown in the original picture, or pick two colors that will harmonize with your color scheme.

Design revised by Maggie Petsch Chasalow

SKILL LEVEL: INTERMEDIATE

SIZE: 13 x 19 inches

MATERIALS
➤ Crochet cotton size 10 (300 yards per ball): 1 ball each (MC) and shaded purples (CC)
➤ Size 7 steel hook or size needed to obtain guage

GAUGE: Rnd 1 pg center motif = 4½ inches in diameter

Check guage to save time

PATTERN NOTES
Weave in loose ends as work progresses.

PATTERN STITCHES
LARGE SHELL (LG SHELL): [Dc, {ch 2, dc} 5 times] in indicated sp.

BEG LG SHELL: Ch 5, [dc, {ch 2, dc} 4 times] in same sp as ch-5.

V-ST: [Dc, ch 2, dc] in indicated sp

SMALL SHELL (SM SHELL): [Dc, {ch 2, dc} 3 times] in indicated sp.

BORDER SHELL 1 (BDR SHELL 1): [4 dc, ch 3, 4 dc] in indicated sp.

SPLIT SHELL (SPL SHELL): 4 dc in next sp, ch 3, 4 dc in next sp.

BORDER SHELL 2 (BDR SHELL 2): [{Dc, ch 2} twice, dc, ch 3, {dc, ch 2} twice, dc] in indicated sp.

BEG BDR SHELL 2: [Ch 5, dc, ch 2, dc, ch 3, {dc, ch 2} twice, dc] in indicated sp.

BDR SHELL 3: [5 dc, ch 3, 5 dc] in indicated sp.

BEG BDR SHELL 3: [Ch 3, 4 dc, ch 3, 5 dc] in indicated sp.

CENTER MOTIF
RND 1: With CC, ch 9, join to form a ring, ch 18 (foundation ch), ch 3 (counts as first dc), dc in 4th ch from hook, dc in each of next 3 chs, 2 dc in next ch, dc in each of next 4 chs, 2 dc in next ch, dc in each of next 8 chs, sc in ring (first spoke made), *turn, ch 18, dc in 12th dc from base of previous spoke, [ch 2, sk 2 dc, dc in next dc] 3 times, turn; ch 5, dc in next dc, [ch 2, dc in next dc] twice, dc in each of next 4 chs, 2 dc in next ch] twice, dc in each of next 8 chs, sc in ring, rep from * 10 times (12 spokes made), ch 1, turn, sl st in each of first 12 dc of last spoke, ch 3, sl st in rem lp of foundation ch at base of first dc on first spoke, [ch 2, sk next 2 dc on 12th spoke, dc in next dc] 3 times, turn (RS facing), ch 5, dc in next dc, ch 2, dc in next dc, ch 2, sl st in top of first dc on first spoke, fasten off.

RND 2: With RS facing, attach MC with a sl st over ch-5 sp at tip of any spoke, beg lg shell in same sp, ch 5, [lg shell in next sp, ch 5] rep around, join in 3rd ch of beg ch-5. (12 shells)

RND 3: Sl st in first ch-2 sp of lg shell, ch 5, *dc in next ch-2 sp, ch 2, V-st in next ch-2 sp, [ch 2, dc in next ch-2 sp] twice, ch 3, dc in next ch-5 sp, ch 3 **, dc in first ch-2 sp of next lp shell, ch 2, rep from * around, ending last rep at **, join in 3rd ch of beg ch-5 sp.

RND 4: Sl st in next ch-2 sp, ch 1, sc in same sp, ch 3, sc in next sp, *ch 3, [sc, ch 3, sc] in V-st sp **, [ch 3, sc in next sp] 6 times, rep from * around, ending last rep at **, [ch 3, sc in next sp] 4 times, ch 3, join in beg sc, fasten off. (96 ch-3 sps)

FIRST END MOTIF
RND 1: With CC, ch 9, join to form a ring, ch 1, 20 sc in ring, join in beg sc. (20 sc)

RND 2: Ch 1, sc in same st as joining, [ch 18, sc in next sc] 12 times, ch 3, sk next 3 sc, sc in next sc, ch 5, sl st in any ch-3 sp directly above a V-st sp on last rnd of center motif, ch 5, sc in same st on end motif as last sc made, ch 3, join in beg sc, fasten off.

ROW 3: With RS facing, sk next 2 ch-3 sps on last rnd of center motif, attach MC with a sl st in next ch-3 sp, ch 5, 3 dc in first ch-18 lp of last rnd, [ch 3, 3 dc in next ch-18 lp] 11 times, ch 5, sk next 2 ch-3 sps on last rnd of center motif, sl st in next ch-3 sp, turn.

ROW 4: Ch 5, sm shell in next ch-3 sp, [ch 2, sm shell in next ch-3 sp] 10 times, ch 5, sl st in same ch-3 sp on last rnd of center motif as beg sl st of Row 3, turn.

ROW 5: Ch 5, sc in first ch-2 sp on last row, [ch 3, sc in next ch-2 sp] rep across to ch-5 sp, ch 5, sl st in same ch-5 sp on center motif as last ch-5, turn. (42 ch-3 sps; 2 ch-5 sps)

ROW 6: Ch 3, sc in next ch-5 sp, [ch 3, sc in next ch-3 sp] rep across to next ch-5 sp, ch 3, sc in ch-5 sp, ch 3, sl st in ch-3 sp on center motif at base of ch-5, fasten off. (45 ch-3 sps)

SECOND END MOTIF

RND 1: Rep Rnd 1 of first end motif.

RND 2: Rep Rnd 2 of first end motif, joining to center motif in ch-3 sp above V-st sp which is directly opposite joining sl st of first end motif.

ROWS 3–6: Rep Rows 3–6 of first end motif.

BORDER

RND 1: With RS facing, attach MC with a sl st in first free ch-3 sp directly above first V-st sp at right-hand edge of either edge of center motif, ch 12 (counts as first tr, ch 8), *sk 3 ch-3 sps, dc in next sp, [ch 8, sk 3 ch-3 sps, dc in next ch-3 sp] 6 times, ch 8, sk 3 ch-3 sps, tr in next sp, ch 5, tr in 3rd ch-3 sp on end motif, [ch 5, sk next ch-3 sp, dc in next ch-3 sp] 19 times, ch 5, sk next ch-3 sp, tr

in next ch-3 sp, ch 5 **, tr in first free ch-3 sp directly above first V-st sp on center motif, ch 8, rep from * around, ending last rep at **, join in 4th ch of beg ch-12, fasten off.

RND 2: With RS facing, attach CC with a sl st in same st as joining, ch 3; working in each rem dc, tr and ch st around, *dc in each of next 8 chs, [dc in next dc, dc in each of next 8 chs] 7 times, [dc dec] 3 times, dc in next tr, dc in each of next 5 chs, [dc in next dc, dc in each of next 5 chs] 19 times, [dc dec] 3 times **, dc in next tr, rep from * around, ending last rep at **, join in 3rd ch of beg ch-3, fasten off. (396 sts)

RND 3: With RS facing, attach MC with a sl st in same st as joining, ch 1; working in back lps for this rnd only and beg in same st as joining, *sc in each of next 71 sts, [sc dec] 3 times, sc in each of next 115 sts, [sc dec] 3 times, rep from * around, join in beg sc.

RND 4: Ch 1, sc in same st as joining, [ch 9, sk 5 sts, sc in next st]

rep around, ending with ch 5, tr in beg sc to form last ch-9 sp. (64 ch-9 sps)

RND 5: Ch 1, sc in sp just formed, *sc in center ch of next ch-9, [ch 9, sc in center ch of next ch-9] 11 times, sc in center ch of next ch-9 *, [ch 9, sc in center ch of next ch-9] 19 times, rep from * to *, [ch 9, sc in center ch of next ch-9] 18 times, ch 9, join in beg sc. (60 ch-9 sps)

RND 6: Sl st in next sc and in each of first 3 chs of ch-9 sp, ch 3, 3 dc in same ch-9 sp, *[bdr shell 1 in next sp] 9 times, spl shell, [bdr shell 1 in next sp] 17 times *, spl shell, rep from * to *, 4 dc in next sp, ch 3, join in 3rd ch of beg ch-3.

RND 7: Sl st in each of next 7 dc and in ch-3 sp, beg bdr shell 2 in same sp, [bdr shell 2 in next ch-3 sp] rep around, join in 3rd ch of beg ch-5. (56 bdr shells 2)

RND 8: [Sl st in each of next 2 chs and in next dc] twice, sl st in next ch-3 sp, beg bdr shell 2 in same sp, [bdr shell 2 in next ch-3 sp] 8

Continued on page 16

Hairpin Doily

The inspiration for this delicate doily came from a rather forlorn and dingy little hairpin lace doily discovered at a flea market.

Design revised by Maggie Petsch Chasalow

SKILL LEVEL: INTERMEDIATE

SIZE
12 inches in diameter

MATERIALS
➤ Crochet cotton size 10 (350 yds per ball): 1 ball dusty blue
➤ Size 7 steel crochet hook or size needed to obtain gauge
➤ 2-inch-wide hairpin frame
➤ Tapestry needle

GAUGE
Center through Rnd 2 of outer edge = 5⅝ inches in diameter
Check gauge to save time.

PATTERN NOTES
Weave in loose ends as work progresses.

Join rnds with a sl st unless otherwise stated.

PATTERN STITCHES
OPEN SHELL: [Tr, ch 2, tr, ch 3, tr, ch 2, tr] in indicated sp or st.

BEG OPEN SHELL: [Ch 6, tr, ch 3, tr, ch 2, tr] in indicated sp or st.

V-ST: [Tr, ch 1, tr] in indicated sp or st.

JOINING OPEN SHELL (J OPEN SHELL): [Tr, ch 2, tr, ch 1] in indicated st on doily center, sl st in indicated group of lps on hairpin strip, ch 1, [tr, ch 2, tr] in same st on doily center as last tr made.

BEG J OPEN SHELL: [Ch 6, tr, ch 1] in indicated st on doily center, sl st in indicated group of lps on hairpin strip, ch 1, [tr, ch 2, tr] in same st on doily center as last tr made.

JOINING V-ST (J V-ST): Tr in indicated st on doily center, ch 1, sl st in indicated group of lps on hairpin strip, ch 1, tr in same st on doily center as last tr made.

PICOT: Ch 4, dc in last tr made.

BEG P: Ch 8, dc in 5th ch from hook.

P SHELL: [{Tr, p} twice, tr] in indicated st or sp.

BEG P SHELL: [Beg p, tr, p, tr] in indicated st or sp.

Doily

Make 1 strip of hairpin lace with a 1-hdc spine and 36 lps on each side and 1 strip with a 1-hdc spine and 162 lps on each side.

CENTER
Inner Edge

RND 1: Retaining twist in lps of smaller hairpin lace strip, attach thread with a sl st in 4 lps held tog, ch 1, sc in same 4-lp group, [sc next 4 lps tog] rep around, join in beg sc, fasten off. (9 sc)

With tapestry needle, sew ends of spine tog.

Outer edge

RND 1 (RS): Retaining twist in lps, attach thread with a sl st in any lp, ch 1, sc in same lp, [ch 7, sc in next lp] rep around, ending with ch 3, tr in beg sc to form last ch-7 sp. (36 ch-7 sps)

RND 2: Beg open shell in top of last tr made, *V-st in center ch of next ch-7 **, open shell in center ch of next ch-7, rep from * around, ending last rep at **, join in 4th ch of beg ch-6.

RND 3: Sl st in each of next 2 chs, in next tr and in each of next 2 chs, [ch 1, sc] in next ch, ch 7, sc in next ch-1 sp, [ch 7, sc in center ch of next ch-3, ch 7, sc in next ch-1 sp] rep around, ending with ch 3, tr in beg sc to form last ch-7 sp, do not fasten off. (36 ch-7 sps)

BORDER

RND 1: Beg j open shell in last tr made to first 12 lps on longer hairpin lace strip, *j V-st in center ch of next ch-7 to next 2 lps on hairpin lace strip, j open shell in center ch of next ch-7 to next 2 lps on hairpin lace strip, j V-st in center ch of next ch-7 to next 2 lps on hairpin lace strip **, j open shell in center ch of next ch-7 to next 12 lps on hairpin lace strip, rep from * around, ending last rep at **, join in 4th ch of beg ch-6, fasten off.

With tapestry needle, sew ends of spine tog.

RND 2: With RS facing, retaining twist in lps, attach thread with a sl st in first 2 unworked lp on opposite side of hairpin lace strip, ch 1, sc in same 2-lp group, *[ch 5, sc next 2 lps tog] 5 times, ch 5, sc next 6 lps tog **, ch 5, sc next 2 lps tog, rep from * around, ending last rep at **, ch 2, dc in beg sc to form last ch-5 sp. (63 ch-5 sps)

RND 3: Beg p shell in last dc made, p shell in center ch of each ch-5 sp around, join in 4th ch of beg ch-8, fasten off. ✧

Rickrack Doily

Crocheters have used rickrack and other novelty braids in their work almost from the first day that they were made available to the public. This type of crochet was very popular in the Victorian era and had a resurgence of popularity in the mid-1950s, when the pattern for this rickrack doily was printed in a widely-circulated needlework magazine. Although a great many of the novelty braids can only be found at antique shops or estate sales today, that old standby rickrack is still readily available.

Design revised by
Maggie Petsch Chasalow

SKILL LEVEL: INTERMEDIATE

SIZE
15¾ inches in diameter

MATERIALS
➤ Crochet cotton size 20: 500-yd ball white
➤ Size 9 crochet hook or size needed to obtain gauge
➤ 2 packages Wrights medium printed rickrack (2½ yds per package)
➤ Sewing needle and thread
➤ Fray Check fray deterrent (optional)

GAUGE
Rnds 1–3 = 1¾ inches in diameter
Check gauge to save time.

PATTERN NOTES
Weave in loose ends as work progresses.

Join rnds with a sl st unless otherwise stated.

PATTERN STITCHES
RICKRACK JOINING (RRJ):
Remove hook from lp, insert hook from RS to WS in indicated tip on rickrack, pick up dropped lp, draw through to RS of rickrack,

DTR CL: *Yo hook 3 times, insert hook in indicated st, yo, draw up a lp, [yo, draw through 2 lps on hook] 3 times, rep from * twice, yo, draw through all 4 lps on hook.

TRIPLE TREBLE (TRTR): Yo hook 4 times, insert hook in indicated st, yo, draw up a lp, [yo, draw through 2 lps on hook] 5 times.

TR CL: *Yo hook twice, insert hook in indicated st, yo, draw up a lp, [yo, draw through 2 lps on hook] twice, rep from * twice, yo, draw through all 4 lps on hook,

BEG TR CL: Ch 3 (counts as first tr), *yo hook twice, insert hook in indicated st, yo, draw up a lp, [yo, draw through 2 lps on hook] twice, rep from * once, yo, draw through all 3 lps on hook.

RICKRACK PUFF ST (RR PUFF ST): [Sl st in tip of next free point on rickrack] twice, push rr puff st to RS of work.

DOILY
Note: Cut length of rickrack with 10 points. Fold 1 end back to WS. Overlap 2 points and blind stitch with sewing needle and thread to form 8-point circle. Apply fray deterrent to ends if desired.

RND 1 (RS): Ch 5, sl st to join to form a ring, ch 1, 8 sc in ring, join in beg sc. (8 sc)

RND 2: Ch 1, beg in same st as joining, 2 sc in each sc around, join in beg sc. (16 sc)

RND 3: Ch 1, sc in same st as joining, ch 3, rrj to tip of any point on inner edge of rickrack circle, *ch 3, sk next sc **, sc in next sc, ch 3, rrj to tip of next free point on inner edge of rickrack circle, rep from * around, ending last rep at **, join in beg sc, fasten off. (8-point center)

Note: Cut length of rickrack with 98 points.

RND 4: With RS facing, attach thread with sl st to tip of any point on outer edge of 8-point center, ch 3, rrj to tip of first point on 98-point length, *[ch 9, rrj to tip of next free point on 98-point length] 4 times, [ch 2, rrj to tip of next free point on 98-point length] 3 times, [ch 4, sl st in center ch of next ch-9, ch 4, rrj to tip of next free point on 98-point length] 4 times, ch 3 **, sl st in tip of next free point on 8-point center, ch 3, rrj to tip of next free point on 98-point length, rep from * around, ending last rep at **, join at base of beg ch-3, fasten off. (8 spokes)

Fold end of rickrack back to WS. Overlapping points to form one free point between last spoke and first spoke, blind stitch ends of rickrack tog with sewing needle and thread. Apply fray deterrent if desired.

RND 5: With RS facing, attach thread with a sl st in tip of free point at top of any spoke, [ch 12, sl st in tip of next free point] 3 times, *ch 5; holding back on hook last lp of each st, tr in tip of next free point, sk next 3 points, tr in tip of next point, yo, draw through all 3 lps on hook, ch 5, sl st in tip of next free point **, [ch 12, sl st in tip of next free point] 6 times, rep from * around, ending last rep at **, [ch 12, sl st in tip of next free point] twice, ch 6, trtr at base of beg ch-12 to form last ch-12 sp.

RND 6: Ch 1, sc in sp just formed, [ch 12, sc in next ch-12 sp] twice, *ch 12, dtr cl in each of next 2 ch-12 sps **, [ch 12, sc in next ch-12 sp] 4 times, rep from * around, ending last rep at **, ch 12, sc in next ch-12 sp, ch 6, trtr in beg sc to form last ch-12 sp.

RND 7: Ch 1, sc in lp just formed, [ch 14, sc in next ch-12 sp] twice, *ch 14, dtr cl in each of next 2 ch-12 sps **, [ch 14, sc in next ch-12 sp] 3 times, rep from * around, ending last rep at **, ch 7, trtr in beg sc to form last ch-14 sp.

RND 8: Beg tr cl in top of trtr just made, *ch 15, sc in next sp, ch 13, sc in next sp **, [ch 15, tr cl in next sp] twice, rep from * around, ending last rep at **, ch 15, tr cl in next sp, ch 8, trtr in top of beg tr cl to form last ch-15 sp.

RND 9: Beg tr cl in top of trtr just made, [ch 15, tr cl in next sp] rep around, ending with ch-11, tr in top of beg tr cl to form last ch-15 lp. (32 ch-15 sps)

Note: Cut a length of rickrack with 98 points.

RND 10: Ch 4, beg in first point of rickrack, *rr puff st, ch 4, sl st in 5th ch of next ch-15, ch 4, sl st in tip of next free point on rickrack, ch 4, sk next 4 chs of same ch-15 **, sl st in next ch, ch 4, rep from * around, ending last rep at **, join in top of tr at base of beg ch-4, fasten off.

Fold end of rickrack back to WS. Overlapping points, blind stitch ends of rickrack strip tog with sewing needle and thread. Apply fray deterrent if desired.

Continued on next page

Rickrack Doily continued from previous page

RND 11: With RS facing, attach thread with a sl st on opposite edge of rickrack at tip of first free point immediately to the left of any rr puff st; working behind rr puff st, ch 1, sc in same st, *ch 9, sc at tip of next free point on rickrack, ch 9, sk rr puff st **, sc at tip of next free point on rickrack, rep from * around, ending last rep at **, join in beg sc. (64 ch-9 sps)

RND 12: Ch 1, [11 sc in next ch-9 sp] twice, *5 sc in first half of next sp, turn, [ch 10, sk next 10 sc, sl st in next sc] twice, **ch 1, turn, 12 sc in next ch-10 sp, 6 sc in first half of next ch-10 sp, ch 1, turn, sk 12 sc, sl st in next sc, ch 1, turn, [6 sc, ch 4, 6 sc] in next ch-11 sp **, [6 sc in rem half of next sp] twice, 11 sc in next ch-9 sp, rep from * around ending with sl st in each of first 5 sc, ch 10, turn, sk 5 sl st and 5 sc, sl st in next sc, ch 10, sk 10 sc, sl st in

next sc, rep from ** to **, 6 sc in rem half of next sp, join in next sl st, fasten off.

FINISHING
Working with center point of 3 free rickrack point between spokes at base of any pair of spokes, push point up and to RS of work to form rickrack puff. With sewing needle and thread, tack sides of puff tog in "V" at base of point. Rep for each of 7 rem rickrack points. ✧

1914 Oval Doily continued from page 11

times, dc in next ch-3 sp, *bdr shell 2 in next ch-3 sp, [ch 1, bdr shell 2 in next ch-3 sp] 6 times, [ch 2, bdr shell 2 in next ch-3 sp] 4 times, [ch 1, bdr shell 2 in next ch-3 sp] 6 times, dc in next ch-3 sp *, [bdr shell 2 in next ch-3 sp] 9 times, dc in next ch-3 sp, rep from * to *, join in 3rd ch of beg ch-5. (52 bdr shells 2)

RND 9: [Sl st in each of next 2 chs and in next dc] twice, sl st in next ch-3 sp, beg bdr shell 2 in same sp, [bdr shell 2 in next ch-3 sp] 9

times, *[ch 1, bdr shell 2 in next ch-3 sp] 6 times, [ch 2, bdr shell 2 in next ch-3 sp] 4 times, [ch 1, bdr shell 2 in next ch-3 sp] 6 times *, [bdr shell 2 in next ch-3 sp] 10 times, rep from * to *, join in 3rd ch of beg ch-5, fasten off.

RND 10: With RS facing, attach CC with a sl st in first ch-3 sp after joining st, beg bdr shell 3 in same sp, [bdr shell 3 in next ch-3 sp] 8 times, *[ch 1, bdr shell 3 in next ch-3 sp] 7 times, [ch 2, bdr shell 3 in next ch-3 sp] 4 times, ch 1, [bdr

shell 3 in next ch-3 sp, ch 1] 6 times *, [bdr shell 3 in next ch-3 sp] 9 times, rep from * to *, join in 3rd ch of beg ch-3, fasten off. (52 bdr shells 3)

RND 11: With RS facing, attach MC with a sl st in same st as joining, ch 1; beg in same st as joining, sc in each rem dc and ch-1 sp, 2 sc in each ch-2 sp and [2 sc in first ch, ch 5, sk next ch, 2 sc in next ch] in each ch-3 sp around, join in beg sc, fasten off. ✧

Silver Bells Doily continued from page 8

ROWS 2–8: Rep Rows 2–8 of first bell; at the end of Row 8, join in top of first st of last row of previous bell, fasten off. (4 ch-9 sps at end of Row 8)

Next 11 Bells

ROWS 1–8: Rep Rows 1–8 of 2nd bell.

Last Bell

ROWS 1–7: Rep Rows 1–7 of 2nd bell.

ROW 8: Ch 3, sl st in top of last st on last row of first bell, continue across as for Row 8 of 2nd bell, do not fasten off, turn.

RND 9: Ch 1, sc in same st as joining, ch 9, sc in each of next 2 dc, *9 sc in next ch-9 sp, [sc in next dc, ch 9, sc in next dc, 9 sc in next ch-9 sp] 3 times **, sc in each of next 2 dc, ch 9, sc in each of next 2 dc, rep from * around,

ending last rep at **, sc in next dc, join in beg sc, fasten off.

FINISHING
With sewing needle and thread, sew one jingle bell to center ch-9 sp on each bell of inner and outer bands. ✧

The Song
of the Hope Chest

By Elba Stratton

In a simple chest of cedar,
With its sweet and spicy scent,
Lies a hoard of needle tokens,
Proof of happy hours well spent.
Here, a robe of lace-trimmed satin,
There, a study pinafore;
Doilies, runners, centerpieces
Aid to make this wondrous store.

Aprons meant for household service,
Coveralls so crisp and clean,
Dainty caps of lace and ribbon—
Fitting crowns for any queen.
Lunch cloths, napkins and buffet sets
With bright flowers embroidered o'er,
Scarfs and trinkets for the dresser,
Sheets and pillow slips galore.

Pretty curtains for the windows
That the sun comes peeping through
Simple, dainty, soft in color,
White and cream, with touch of blue.
Towels of all sorts and uses—
Which we well can understand—
For the kitchen and the bathroom,
And the guest room wisely planned.

Just to hint at all the treasures
Garnered here, would take so long
That I fear, before t'was finished,
You would weary of my song.
Close your hope chest, with its visions,
To await the perfect day
Fraught with love and joy and sunshine
When Prince Charming comes your way.

Nanny's Zinnias

Linen and zinnias speak to us of a bygone era, a lazy summer afternoon, a vase full of freshly cut flowers set on a doily in Grandmother's parlor.

Design Revised by
Maggie Petsch Chasalow

SKILL LEVEL: INTERMEDIATE

SIZE
14½ x 18 inches

MATERIALS
➢ South Maid crochet cotton size 10 (300 yds per ball):1 ball each cream #430 (A), shaded yellows #19 (B), spruce #479 (C)
➢ Size 7 crochet hook or size needed to obtain gauge
➢ 1 yd beige linen fabric
➢ Sewing needle and thread

GAUGE
Small zinnia = 1³⁄₁₆ inches in diameter
Check gauge to save time.

PATTERN NOTES
Weave in loose ends as work progresses.

Join rnds with a sl st unless otherwise stated.

PATTERN STITCHES
PICOT(P): [Sc, ch 3, sc] in indicated st.

JOINING CH-6 (JCH): Ch 3, remove hook from lp, insert hook from RS to WS in indicated ch-6 sp on previous motif, pick up dropped lp, draw through ch-6 sp, ch 3.

LINEN RECTANGLE (make 4)
Cut 5 x 7 inch linen rectangle. On each edge, turn under ⅛ inch, then ¼ inch. Hemstitch in place.

FIRST MOTIF
RND 1: Attach A with a sl st approximately ¼ inch from edge at right-hand corner of either longer edge of any linen rectangle, ch 1, *3 sc in corner, 51 sc evenly sp across to next corner, 3 sc in corner, 31 sc evenly sp across to next corner, rep from * around, join in beg sc.

RND 2: Ch 1, sc in same st as joining, *ch 5, sk next corner sc, sc in 3rd corner sc, ch 3, sk next sc, sc in next sc, [ch 5, sk 2 sc, sc in next sc, ch 3, sk next sc, sc in next sc] rep across to first sc of next 3-sc corner group, rep from * around, ending with ch 3, join in beg sc.

RND 3: Sl st in first ch of first ch-5 sp, ch 1, beg in same sp, *[p, ch 6, p] in corner sp, [ch 6, p in next ch-5 sp] rep across to last ch-5 sp before next corner ch-5 sp **, ch 6, rep from * around, ending last rep at **, ch 3, dc in beg sc to form last ch-6 sp.

RND 4: Ch 1, p in sp just formed, *ch 6, [p, ch 6, p] in corner ch-6 sp, [ch 6, p in next ch-6 sp] rep across to last ch-6 sp before next corner ch-6 sp, rep from * around, ending with ch 3, dc in beg sc to form last ch-6 sp, fasten off.

RND 5: With RS facing, attach B with a sl st in top of dc just made, ch 1, p in sp just made, ch 6, p in next ch-6 sp, *ch 6, [p, ch 6, p] in corner ch-6 sp, [ch 6, p in next ch-6 sp] rep across to last ch-6 sp before next corner ch-6 sp, rep form * around, ending with ch 3, dc in beg sc to form last ch-6 sp, fasten off.

RND 6: With RS facing, attach A with a sl st in first corner ch-6 sp after joining st, beg in same sp, *[p, ch 6, p] in corner ch-6 sp, [ch 6, p in next ch-6 sp] rep across to last ch-6 sp before next corner ch-6 sp, ch 6, rep from * around, join in beg sc, fasten off.

SECOND MOTIF
RNDS 1–5: Rep Rnds 1–5 of first motif.

RND 6: With RS facing, attach A with a sl st in first corner ch-6 sp after joining st, p in same sp, jch to corresponding corner ch-6 sp on previous motif, p in same sp as last p made, [jch to next ch-6 sp on previous motif, p in next ch-6 sp on working motif] rep across to last ch-6 sp on working motif before next corner ch-6 sp, jch to last ch-6 sp on previous motif before corner ch-6 sp, p in corner ch-6 sp on working motif, jch to corner ch-6 sp on previous motif, p in same corner ch-6 sp on working motif as last p made (one side joined), continue around as for Rnd 6 of first motif.

REM TWO MOTIFS
RNDS 1–6: Rep Rnds 1–6 of 2nd motif, joining on as many sides as necessary to form a rectangle of two rows of two motifs each.

BORDER
RND 1: With RS facing, attach A with sl st in ch-6 sp at upper right corner, [p, ch 6, p] in same sp, *[ch 6, p in next ch-6 sp] 14 times *, ch 6, p in jch, rep from * to *, ch 6, [p, ch 6, p] in corner ch-6 sp, **[ch 6, p in next ch-6 sp] 10 times **, ch 6, [p, ch 6, p] in jch, rep from ** to **, ch 6, [p, ch 6, p] in corner ch-6 sp, rep from * around, ending with ch 6, join in beg sc, fasten off.

RND 2: With RS facing, attach C with a sl st in ch-6 sp at upper right corner, ch 1, beg in same sp, *[p, ch 6, p] in corner ch-6 sp, ch 6, [p in next ch-6 sp, ch 6] rep across to next corner ch-6 sp, rep from * around, join in beg sc, fasten off.

RND 3: With RS facing, attach A with a sl st in any ch-6 sp, ch 1, sc in same sp, *ch 2, [dc, ch 3, hdc in

Continued on page 23

Star With Cluny Border

This pattern first appeared in August 1915. In the early 1900s, needlework magazines frequently published patterns for crocheted doilies that were meant to resemble doilies worked in other types of lace — reticella, Cluny, Armenian, tatted, to name just a few.

SKILL LEVEL: INTERMEDIATE

SIZE

12 inches in diameter

MATERIALS

➤ Crochet cotton size 20: 350 yds ecru

➤ Size 9 steel crochet hook or size needed to obtain gauge

GAUGE

Rnds 1 and 2 = ⅝ inch

Check gauge to save time.

PATTERN NOTES

Weave in loose ends as work progresses.

Join rnds with a sl st unless otherwise stated.

PATTERN STITCHES

TR 3 TOG: Holding back on hook last lp of each st, tr in each of next 3 dc, yo, draw through all 4 lps on hook.

BEG TR 3 TOG: Ch 3, holding back on hook last lp of each st, tr in each of next 2 dc, yo, draw through all 3 lps on hook.

TR CL: Holding back on hook last lp of each st, 3 tr in indicated st, yo, draw through all 4 lps on hook.

TRTR: Yo hook 4 times, insert hook in indicated st, yo, draw up a lp, [yo, draw through 2 lps on hook] 5 times.

DC 3 TOG: Holding back on hook last lp of each st, dc in last dc of next 3-dc group, dc in next sp, dc in first dc of next 3-dc group, yo, draw through all 4 lps on hook.

BEG DC 3 TOG: Ch 2, holding back on hook last lp of each st, dc in next sp, dc in first dc of next 3-dc group, yo, draw through all 3 lps on hook.

DTRTR: Yo hook 5 times, insert hook in indicated st, yo, draw up a lp, [yo, draw through 2 lps on hook] 6 times.

DOILY

RND 1: Ch 10, sl st to join to form a ring, ch 1, 15 sc in ring, join in beg sc. (15 sc)

RND 2: Ch 1, beg in same st as joining, 2 sc in each sc around, join in beg sc. (30 sc)

RND 3: Ch 1, sc in same st as joining, ch 4, sk next 4 sc, [sc in next sc, ch 4, sk next 4 sc] rep around, join in beg sc. (6 ch-4 sps)

RND 4: Ch 1, sc in same st as joining, *sc in first ch of next ch-4, ch 4, sk next 2 ch, sc in next ch **, sc in next sc, rep from * around, ending last rep at **, join in beg sc. (6 groups 3-sc)

RNDS 5–9: Ch 1, beg in same st as joining, *sc in each sc across to next ch-4, sc in first ch of ch-4, ch 4, sk next 2 chs, sc in next ch, rep from * around, ending with sc in each sc across to beg sc, join in beg sc. (6 groups of 13 sc at the end of Rnd 9)

RND 10: Ch 1, beg in same st as joining, *sc in each sc across to last sc of same sc group, leave last sc unworked, ch 7, sk first sc of next sc group, rep from * around, ending with sc in each rem sc of same sc group across to beg sc, join in beg sc. (6 groups 11-sc)

RND 11: Ch 1, beg in same st as joining, *sc in each sc across to last sc of same sc group, leave last sc unworked, ch 4, sc in center ch of next ch-7 sp, ch 4, sk first sc of next sc group, rep from * around, ending with sc in each rem sc of same sc group across to beg sc, join in beg sc. (6 groups of 9-sc)

RND 12: Ch 1, beg in same st as joining, *sc in each sc across to last sc of same sc group, leave last sc unworked, ch 5, sk ch-4, [{dc, ch 1} twice, dc] in next sc, ch 5, sk first sc of next sc group, rep from * around, ending with sc in each sc of same sc group across to beg sc, join in beg sc. (6 groups 7-sc)

RND 13: Ch 1, beg in same st as joining, *sc in each sc across to last sc of same sc group, leave last sc unworked, ch 5, 3 dc in next ch-1 sp, ch 3, 3 dc in next ch-1 sp, ch 5, sk first sc of next sc group, rep from * around, ending with sc in each sc of same sc group across to beg sc, join in beg sc. (6 groups 5-sc)

RND 14: Ch 1, beg in same st as joining, *sc in each sc across to last sc of same sc group, leaving last sc unworked, ch 6, dc in each of next 3 dc, ch 3, 3 dc in center ch of next ch-3, ch 3, dc in each of next 3 dc, ch 6, sk first sc of next sc group, rep from * around, ending with sc in each sc across to beg sc, join in beg sc. (6 groups 3-sc)

RND 15: Ch 1, sc in same st as joining, *ch 6, dc in each of next 3 dc, ch 3, 3 dc in first dc of next 3-dc group, ch 3, sk next dc, 3 dc in next dc, ch 3, dc in each of next 3 dc, ch 6 **, sc in center sc of next 3-sc group, rep from * around, ending last rep at **, join in beg sc.

RND 16: Ch 1, sc in same st as joining, *ch 6, dc in each of next 3 dc, ch 3, dc in each of next 3 dc, ch 3, 3 dc in center ch of next ch-3, [ch 3, dc in each of next 3 dc] twice, ch 6 **, sc in next sc, rep from * around, ending last rep at **, join in beg sc.

RND 17: Sl st in each of next 6 chs and in next dc, beg tr 3 tog, *ch 6, tr 3 tog over next 3 dc, ch 6, tr cl in first dc of next 3-dc group, ch 6, sk next dc, tr cl in next dc, [ch 6, tr 3 tog over next 3 dc] twice, ch 6 **, tr 3 tog over next 3 dc, rep from * around, ending last rep at **, join in top of beg tr 3 tog.

RND 18: Ch 5 (counts as first tr, ch 1 throughout), sk next ch, *dc in next ch, [ch 1, sk next ch, dc in next ch] twice, ch 1, sk first ch of next ch-6, dc in next ch, [ch 1, sk next ch, dc in next ch] twice, ch 1, sk first ch of next ch-6, hdc in next ch, [ch 1, hdc in next ch] twice, ch 1, dc in top of next tr cl, ch 1, sk first 2 chs of next ch-6, dc in next ch, ch 1, sk next ch, dc in next ch, ch 1, dc in first ch of next ch-6, [ch 1, sk next ch, dc in next ch] twice, ch 1, tr in top of next tr 3 tog, ch 1 **, sk first ch of next

Continued on next page

ch-6, tr in next ch, [ch 1, sk next ch, tr in next ch] twice, ch 1, sk first ch of next ch-6, rep from * around to last ch-6 sp, ending last rep at **, sk first 2 chs of next ch-6, tr in next ch, ch 1, sk next ch, tr in next ch, ch 1, join in 4th ch of beg ch-5. (114 ch-1 sps)

RND 19: Ch 7 (counts as first tr, ch 3), *sk next sp, dc in next sp, ch 2, sk next dc, dc in next dc, ch 2, sk next sp, dc in next sp, ch 3, sk next dc, tr in next dc, sk next sp, tr in next sp, ch 7, tr in next sp, sk next sp, tr in next dc, ch 3, sk next sp, dc in next sp, ch 2, sk next dc, dc in next dc, ch 2, sk next sp, dc in next sp, ch 3, sk next sp, tr in each of next 2 tr, ch 7 **, tr in each of next 2 tr, ch 3, rep from * around, ending last rep at **, tr in last tr, join in 4th ch of beg ch-7.

RND 20: Ch 3, 2 dc in same st as joining, ch 2, *[3 tr in next dc, ch 1] twice, 3 tr in next dc, ch 2, sk next tr, 3 dc in next tr, ch 5, trtr in 4th ch of next ch-7, ch 5 **, 3 dc in next tr, ch 2, rep from * around, ending last rep at **, join in 3rd ch of beg ch-3.

RND 21: Ch 3, dc in each of next 2 dc, *ch 1, dc in each of next 3 tr, ch 1, dc in center tr of next 3-tr group, ch 1, sk next tr, dc in each of next 3 tr, ch 1, dc in each of next 3 dc, ch 5, sk first 4 chs of next ch-5, 2 sc in next ch, sc in trtr, 2 sc in first ch of next ch-5, ch 5 **, dc in each of next 3 dc, rep from * around, ending last rep at **, join in 3rd ch of beg ch-3.

RND 22: Ch 3, dc in each of next 2 dc, *ch 1, dc in each of next 3 dc, ch 1, sk next dc, dc in each of next 3 dc, ch 1, dc in each of next 3 dc, ch 5, sk first 4 chs of next ch-5, 2 sc in next ch, sc in each of next 5 sc, 2 sc in next ch, ch 5 **,

dc in each of next 3 dc, rep from * around, ending last rep at **, join in 3rd ch of beg ch-3.

RND 23: Ch 3, dc in each of next 2 dc, *ch 1, sk next 2 dc, dc in next dc, dc in next sp, dc in first dc of next 3-dc group, ch 1, sk 2 dc, dc in each of next 3 dc, ch 5, sk first 4 chs of next ch-5, 2 sc in next ch, sc in each of next 9 sc, 2 sc in first ch of next ch-5, ch 5 **, dc in each of next 3 dc, rep from * around, ending last rep at **, join in 3rd ch of beg ch-3.

RND 24: Ch 3, dc in each of next 2 dc, *ch 1, sk next 3 dc, dc in each of next 3 dc, ch 3, sk first 4 chs of next ch-5, 2 sc in next ch, sc in each of next 13 sc, 2 sc in first ch of next ch-5, ch 3 **, dc in each of next 3 dc, rep from * around, ending last rep at **, join in 3rd ch of beg ch-3.

RND 25: Sl st in each of next 2 dc, beg dc 3 tog, *ch 5, sk first 2 chs of next ch-3, 2 sc in next ch, sc in each of next 17 sc, 2 sc in first ch of next ch-3, ch 5, sk first 2 dc of next 3-dc group **, dc 3 tog, rep from * around, ending last rep at **, join in top of beg dc 3 tog.

RND 26: Ch 4 (counts as first dc, ch 1), [dc, ch 1, dc] in same st as joining, *ch 5, sk first 2 sc of next 21-sc group, sc in each of next 17 sc, ch 5 **, [[{dc, ch 1} twice, dc] in top of next dc 3 tog, rep from * around, ending last rep at **, join in 3rd ch of beg ch-4, turn.

RND 27: Sl st in last ch of last ch-5 made, turn, ch 3 (counts as first dc), dc in same st as joining, *dc in next sp, ch 3, dc in next sp, dc in next dc, dc in first ch of next ch-5, ch 6, sk first 2 sc of next 17-sc group, sc in each of next 13 sc, ch 6 **, sk first 4 chs of next ch-5, dc in next ch, dc in next dc, rep

from * around, ending last rep at **, join in 3rd ch of beg ch-3.

RND 28: Ch 3, dc in each of next 2 dc, *ch 3, 3 dc in center ch of next ch-3, ch 3, dc in each of next 3 dc, ch 6, sk first 2 sc of next 13-sc group, sc in each of next 9 sc, ch 6 **, dc in each of next 3 dc, rep from * around, ending last rep at **, join in 3rd ch of beg ch-3.

RND 29: Ch 3, dc in each of next 2 dc, *ch 3, 3 dc in first dc of next 3-dc group, ch 3, sk next dc, 3 dc in next dc, ch 3, dc in each of next 3 dc, ch 6, sk first 2 sc of next 9-sc group, sc in each of next 5 sc, ch 6 **, dc in each of next 3 dc, rep from * around, ending last rep at **, join in 3rd ch of beg ch-3.

RND 30: Ch 3, dc in each of next 2 dc, *ch 3, dc in each of next 3 dc, ch 3, 3 dc in center ch of next ch-3, [ch 3, dc in each of next 3 dc] twice, ch 7, sk first sc of next 5-sc group, sc in each of next 3 sc, ch 7 **, dc in each of next 3 dc, rep from * around, ending last rep at **, join in 3rd ch of beg ch-3.

RND 31: Beg tr 3 tog, *ch 5, tr 3 tog, ch 5, tr cl in first dc of next 3-dc group, ch 5, sk next dc, tr cl in next dc, [ch 5, tr 3 tog] twice, ch 5, dtrtr in center sc of next 3-sc group, ch 5 **, tr 3 tog, rep from * around, ending last rep at **, join in top of beg tr 3 tog.

RND 32: *Ch 11, sl st in 6th ch from hook, ch 5, sl st in top of next tr 3 tog, [ch 11, sl st in 6th ch from hook, ch 5, sl st in top of next tr cl] twice, [ch 11, sl st in 6th ch from hook, ch 5, sl st in top of next tr 3 tog] twice, ch 11, sl st in 6th ch from hook, ch 5, sl st between pair of dtrtr, ch 11, sl st in 6th ch from hook, ch 5 **, sl st in top of next tr 3 tog, rep from * around, ending last rep at **, join in top of beg tr 3 tog, fasten off. ✧

Nanny's Zinnias continued from page 18

top of last dc made, dc] in next p, ch 2 **, sc in next ch-6 sp, rep from * around, ending at ** join in beg sc, fasten off.

SMALL ZINNIA *(make 4)*
RND 1: With B, ch 2, 6 sc in 2nd ch from hook, join in beg sc. (6 sc)

RND 2: Ch 1, sc in same st as joining, ch 2, [sc in next sc, ch 2] rep around, join in beg sc. (6 ch-2 sps)

RND 3: [Sl st, ch 2, 3 hdc, ch 2, sl st] in each ch-2 sp around, do not join. (6 petals)

RND 4: Working behind petals of last rnd, sc in beg sc of Rnd 2, ch 3, [sc in next unworked sc of Rnd 2, ch 3] rep around, join in beg sc. (6 ch-3 sps)

RND 5: [{Sl st, ch 3, 2 dc, ch 3} twice, sl st] in each ch-3 sp around, fasten off. (12 petals)

LARGE ZINNIA
RNDS 1 & 2: Rep Rnds 1 and 2 of small zinnia.

RND 3: [Sl st, ch 3, 3 dc, ch 3, sl st] in each ch-2 sp around, do not join. (6 petals)

RND 4: Rep Rnd 4 of small zinnia.

RND 5: [{Sl st, ch 4, 2 tr, ch 4} twice, sl st] in each ch-3 sp around, do not join. (12 petals)

RND 6: Working behind petals of last rnd, sc in beg sc of Rnd 4, ch 4, [sc in next unworked sc of Rnd 4, ch 4] rep around, join in beg sc. (6 ch-4 sps)

RND 7: [{Sl st, ch 4, 3 tr, ch 4} twice, sl st] in each ch-4 sp around, do not join. (12 petals)

RND 8: Working behind petals of last rnd, sc in beg sc of Rnd 6, ch 5, [sc in next unworked sc of Rnd 6, ch 5] rep around, join in beg sc. (6 ch-5 sps)

RND 9: [{Sl st, ch 5, 3 dtr, ch 5} twice, sl st] in each ch-5 sp, do not join. (12 petals)

RND 10: Working behind petals of last rnd, sc in beg sc of Rnd 8, ch 5, [sc in next unworked sc of Rnd 8, ch 5] rep around, join in beg sc, fasten off.

LARGE LEAF *(make 6)*
With C, ch 8, 2 sc in 2nd ch from hook, *dc in next ch, tr in next ch, 2 tr in next ch, tr in next ch, dc in next ch *, 3 sc in last ch, working on opposite side of foundation ch, rep from * to *, sc in same ch as beg sc, join in beg sc, sl st in center of any unworked ch-5 on Rnd 10 of large zinnia.

LARGE STEM *(make 4)*
With C, ch 66, sl st in 2nd ch from hook and in each rem ch across, fasten off.

SMALL STEM *(make 4)*
With C, ch 41, sl st in 2nd ch from hook and in each rem ch across, fasten off.

LEAF PAIR *(make 8)*
With C, ch 7, *sc in 2nd ch from hook, dc in next ch, 2 dc in next ch, dc in next ch, sc in next ch *, sl st in next ch, ch 6, rep from * to *, sl st at base of first leaf, fasten off.

SMALL LEAF *(make 20)*
With C, ch 6, sc in 2nd ch from hook, dc in next ch, 2 dc in next ch, dc in next ch, sc in next ch, fasten off.

FINISHING
Press doily. With sewing needle and thread, using photo as a guide, sew zinnias, stems and leaves to doily. ✧

Mayrain

By Harry Elmore Hurd

*Despite the cold,
ignoring the rain,*

*She said, "I shall walk
this afternoon."*

*I glanced at a nearby
weather vane,*

*Protesting, in words
that were out of tune,*

*"The wind is north by
raw northwest,"*

*And the arrow
vouched that my
words were true.*

*My Lady was not dis-
turbed in the least,*

*For her heart and
every blossom knew*

*That falling rain was
life and friend.*

*It is best that a
woman have her way*

*Through petaled time
to the garden's end,*

*For a woman's ways
are the ways of May.*

Pineapple Doily

No collection of old-time doilies is complete without the perennial pineapple, the symbol of hospitality since Colonial days and one of the most beloved crochet motifs. This dainty combination of pineapples and daisy-like blossoms is a real eye-pleaser.

Design revised by Maggie Petsch Chasalow

SKILL LEVEL: INTERMEDIATE

SIZE
11 inches in diameter

MATERIALS
➤ Crochet cotton size 30: 500 yds white

➤ Size 10 steel crochet hook or size needed to obtain gauge

GAUGE
First motif = 1¾ inches in diameter

Check gauge to save time.

PATTERN NOTES
Weave in loose ends as work progresses.

Join rnds with a sl st unless otherwise stated.

PATTERN STITCHES
CL: Holding back on hook last lp of each st, 3 tr in indicated sp or st, yo, draw through all 4 lps on hook.

BEG CL: Ch 3, holding back on hook last lp of each st, 2 tr in same st as ch-3, yo, draw through all 3 lps on hook.

JOINING SP (JSP): Ch 3, sl st in indicated sp on previous motif, ch 3.

TRTR: Yo hook 4 times, insert hook in indicated sp or st, yo, draw up a lp, [yo, draw through 2 lps on hook] 5 times.

QUINTUPLE TR (QNTR): Yo hook

6 times, insert hook in indicated st or sp, yo, draw up a lp, [yo, draw through 2 lps on hook] 7 times.

Doily Center

FIRST MOTIF
RND 1 (RS): Ch 12, sl st to join to form a ring, ch 4 (counts as first tr throughout) 31 tr in ring, join in 4th ch of beg ch-4. (32 tr)

RND 2: Ch 1, sc in same st as joining, [ch 5, sk next sc, sc in next sc] rep around, ending with ch 2, dc in beg sc to form last ch-5 sp. (16 ch-5 sps)

RND 3: Beg cl in sp just formed, ch 7, [cl in next sp, ch 7] rep around, join in top of beg cl, fasten off. (16 ch-7 sps)

SECOND MOTIF
RNDS 1 & 2: Rep Rnds 1 and 2 of first motif.

RND 3: Beg cl in sp just formed, jsp to any ch-7 sp on previous motif, cl in next sp on working motif, jsp to next ch-7 sp on previous motif (one side joined), cl in next sp on working motif, continue around as for Rnd 3 of first motif, fasten off.

REM TWO MOTIFS
RNDS 1–3: Rep Rnds 1–3 of 2nd motif, joining to form a square if two rows of two motifs each, leaving 2 ch-7 sps free between each pair of joined sps, joining 4th motif on two sides.

FILL-IN MOTIF
With RS facing, attach thread with a sl st in first ch-7 sp to the left of any joining on inner edge of doily center, ch 6 (counts as first trtr), trtr

in next unworked ch-7 sp, [qntr in next joining, trtr in each of next 2 unworked ch-7 sps] rep around, ending with qntr in last joining, join in 6th ch of beg ch-6, fasten off.

Pineapple Border

FIRST PINEAPPLE CORNER
First Pineapple

ROW 1: With WS facing, sk first 3 unworked ch-7 sps to the right of a joining sp on Rnd 3 of any motif, attach thread with a sl st in center ch of next sp, ch 7, sl st in center ch of last skipped sp, turn.

ROW 2: Ch 4 (counts as first tr throughout), 10 tr in ch-7 sp, tr at base of ch-7, turn. (12 tr)

ROW 3: Ch 5 (counts as first tr, ch 1), [tr in next tr, ch 1] 10 times, tr in 4th ch of turning ch-4, turn. (11 ch-1 sps)

ROW 4: Ch 6 (counts as first tr, ch 2), [tr in next tr, ch 2] 10 times, tr in 4th ch of turning ch-5, turn. (11 ch-2 sps)

ROW 5: Ch 5, sc in first ch-2 sp, [ch 5, sc in next ch-2 sp] 10 times, turn. (11 ch-5 sps)

ROW 6: Ch 5, sc in first ch-5 sp, [ch 5, sc in next ch-5 sp] 9 times, turn. (10 ch-5 sps)

ROWS 7–14: Ch 5, sc in first ch-5 sp, [ch 5, sc in next ch-5 sp] rep across to last sp, leave last sp unworked, turn. (2 ch-5 sps at the end of Row 14)

ROW 15: Ch 5, sk first ch of first ch-5 sp, sc in next ch, ch 5, sk next ch of same ch-5 sp, sc in next ch, fasten off.

Continued on next page

Second Pineapple

ROW 1: With WS facing, sk next unworked ch-7 sp on Rnd 3 of same motif, attach thread with a sl st in center ch of next sp, ch 7, sl st in center ch of skipped sp, turn.

ROW 2: Ch 4, sl st in top of end st of Row 2 of previous pineapple, 6 tr in ch-7 sp, tr in st at base of ch-7, turn. (8 tr)

ROW 3: Ch 5 (counts as first tr, ch 1), [tr in next tr, ch 1] 6 times, tr in 4th ch of turning ch-4, sl st in top of end st of Row 3 of previous pineapple, turn. (7 ch-1 sps)

ROW 4: Ch 4, sl st in top of end st of Row 4 of previous pineapple, ch 2, sk first ch-1 sp, [tr in next tr, ch 2] 6 times, tr in 4th ch of turning ch-5, turn. (7 ch-2 sps)

ROW 5: Ch 5, sc in first ch-2 sp, [ch 5, sc in next ch-2 sp] 6 times, ch 2, sl st in ch-5 sp at end of Row 7 on previous pineapple, turn. (7 ch-5 sps)

ROW 6: Ch 2, sc in first ch-5 sp, [ch 5, sc in next ch-5 sp] 6 times, turn. (6 ch-5 sps)

ROW 7: Ch 5, sc in first ch-5 sp, [ch 5, sc in next ch-5 sp] 5 times, turn. (6 ch-5 sps)

ROWS 8–11: Ch 5, sc in first ch-5 sp, [ch 5, sc in next ch-5 sp] rep across to last ch-5 sp, leave last ch-5 sp unworked, turn. (2 ch-5 sps at the end of Row 11)

ROW 12: Rep Row 15 of first pineapple.

Third Pineapple

ROW 1: Rep Row 1 of 2nd pineapple.

ROW 2: Ch 4, sl st in top of end st of Row 2 of previous pineapple, 10 tr in ch-7 sp, tr in st at base of ch-7, turn. (12 tr)

ROW 3: Ch 5 (counts as first tr, ch 1), [tr in next tr, ch 1] 10 times, tr in 4th ch of turning ch-4, sl st in top of end st of Row 3 of previous pineapple, turn. (11 ch-1 sps)

ROW 4: Ch 4, sl st in top of end st of Row 4 of previous pineapple, ch 2, sk first ch-1 sp, [tr in next tr, ch 2] 10 times, tr in 4th ch of turning ch-5, turn. (11 ch-2 sps)

ROW 5: Ch 5, sc in first ch-2 sp, [ch 5, sc in next ch-2 sp] 10 times, ch 2, sl st in end sp on Row 5 of previous pineapple, turn. (11 ch-5 sps)

ROW 6: Ch 2, sc in first ch-5 sp, [ch 5, sc in next ch-5 sp] 9 times, turn. (9 ch-5 sps)

ROW 7: Ch 5, sc in first ch-5 sp, [ch 5, sc in next ch-5 sp] 8 times, ch 2, sl st in ch-5 sp at end of Row 7 on previous pineapple, turn. (9 ch-5 sps)

ROW 8: Ch 2, sc in first ch-5 sp, [ch 5, sc in next ch-5 sp] 7 times, turn. (7 ch-5 sps)

ROW 9: Ch 5, sc in first ch-5 sp, [ch 5, sc in next ch-5 sp] 6 times, turn. (7 ch-5 sps)

ROWS 10–14: Ch 5, sc in first ch-5 sp, [ch 5, sc in next ch-5 sp] rep across to last ch-5 sp, leave last ch-5 sp unworked, turn. (2 ch-5 sps at end of Row 14)

ROW 15: Rep Row 15 of first pineapple.

SECOND PINEAPPLE CORNER

First Pineapple

ROW 1: With WS facing, sk first 3 unworked ch-7 sps to the right of joining sp on Rnd 3 of next motif to the right, attach thread with a sl st in center ch of next sp, ch 7, sl st in center ch of last skipped sp, turn.

ROWS 2–5: Rep Rows 2–5 of first pineapple for first pineapple corner; at the end of Row 5, ch 2, sl st in end sp of Row 5 of 3rd pineapple on previous pineapple corner, turn. (11 ch-5 sps at the end of Row 5)

ROW 6: Ch 2, sc in first ch-5 sp, [ch 5, sc in next ch-5 sp] 9 times, turn. (9 ch-5 sps)

ROW 7: Ch 5, sc in first ch-5 sp, [ch 5, sc in next ch-5 sp] 8 times, ch 2, sl st in sp at end of Row 7 of 3rd pineapple on previous pineapple corner, turn. (9 ch-5 sps)

ROW 8: Ch 2, sc in first ch-5 sp, [ch 5, sc in next ch-5 sp] 7 times, turn. (7 ch-5 sps)

ROW 9: Ch 5, sc in first ch-5 sp, [ch 5, sc in next ch-5 sp] 6 times, turn. (7 ch-5 sps)

ROWS 10–14: Ch 5, sc in first ch-5 sp, [ch 5, sc in next ch-5 sp] rep across to last ch-5 sp, leave last ch-5 sp unworked, turn.

ROW 15: Rep Row 15 of first pineapple corner.

Second Pineapple

ROWS 1–12: Rep Rows 1–12 of 2nd pineapple for first pineapple corner.

Third Pineapple

ROWS 1–15: Rep Rows 1–15 of 3rd pineapple for first pineapple corner.

THIRD PINEAPPLE CORNER

Rep instructions for 2nd pineapple corner.

FOURTH PINEAPPLE CORNER

First Pineapple

ROWS 1–15: Rep Rows 1–15 of first pineapple.

Second Pineapple

ROWS 1–12: Rep Rows 1–12 of 2nd pineapple for 2nd pineapple corner.

Third Pineapple

ROWS 1–4: Rep Rows 1–4 of 3rd pineapple for 2nd pineapple corner; at the end of Row 4, ch 2, sl st in end sp of Row 5 of first pineapple on first pineapple corner, turn.

ROW 5: Ch 2, sc in first ch-2 sp, [ch 5, sc in next ch-2 sp] 10 times, ch 2, sl st in end sp on Row 5 of previous pineapple, turn.

ROW 6: Ch 2, sc in first ch-5 sp, [ch 5, sc in next ch-5 sp] 9 times, ch 2, sl st in end sp of Row 7 on first pineapple of first pineapple corner, turn. (9 ch-5 sps)

ROW 7: Ch 2, sc in first ch-5 sp, [ch 5, sc in next ch-5 sp] 8 times, ch 2, sl st in ch-5 sp at end of Row 7 on previous pineapple, turn. (8 ch-5 sps)

ROWS 8–15: Rep Rows 8–15 of 3rd pineapple for 2nd pineapple corner.

FILL-IN MOTIFS (*make 4*)

With RS facing, attach thread with a sl st in center ch of first unworked ch-7 sps on Rnd 3 of motif below 3rd pineapple on any pineapple corner, ch 6 (counts as first trtr), trtr in center ch of next ch-7 sp, qntr in joining st between motifs, trtr in center ch of each of next 2 unworked ch-7 sps on next motif, trtr in top of end st of Row 2 on next pineapple, trtr in top of end st of next row on same pineapple, qntr in joining st between 2 pineapples, trtr in top of end st of Row 3 on next pineapple, trtr in top of end st of next row on same pineapple, join in 6th ch of beg ch-6, fasten off. Rep for 3 rem sps.

BORDER

RND 1: With RS facing, attach thread with a sl st in lowest of 3 unworked ch-5 sps along right edge of first pineapple of any pineapple corner, beg cl in same sp, *ch 7, [cl in next unworked ch-5 sps, ch 7] twice, [{cl, ch 7} twice in next ch-5 sp at tip of pineapple] twice, cl in next unworked ch-5 sp on next side of same pineapple, [ch 7, cl in next unworked ch-5 sp] twice *, cl in first unworked ch-5 sp on 2nd pineapple, ch 7, cl in next unworked ch-5 sp, ch 7, [{ch, ch 7} twice in next ch-5 sp at tip of pineapple] twice, cl in next unworked ch-5 sp on next side of same pineapple, ch 7, sl in next unworked ch-5 sp, cl in first unworked ch-5 sp on 3rd pineapple, rep from * to *, cl in first unworked ch-5 sp on first pineapple of next pineapple corner, rep from * around, join in top of beg cl.

RND 2: Sl st in each of first 4 chs of first ch-7 sp, ch 7 (counts as first tr, ch 3 throughout), sc in next ch-7 sp, *[ch 7, sc in next ch-7 sp] 22 times, ch 3 **, tr in each of next 2 sps, ch 3, sc in next ch-7 sps *, rep from * around, ending last rep at **, ch 3, tr in next sp, join in 4th ch of beg ch-7.

RND 3: Ch 7, sc in next sp, *[ch 9, sc in next sp] 21 times, ch 3 **, tr in each of next 2 tr, ch 3, sc in next ch-7 sp, rep from * around, ending last rep at **, tr in next tr, join in 4th ch of beg ch-7.

RND 4: Ch 5 (counts as first tr, ch 1), sc in next sp, *[{ch 11, sc in next sp} 6 times, sc in next sp] twice, [ch 11, sc in next sp] 6 times, ch 1 **, tr in each of next 2 tr, ch 1, sc in next ch-9 sp, rep from * around, ending last rep at **, tr in next tr, join in 4th ch of beg ch-5.

RND 5: Sl st in next ch-1 sp, next sc and in each of next 5 chs of first ch-11 sp, ch 1, sc in same sp, *[ch 13, sc in next ch-11 sp] 5 times **, sc in next ch-11 sp, rep from * around, ending last rep at **, join in beg sc, fasten off. ✧

Left-Handed Filet Crochet

By Agnes Russell

If you're left-handed, here's a simple rule to remember: Right means left and left means right. Simply work first row from left to right.

Most filet-crocheted pieces will not be affected in appearance by left-handed crocheters. However, if the crocheted design has a definite right side (as with lettering or numbers), it will be backwards

Kaleidoscope Doily

The kaleidoscope is a favorite childhood toy. Its colorful, ever-changing, lacey patterns, reminiscent of crocheted lace, are probably responsible for the designer's fascination with doilies today. The pattern stitch for this doily is based on a swatch found in a collection of antique swatches made by an ambitious and talented crocheter many years ago. It's called briar rose lace and was very popular in 1917.

Design revised by Maggie Petsch Chasalow

SKILL LEVEL: INTERMEDIATE

SIZE
11½ inches in diameter

MATERIALS
➤ Clarks Big Ball 3 cord crochet cotton size 20 (300 yds per ball): 1 ball each pastels #165 (A) and new ecru #61 (B)
➤ Size 9 steel crochet hook or size needed to obtain gauge

GAUGE
Full motif = 2¾ inches in diameter
Check gauge to save time.

PATTERN NOTES
Weave in loose ends as work progresses.
Join rnds with a sl st unless otherwise stated.

PATTERN STITCHES
PICOT (P): Ch 4, sl st in top of last dc made.

JOINING P (JP): Ch 2, remove hook from lp, insert hook from RS to WS in indicated p on previous circle, pick up dropped lp, draw through st on hook, ch 2, sl st in top of last dc made.

V-ST: [Tr, ch 2, tr] in indicated st.

FULL MOTIF BORDER
First Circle
(RS): Beg at upper right corner of doily, ch 8, sl st to join to form a ring, ch 3 (counts as first dc

throughout), [2 dc, p, {3 dc, p} 7 times] in ring, join in 3rd ch of beg ch-3, fasten off. (24 dc; 8 p)

Second Circle
(RS): Ch 8, sl st to join to form a ring, ch 3, 2 dc in ring, jp to any p on first circle, [3 dc, p] 7 times in ring, join in 3rd ch of beg ch-3, fasten off. (24 dc; 8 p)

Third Circle
Rep instructions for 2nd circle, sk 2 p on inner edge of previous circle before working jp.

Rem Five Circles
Rep instructions for 3rd circle, joining last circle to p on previous circle and to corresponding p on first circle.

CENTER
With B, ch 8, sl st to join to form a ring, ch 8, sl st in first p on inner edge of any circle, ch 8, sl st in ring, [ch 8, sl st in first free p on inner edge of next circle, ch 8, sl st in ring] 7 times, fasten off.

PARTIAL MOTIF BORDER
First Motif
(RS): Ch 8, sl st to join to form a ring, ch 3, 2 dc in ring, jp on full motif border at point A on joining diagram, [3 dc, p] 7 times in ring, join in 3rd ch of beg ch-3, fasten off.

Rem Circles
Following joining diagram for placement, rep instructions for 3rd circle of full motif border as many times as necessary to complete partial motif.

CENTER
Rep instructions for center for full motif.

REM NINETEEN MOTIFS
Following joining diagram for placement of motifs and jp, work full and partial motifs as indicated.

CORNER FILL-IN MOTIFS *(make 4)*
With B, ch 8, sl st to join to form a ring, ch 8, with RS facing, sl st in p of circle at right-hand edge of any corner opening (point B on joining diagram), ch 8, sl st in ring, [ch 8, sl st in first free p of next circle, ch 8, sl st in ring] twice, ch 8, sk next free p on next circle, sl st in next p (point C on joining diagram), ch 8, sl st in ring, fasten off.

EDGING
RND 1 (RS): Attach B with sl st in p at point D on joining diagram, *[ch 5, sl st in next p] 3 times, ch 5, sl st in first free p on next motif, [ch 5, sl st in next free p] 3 times, V-st in next free p on circle between same motif and next motif, sl st in next free p on next motif, rep from * once, [{ch 5, sl st in next free p} 3 times, ch 5, sl st in next free p on next circle] twice, ch 5, sl st in next free p, ch 5, sl st in first ch of next ch-8, [ch 5, sk 2 ch, sl st in next ch] twice, ch 5, sl st in ch-8 ring, ch 5, sk next ch of next ch-8, sl st in next ch, [ch 5, sk 2 ch, sl st in next ch] twice, [ch 5, sl st in next free p] twice, ch 5 **, sl st in first free p on next circle, rep from * around, ending last rep at **, join in same p as beg sl st, fasten off.

RND 2 (RS): Attach A with a sl st in first ch-5 sp after joining, *[{ch 5, sl st in next sp} 6 times, ch 2, sk V-st sp, sl st in next ch-5 sp]

twice, [ch 5, sl st in next ch-5 sp] 19 times, rep from * around, ending with join in same sp as beg sl st, fasten off.

RND 3 (RS): Attach B with sl st in center of first ch-5 sp after joining, [ch 6, sl st] in same ch, [ch 5, sl st in center ch of next ch-5 , ch 5, {sl st, ch 6, sl st} in center ch of next ch-5] rep around, ending with ch 5, join in same ch as beg sl st, fasten off. ✧

Kaleidoscope Doily

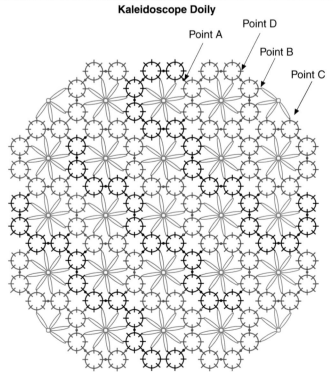

Point A
Point D
Point B
Point C

Plentiful Petals

Originally created in 1914, this lovely doily was first published as a bread-and-butter plate doily. Dozens of delicate petals radiate from the center of the doily, and are then framed by an exquisite edging. Crochet this masterpiece from yesterday to showcase your crocheting skills of today.

Design revised by Maggie Petsch Chasalow

SKILL LEVEL: INTERMEDIATE
SIZE: 13 inches in diameter

MATERIALS
➤ Crochet cotton size 20: 400 yds white
➤ Size 9 steel crochet hook or size needed to obtain gauge

GAUGE
Rnds 1–5 = 4 inches in diameter
Check gauge to save time.

PATTERN NOTES
Weave in loose ends as work progresses.

Join rnds with a sl st unless otherwise stated.

DOILY

RND 1 (RS): Ch 7, sl st to join to form a ring, ch 3 (counts as first dc throughout), 27 dc in ring, join in 3rd ch of beg ch-3. (28 dc)

RND 2: Ch 5 (counts as first dc, ch 2), sk next dc, [dc in next dc, ch 2, sk next dc] rep around, join in 3rd ch of beg ch-5. (14 ch-2 sps)

RND 3: [Ch 17, dc in 4th ch from hook, dc in each of next 13 chs, sl st in next dc] 13 times, ch 17, dc in 4th ch from hook, dc in each of next 13 chs, sl st in same st as joining (14 front petals made); working behind front petals for back petals, sl st in next ch-2 sp, [ch 17, dc in 4th ch from hook, dc in each of next 13 chs, sl st in next ch-2 sp] 13 times, ch 17, dc in 4th ch from hook, dc in each of next 13 chs, join in same sp as first back petal, fasten off. (28 petals)

RND 4: With RS facing, attach thread with a sl st in ch-3 sp at tip of first front petal, ch 5, [sl st in ch-3 sp at tip of next back petal, ch 5, sl st in ch-3 sp at tip of next front petal] rep around, ending with ch 5, join at base of beg ch-5. (28 ch-5 sps)

RND 5: Sl st into first ch-5 sp, ch 3, 5 dc in same sp, 6 dc in each rem ch-5 sp around, join in 3rd ch of beg ch-3, ch 1, turn. (28 groups 6-dc)

RND 6: Sl st in sp between last dc made and beg ch-3, ch 6 (counts as first dc, ch 3), *dc between 3rd and 4th dc of next 6-dc group, ch 3 **, dc between last dc of same 6-dc group and first dc of next 6-dc group, ch 3, rep from * around, ending last rep at **, join in 3rd ch of beg ch-3. (56 ch-3 sps)

RND 7: Sl st in each of first 2 chs of first ch-3 sp, ch 7 (counts as first dc, ch 4), [dc in center ch of next ch-3, ch 4] rep around, join in 3rd ch of beg ch-7. (56 ch-4 sps)

RND 8: Sl st in first ch-4 sp, *ch 14, dc in 4th ch from hook, dc in each of next 10 chs **, sl st in next ch-4 sp, rep from * around, ending last rep at **, join in same sp as beg sl st, fasten off. (56 petals)

RND 9: With RS facing, attach thread with a sl st in ch-3 sp at tip of any petal, ch 5, [sl st in ch-3 sp at tip of next petal, ch 5] rep around, join in base of beg ch-5. (56 ch-5 sps)

RND 10: Sl st into first ch-5 sp, ch 3, 4 dc in same sp, 5 dc in each rem sp around, join in 3rd ch of beg ch-3, ch 1, turn. (56 groups 5-dc)

RND 11: Sl st in sp between last dc made and beg ch-3, turn, *ch 8, sl st between next two 5-dc groups, ch 6 **, sl st between next two 5-dc groups, rep from * around to last 5-dc group, ending last rep at **, join in beg sl st. (28 ch-8 sps; 28 ch-6 sps)

RND 12: Sl st in first ch-8 sp, ch 1, 9 sc in same sp, *ch 5, sk ch-6 sp, 9 tr in next ch-8 sp, ch 5, sk next ch-6 sp **, 9 sc in next ch-8 sp, rep from * around, ending last rep at ** join in beg sc. (14 groups 9-tr)

RND 13: Sl st in next sc, ch 1, sc in same st, sc in each of next 6 sc, *ch 4, [dc in next tr, ch 1] 8 times, dc in next tr, ch 4 **, sk first sc of next 9-sc group, sc in each of next 7 sc, rep from * around, ending last rep at **, join in beg sc.

RND 14: Sl st in next sc, ch 1, sc in same st, sc in each of next 4 sc, *ch 4, [dc in next dc, ch 2] 8 times, dc in next dc, ch 4 **, sk first sc of next 7-sc group, sc in each of next 5 sc, rep from * around, ending last rep at **, join in beg sc.

RND 15: Sl st in next sc, ch 1, sc in same st, sc in each of next 2 sc, *ch 4, [dc in next dc, ch 3] 8 times, dc in next dc, ch 4 **, sk *Continued on page 34*

Pansy Doily

In the late 1940s and early 1950s floral doilies were all the rage. Pansy doilies were particularly sought after and pattern booklets kept coming out with new versions of this old favorite. The classic doily featured here first appeared in a late 1940s instruction booklet. These lovely, colorful pansies look so real they'll bring a touch of springtime to whatever room you put them in.

Design revised by Maggie Petsch Chasalow

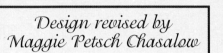

SKILL LEVEL: INTERMEDIATE

SIZE:
13¼ inches in diameter

MATERIALS
- Crochet cotton size 10: 225-yd ball white (A), 150-yd ball each shaded purples (B), shaded yellows (C) and green (D)
- Size 7 steel crochet hook or size needed to obtain gauge

GAUGE
Rnds 1 and 2 = 1½ inches in diameter
Check gauge to save time.

PATTERN NOTES
Weave in loose ends as work progresses.

Join rnds with a sl st unless otherwise stated.

PATTERN STITCHES
SPLIT TR CL: Holding back on hook last lp of each st, [3 tr in same sp] twice, yo, draw through all 7 lps on hook.

SHELL: [3 tr, ch 3, 3 tr] in indicated st or sp.

2-TR CL: Holding back last lp of each st, 2 tr in indicated st or sp, yo, draw through all 3 lps on hook.

PICOT (P): Ch 3, sl st in top of last 2-tr cl made.

LEAF: [Ch 4, 2-tr cl, p, ch 4, sl st] in indicated st or sp.

DOILY
RND 1 (RS): With A, ch 8, sl st to join to form a ring, ch 4 (counts as first dc, ch 1), [dc in ring, ch 1] 15 times, join in 3rd ch of beg ch-4. (16 ch-1 sps)

RND 2: Sl st into first sp, ch 4 (counts as first tr throughout), 2 tr in same sp, ch 5, [sk next sp, 3 tr in next sp, ch 5] rep around, join in 4th ch of beg ch-4. (8 ch-5 sps)

RND 3: [Sl st, ch 4, 2 tr] in next tr, *ch 3, sc in center ch of next ch-5, ch 3 **, 3 tr in center tr of next 3-tr group, rep from * around, ending last rep at **, join in 4th ch of beg ch-4.

RND 4: [Sl st, ch 1, sc] in next tr, *ch 7, split tr cl, ch 7 **, sc in center tr of next 3-tr group, rep from * around, ending last rep at **, join in beg sc.

RND 5: Ch 9 (counts as first tr, ch 5), *sc in next sp, ch 7, sc in next sp **, ch 5, tr in next sc, ch 5, rep from * around, ending last rep at **, ch 2, dc in 4th ch of beg ch-9 to form last ch-5 sp.

RND 6: Ch 1, sc in sp just formed, *ch 5, sc in next sp, [ch 9, sc in next sp] twice, rep from * around, ending with ch 5, sc in next sp, ch 9, sc in next sp, ch 4, dtr in beg sc to form last ch-9 sp.

RND 7: Ch 1, sc in sp just formed, *ch 3, shell in center ch of next ch-5, ch 3, sc in next sp **, ch 7, sc in next sp, rep from * around, ending last rep at **, ch 3, tr in beg sc to form last ch-7 sp. (8 shells)

RND 8: Ch 1, sc in sp just formed, *ch 8, sc in next ch-3 sp, ch 8, sc in next shell sp, ch 8, sc in next ch-3 sp **, ch 8, sc in next ch-7 sp, rep from * around, ending last rep at **, ch 4, tr in beg sc to form last ch-8 sp. (32 ch-8 sps)

RND 9: Ch 1, sc in sp just formed, [ch 9, sc in next ch-8 sp] rep around, ending ch 4, dtr in beg sc to from last ch-9 sp. (32 ch-9 sps)

RND 10: Ch 1, sc in sp just formed, *ch 4, shell in center ch of next ch-9, ch 4, sc in next ch-9 sp **, [ch 9, sc in next ch-9 sp] twice, rep from * around, ending last rep at **, ch 9, sc in next ch-9 sp, ch 4, dtr in beg sc to form last ch-9 sp.

RND 11: Ch 1, sc in sp just formed, *ch 8, sc in next ch-4 sp, ch 8, sc in next shell sp, ch 8, sc in next ch-4 sp **, [ch 8, sc in next ch-9 sp] twice, rep from * around, ending last rep at **, ch 9, sc in next ch-8 sp, ch 4, tr in beg sc to form last ch-8 sp. (40 ch-8 sps)

RND 12: Rep Rnd 9. (40 ch-9 sps)

RND 13: Ch 3, 2 dc in last tr made, ch 6, [3 dc in center ch of next ch-9, ch 6] rep around, join in 3rd ch of beg ch-3.

Continued page 34

Pansy Doily continued from previous page

RND 14: [Sl st, ch 4, 2 tr] in next dc, *ch 3, sc in next sp, ch 3 **, 3 tr in center dc of next 3-dc group, rep from * around, ending last rep at **, join in 4th ch of beg ch-4.

RND 15: [Sl st, ch 1, sc] in next tr *[ch 7, split tr cl, ch 7, sc in next sp, ch 5, sc in next sp] twice, ch 7, split tr cl, ch 7 **, sc in center tr of next 3-tr group, rep from * around, ending last rep at **, join in beg sc, fasten off.

PANSY *(make 8 each B & C)*
RND 1: Ch 7, sl st to join to form a ring, ch 3 (counts as first dc throughout), [2 dc, ch 7, {3 dc, ch 7} 4 times] in ring, join in 3rd ch of beg ch-3. (5 ch-7 sps)

RND 2: [Sl st, ch 1, sc] in next dc, sk next dc, [16 dc in next sp, sk next dc, sc in next dc] 3 times, ch 4, [dtr {ch 1, dtr} 11 times, {ch 1, tr} twice, {ch 1, dc} twice] in next sp, sk next dc, sc in next dc, [dc, ch 1, dc, {ch 1, tr} twice, {ch 1, dtr} 12 times] in next sp, ch 4, join in beg sc, fasten off.

BORDER
RND 1: With RS facing, attach D with a sl st in center ch of first ch-5 on Rnd 15 after joining st, leaf in same st, *ch 5, 2 dc in tip of next split tr cl, ch 1, sl st in 8th dc of middle 16-dc petal on any pansy made with B, ch 1, 2 dc in same st as last 2 dc made, ch 5, [sl st, petal in center ch of next ch-5, ch 7, sc in top of next split tr cl, ch 4, sl st in 4th dc of middle 16-dc petal on any pansy made with C, ch 3, 2 dc in next sc of

Rnd 15, ch 1, sk 3 sts on same pansy, sl st in next dc, ch 1, 2 dc in same sc on Rnd 15 as last 2 dc made, ch 3, sk next 3 sts on same pansy, sl st in next dc, ch 4, sc in next split tr cl on Rnd 15, ch 7 **, [sl st, leaf] in center ch of next ch-5, rep from * around, ending last rep at **, join in st at base of first leaf, fasten off.

RND 2: With RS facing, attach A with a sl st in sc between 2 large petals at top of any pansy, ch 1, sc in same st, *[ch 3, sc in next ch-1 sp] 15 times, ch 3, sc in next ch-4 sp on same pansy, ch 3, sc in next ch-4 sp on next pansy, [ch 3, sc in next ch-1 sp] 15 times, ch 3 **, sc in next sc between petals, rep from * around, ending last rep at **, join in beg sc, fasten off. ✧

Plentiful Petals continued from page 30

first sc of next 5-sc group, sc in each of next 3 sc, rep from * around, ending last rep at **, join in beg sc.

RND 16: Sl st in next sc, ch 1, sc in same st, *ch 4, [dc in next dc, ch 3] 8 times, dc in next dc, ch 4 **, sk first sc of next 3-sc group, sc in next sc, rep from * around, ending last rep at **, join in beg sc.

RND 17: Ch 5 (counts as first tr, ch 1), *dc in next dc, [ch 4, dc in

next dc] 8 times, ch 1 **, tr in next sc, ch 1, rep from * around, ending last rep at **, join in 4th ch of beg ch-5.

RND 18: Sl st in next ch, next dc, each of next 4 chs and next dc, ch 8 (counts as first dc, ch 5), dc in next dc, [ch 5, dc in next dc] 5 times, *ch 1, sk next dc, next tr and next dc, dc in next dc, [ch 5, dc in next dc] 6 times, rep from * around, ending with ch 1, join in 3rd ch of beg ch-8.

RND 19: Sl st in each of first 2 chs of first ch-5, ch 1, sc in same ch-5 sp, [ch 6, sc in next ch-5 sp] 5 times, *ch 6, sl st in next ch-1 sp **, [ch 6, sc in next ch-5 sp] 6 times, rep from * around, ending last rep at **, ch 3, dc in beg sc to form last ch-6 sp.

RND 20: [Ch 10, sl st in 6th ch from hook, ch 4, sl st in next ch-6 sp] rep around, ending with ch 4, join in last dc of last rnd, fasten off. ✧

Hairpin Crochet

By Maggie Petsch Chasalow

What prompted that first Victorian lady or gentleman to wrap some crochet thread around a hairpin and proceed to work the first piece of hairpin lace? We will never know, but fortunately for us, she or he did and hairpin, that often under-utilized craft, remains with us today.

Early hairpin crochet was worked, as the name implies, on milady's hairpin. Later on, hairpin forks of wood, metal, bone or tortoise shell were made specifically for the purpose of making hairpin lace. These early hairpin forks were generally in the shape of a real hairpin, an elongated "U-shape", but nowadays most hairpin forks consist of two vertical steel rods held together with adjustable horizontal plastic bars. When hairpins were no longer in fashion, a 1920s needlework magazine instructed crocheters how to make their own hairpin forks by holding "the middle of an ordinary knitting needle over a gas-jet or lamp until it loses its temper sufficiently to bend; then bring the ends together over some object of required size and plunge the heated part into cold water."

The circumstances surrounding my introduction to hairpin are worth mentioning, I think. It was one of those instances where I learned how to do something only because I was forced to, a situation probably familiar to all of us. I was taking a crochet correspondence course from a lovely and talented lady named Pauline Turner, and hairpin crochet was one of the requirements. I approached it with the attitude, "I'll do this and get it over with because I have no choice, but I have no desire to learn hairpin at this point in my life. It's one of those esoteric crafts that are for somebody else, not for me, and I'll probably never use it again."

Funny thing is, I took to it almost as soon as I put thread to hook and frame. It was delightful to watch the hairpin lace strip climbing up the frame (reminded me a little of a centipede, particularly when taken off the frame, allowing its little "legs" to go free!), and there are so many ways of joining the strips and adding to them to make anything from the most delicate, cobweblike lace to a warm and wooly scarf or afghan.

My insatiable curiosity about needlework history led me on a fascinating journey through old needlework magazines for the earliest mention of hairpin I could find: *Embroidery Magazines,* April 1910, page 29, "About 50 years ago, Maltese lace, or hairpin crochet as it is sometimes called, was a decided fad. Since then it seems to have been entirely forgotten. Last year it was revived and this coming season will probably see a return of its past vogue. The process is very simple and produces an effect of daintiness and lacy lightness." Antique shops, flea markets, and auctions are ideal places to find actual samples of old hairpin work and the original implements they were worked on. To this end, I recently made an absolutely mind-boggling find—a long-deceased sister-in-crochet's treasure box replete with genuine Victorian hairpins (the kind meant to be used in the hair, not specifically designed for lace-making) on which some incomplete hairpin work was still attached, and an original paper packet of hairpins that must have been sold in the late 1800s.

If you've been thinking about developing your crochet skills further and hairpin lace is not in your current repertoire, now is as good a time as any to learn it! And if it's something you have already thought of and rejected, now is as good a time as any to reconsider! You may be positively delighted with your newly found skill. ✧

Chapter Two

Keepsake Filet

In days gone by, much of a lady's worth was determined by the quality of her needlework. Many young girls began crocheting items for their hope chests at a tender age. Young ladies practiced their needlework by creating samplers of their family name or the alphabet. This collection of filet patterns includes samplers and an assortment of pretty and practical items to be used around the home.

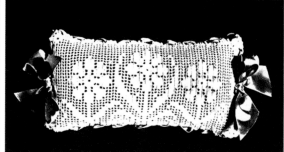

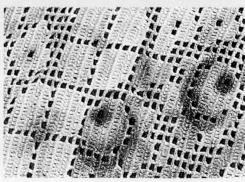

Briar Roses

This dainty table mat or tray cover evokes the garden parties of long ago, held in courtyards on summer evenings amid the sweet fragrances of briar roses.

SKILL LEVEL: INTERMEDIATE

SIZE
51½ x 32½ inches

MATERIALS
➤ Crochet cotton size 10: 6 balls (175 yds per ball) peach
➤ Size 9 steel crochet hook or size needed to obtain gauge

GAUGE
10 dc = 1 inch; 3 dc rows = 1 inch
Check gauge to save time.

PATTERN NOTES
Weave in loose ends as work progresses.

Beg at A-B on the graph for first 14 sps. The 2nd row widens 3 sps at each end. The lacet and bars beg in the 4th row. Continue to follow graph to C-D which is the center row of the mat.

For 2nd half of mat, turn graph around and work into the center row the row beside it, beg it at end farthest from your thread. This is to bring the little leaf at the D end to finish the spray at the C end and give a proper reverse of design.

PATTERN STITCHES
BLOCK (BL): 3 tr.

BL OVER BL: Tr in next 3 tr.

BL OVER SP: 2 tr in sp, tr in next tr.

BL OVER A BAR: 3–5 tr in bar, tr in next st or tr.

SPACE (SP): Ch 2, sk 2 sts, tr in next st.

BEG SP: Ch 6, sk 2 sts, tr in next st or tr.

SP OVER A BL: Ch 2, sk 2 tr, tr in next tr.

SP OVER A SP: Ch 2, tr in next tr.

SP OVER A BAR: Ch 2, sk 2 chs, tr in next ch or tr.

SP INC AT BEG OF ROW: Ch 8, tr in next tr.

ADDITIONAL SP INC AT BEG OF ROW: Ch 8 for first sp, ch 3 for each additional sp.

SP INC AT END OF ROW: Ch 2, dtr in base of tr just made.

ADDITIONAL SP INC AT END OF ROW: Rep sp inc at end of row for desired number of sp inc needed.

LACET: Ch 3, sk 2 sts, dc in next st, ch 3, sk 2 sts, tr in next tr.

BAR: Ch 5, sk 5 sts, tr in next st or tr.

DTR: Yo hook 3 times, insert hook in indicated st, yo, draw up a lp, [yo, draw through 2 lps on hook] 4 times.

DOILY
ROW 1: Beg at lower edge of graph, ch 47, tr in 8th ch from hook (1 sp), [ch 2, sk 2 ch, tr in next ch] 13 times, turn. (14 sps)

ROW 2: Ch 13, tr in 8th ch from hook (first sp), ch 2, sk 2 ch, tr in next ch, ch 2, sk 2 ch, tr in next tr (3 sp inc at beg of row), tr in each of next 43 sts, ch 2, dtr in same st as last tr was made, [ch 2, dtr into middle twist of the previous dtr]

twice (3 sp inc at end of row), turn. (3 sps; 14 bls; 3 sps)

ROW 3: Ch 10, tr in 8th ch from hook, ch 2, sk 2 ch (2 sp inc at beg), tr in each of next 61 sts, ch 2, dtr in same st as last tr was made, ch 2, dtr in middle twist of previous dtr, turn. (2 sps; 20 bls; 2 sps)

ROW 4: Ch 10, tr in 8th ch from hook, ch 2, sk 2 ch, tr in each of next 16 sts, [1 lacet, 1 bar] 3 times, 1 lacet, tr in each of next 16 sts, ch 2, dtr in same st as last tr was made, ch 2, dtr in middle twist of previous dtr, turn. (2 sps; 5 bls; alternate 4 lacets and 3 bars; 5 bls, 2 sps)

Continue following graph (page 45) until you have completed 78th row which is center of mat, then reverse for other half.

BORDER
When the filet is finished, work a rnd of dc around entire outer edge, placing 3 of 4 dc into each sp as needed to keep work flat, with a p of ch 5, sl st in first ch of ch-5 after each 7th dc, fasten off. ✧

Continued on page 45

Pretty Flowers

Pretty flowers accompany you in your sitting room encouraging beauty and femininity to blossom. This pattern was originally stitched in size 40 crochet cotton to create an old-style pincushion.

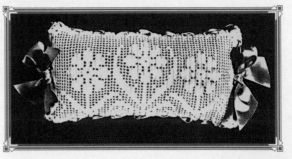

SIZE:

16 inches x 9 inches

MATERIALS

➤ Crochet cotton size 20: 350 yds light blue

➤ Size 10 steel crochet hook or size needed to obtain gauge

GAUGE

13 dc and 5 rows = 1 inch

Check gauge to save time.

PATTERN NOTES

Work over loose ends as work progresses.

Work first 2 rows of 9 end pieces beg at right edge working top to bottom.

PATTERN STITCHES

SPACE (SP): Ch 2, sk 2 sts, dc in next st.

BLOCK (BL): Dc in each of next 3 sts.

DEC 1 BL AT BEG OF A ROW: Sl st across into 4th st.

DEC 1 BL AT THE END OF ROW: Work across row to within last 4 sts of last block, turn.

INC 1 BL AT END OF ROW: Yo, draw up lp in top of turning ch where last dc was worked, yo, draw through 1 lp on hook (base st), [yo, draw through 2 lps on hook] twice (dc), *yo, draw up lp in base st, yo, draw through 1 lp on hook for next base st, yo, draw through 2 lps on hook] twice, rep from * once for 1 bl inc.

FILET PIECE

Note: While working top, center and bottom sections, use care when joining that each section is facing in the proper direction.

Top Section

ROW 1 (RS): Ch 9, dc in 4th ch from hook, dc in each of next 5 chs, turn. (2 bls)

ROW 2 (WS): Ch 5, dc in 4th ch from hook, dc in next ch, dc in next dc, ch 2, sk next 2 sts, dc in

each of next 4 sts, inc 1 bl at end of row, fasten off. (1 bl; 1 sp; 2 bls)

Center Section *(make 7)*

ROW 1 (RS): Ch 6, dc in 4th ch from hook, dc in each of next 2 chs, turn. (1 bl)

ROW 2 (WS): Ch 5, dc in 4th ch from hook, dc in next ch, dc in each of next 4 dc, inc 1 bl at end of row, to join pieces, ch 2, sl st in 5th ch of previous section, fasten off.

Bottom Section

ROW 1 (RS): Ch 9, dc in 4th ch from hook, dc in each of next 5 chs, turn. (2 bls)

ROW 2 (WS): Ch 5, dc in 4th ch from hook, dc in each of next 4 sts, ch 2, sk next 2 sts, dc in next st, inc 1 bl at end of row, ch 2, sl st in 5th ch of previous section, fasten off.

Main Section

Note: Work this row in each st across, including each ch-2 sp between sections.

ROW 3 (RS): Attach cotton in end dc of top section, ch 3 (counts as first dc throughout), dc in each of next 3 sts, ch 2, sk next 2 sts, dc in each of next 100 sts, ch 2, sk next 2 sts, dc in each of next 4 sts, turn.

ROW 4 (WS): Sl st into 4th dc, ch 3, dc in each of next 6 sts, ch 2, sk next 2 sts, dc in each of next 4 sts, [{ch 2, sk next 2 sts, dc in next st}

3 times, dc in each of next 3 sts] 7 times, ch 2, sk next 2 sts, dc in each of next 7 sts, leaving last bl unworked, turn.

ROW 5 (RS): Sl st into 4th dc, ch 3, dc in each of next 6 sts, [ch 2, sk next 2 sts, dc in next st] 29 times, dc in each of next 6 sts, leaving last bl unworked, turn.

ROW 6 (WS): Ch 5, dc in 4th ch from hook, dc in next ch, dc in each of next 4 sts, [ch 2, sk next 2 sts, dc in next st] 7 times, dc in each of next 6 sts, [ch 2, sk next 2 sts, dc in next st] 22 times, dc in each of next 3 sts, inc 1 bl at end of row, turn.

ROW 7 (RS): Ch 5, dc in 4th ch from hook, dc in next ch, dc in each of next 7 dc, [ch 2, sk next 2 sts, dc in next st] 21 times, dc in each of next 3 sts, [ch 2, sk next 2 sts, dc in next st] twice, dc in each of next 3 sts, [ch 2, sk next 2 sts, dc in next st] twice, dc in each of next 3 sts, [ch 2, sk next 2 sts, dc in next st] 3 times, dc in each of next 6 sts, inc 1 bl at end of row turn.

ROWS 8–67: Following graph, turn at the end of each row.

ROWS 68 & 69: Follow graph beg with bottom section on WS, work across each two row section, fasten off at end of each section, sk next 2 sts, attach cotton and rep until all nine sections are completed. ✦

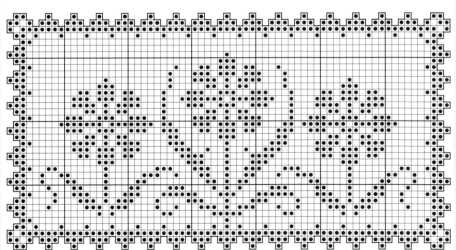

ABC Floral Sampler

The sampler is one of the best-loved keepsakes of the olden days, and is often the first thing that comes to mind when thinking of vintage needlework. Create your own heirloom showpiece with this beautiful pattern inspired by samplers of old.

Design by Nancy Hearne

SKILL LEVEL: INTERMEDIATE

SIZE
14½ x 19½ inches

MATERIALS
➤ DMC Cebelia cotton size 20 (50 grams per ball): 2 balls ecru, 1 ball each sage #524, rose #224 and dark rose #223
➤ Size 10 steel crochet hook or size needed to obtain gauge

GAUGE
16 sts = 1 inch; 5½ rows = 1 inch
Check gauge to save time.

PATTERN NOTES
Weave in loose ends as work progresses.

Designer used bobbins in the following colors to stitch the model: 9 bobbins sage and 8 bobbins rose.

PATTERN STITCHES
BLOCK (BL): 3 dc.

SPACE (SP): Ch 2, sk 2sts, dc in next dc.

POPCORN (PC): 5 dc in indicated st or sp, draw up a lp, remove hook, insert hook in top of first dc of 5-dc group, pick up dropped lp, draw through st on hook, ch 1 to lock.

PUFF: [Yo, insert hook in sp or st, yo, draw up a lp] 4 times, yo, draw lp through, yo, draw through all lps on hook, ch 1 to lock.

LACET: Ch 3, sk next 2 sts, sc in next st, ch 3, sk next 2 sts, dc in next dc.

BAR: Ch 5, sk next 5 sts, dc in next st or dc.

BL OVER BL: Dc in next 3 dc.

BL OVER SP: 2 dc in sp, dc in next dc.

SP OVER BL: Ch 2, sk next 2 dc, dc in next dc.

SP OVER SP: Ch 2, dc in next dc.

SP OVER PC: Ch 2, sk pc, dc in next dc.

SP OVER PUFF: Ch 2, sk puff, dc in next dc.

PC OVER SP: Pc in ch-2 sp, dc in next dc.

PC OVER PC: Pc in top of pc, dc in next dc.

PC OVER PUFF: Pc in top of puff, dc in next dc.

STARTING PUFF: Ch 3, puff in indicated st or sp, dc in next st or dc.

PUFF OVER SP: Puff in ch-2 sp, dc in next dc.

PUFF OVER PC: Puff in top of pc, dc in next dc.

PUFF OVER PUFF: Puff in top of puff, dc in next dc.

PUFF INC AT BEG OF ROW: Ch 5, puff in 5th ch from hook, dc in next dc.

ADDITIONAL PUFF INC AT BEG OF ROW: Ch 5 for first puff, ch 3 for each additional puff inc.

PUFF INC AT END OF ROW: Dc in top of turning ch-3 of previous row, [yo hook, insert hook in base of dc just made] 5 times, yo, draw through all lps on hook, ch 1 to lock, yo, insert hook in base of puff just completed, yo, draw up a lp, [yo, draw through 2 lps] twice.

ADDITIONAL PUFF INC AT END OF ROW: Rep puff inc at end of row for desired number of puffs.

PUFF DEC AT BEG OF ROW: Sl st across top of puff and in next dc.

PUFF DEC AT END OF ROW: Leave last puff of previous row unworked.

OPENWORK: Unworked areas; in areas of openwork, work section of short rows connecting these sections with next long row on graph.

COLOR CHANGE: Change colors within dc as follows: with first color, yo, insert hook in st, yo, draw up a lp, yo, draw through 2 lps on hook, with 2nd color, yo, draw through last 2 lps on hook.

Work dc over dropped cotton, carrying it in the st to its next working area. When a color is finished for the row, wrap over working cotton from RS to WS to position for the next row.

To carry a dropped color through sps, wrap and form sp sts around the dropped cotton. Carry color through 1–3 sps per color section per row, attach new strand of color where desired. It is always wise to work isolated areas with separate strands of cotton.

SHORT ROWS *(make 9)*
ROW 1 (RS): With ecru, ch 9, puff in 5th ch from hook, dc in next ch, sk 1 ch, puff in next ch, dc in last ch, turn.

ROW 2: Puff inc at beg of row, 2 sps over 2 sps, puff inc at end of row, turn.

ROWS 3 & 4: Follow graph, utilizing techniques. At the end of Row 4, fasten off.

At the end of 9th section of short rows, do not fasten off, turn.

ROWS 5–20: Continue as estab-

Continued on page 44

ABC Sampler

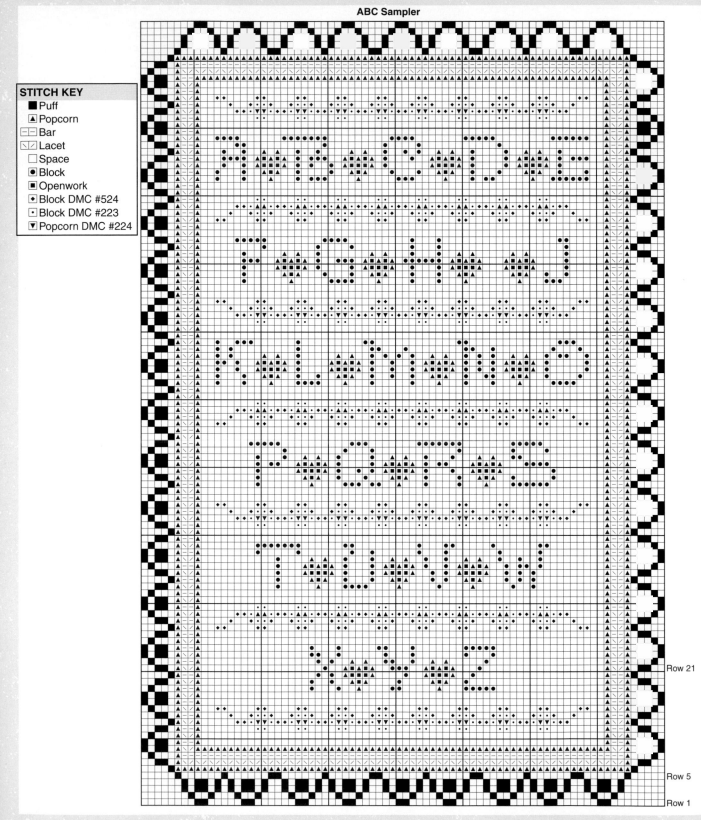

STITCH KEY
- ■ Puff
- ▲ Popcorn
- ⊟ Bar
- ⊠ Lacet
- □ Space
- ● Block
- ■ Openwork
- ◉ Block DMC #524
- ⊡ Block DMC #223
- ▽ Popcorn DMC #224

Row 21

Row 5

Row 1

lished, following graph and utiliz-ing techniques.

ROW 21: Connecting short rows forming openwork hearts: Follow graph to heart. Work suspended heart shaping, pc over pc, ch 9, in 4th ch from hook work 4 dc, draw up a lp, remove hook, counting from pc previously made, insert hook in 3rd ch from that pc and 1 dc of 4 just made, draw lp through and ch 1, yo hook, insert in base of pc just made, yo and draw through 1 lp, [yo, draw through 2 lps] twice, ch 2, dc in next dc (of next section) pc over pc, continue as established, following graph and utilizing techniques.

ROWS 22–112: Follow graph, utilizing techniques.

ROWS 113–116: Work short rows to shape top edge. At the end of last rep, fasten off. ✧

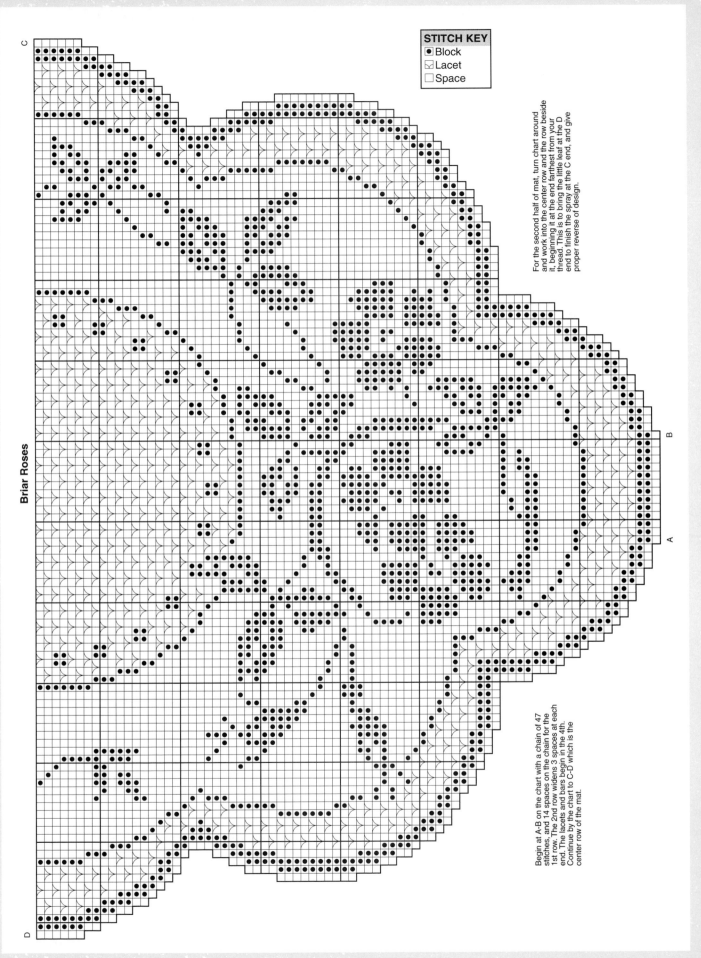

STITCH KEY
- ● Block
- ☑ Lacet
- ☐ Space

Briar Roses

For the second half of mat, turn chart around and work into the center row and the row beside it, beginning it at the end farthest from your thread. This is to bring the little leaf at the D end to finish the spray at the C end, and give proper reverse of design.

Begin at A-B on the chart with a chain of 47 stitches, and 14 spaces on the chain for the 1st row. The 2nd row widens 3 spaces at each end. The lacets and bars begin in the 4th. Continue by the chart to C-D which is the center row of the mat.

Design revised by
Agnes Russell

SKILL LEVEL: BEGINNER

SIZE:

TABLECLOTH:
52 x 69 inches

BLOCK: 17 inches square

MATERIALS
➤ J&P Coats Knit-Cro-Sheen crochet cotton size 10 (325 yds per ball): 16 balls natural #62
➤ Size 6 steel crochet hook or size needed to obtain gauge
➤ Tapestry needle

GAUGE
9 tr = 1 inch; 7 rnds = 3 inches
Check gauge to save time.

Square-A-Day Tablecloth

Combining granny square-style motifs with a fine thread and an elegant openwork design, this handsome tablecloth draws on several of the most time-honored crochet traditions. Enjoy creating an old-fashioned masterpiece, one square at a time.

PATTERN NOTES
Weave in loose ends as work progresses.

Sl st to join each rnd in indicated st.

Tablecloth can be made any size desired. Each square requires one ball of cotton. For larger cloth, allow sufficient cotton for edging.

BLOCK (make 12)
RND 1 (RS): Starting at center, ch 10, sl st to join to form a ring, ch 4 (counts as first tr throughout), 4 tr in ring, ch 7, [5 tr in ring, ch 7] 3 times, join in 4th ch of beg ch-4.

RND 2: Ch 4, tr in each of next 4 tr, *[4 tr, ch 7, 4 tr] in corner ch-7 sp **, tr in each of next 5 tr, rep from * around, ending last rep at **, join in 4th ch of beg ch-4.

RND 3: Ch 7 (counts as first tr, ch-3 throughout), *sk 3 tr, tr in next tr, ch 3, sk 3 tr, [tr, ch 7, tr] in 4th ch of ch-7, ch 3, tr in next tr, ch 3, sk 3 tr **, tr in next tr, ch 3, rep from * around, ending last rep at **, join in 4th ch of beg ch-7.

RND 4: Ch 7, tr in next tr, ch 3, *tr in next tr, 3 tr in next ch-3 sp, tr in next tr, [4 tr, ch 7, 4 tr] in next ch-7 sp, tr in next tr, 3 tr in next

ch-3 sp **, [tr in next tr, ch 2] 3 times, rep from * around, ending last rep at **, tr in next tr, ch 3, join in 4th ch of beg ch-7.

RND 5: Ch 7, *sk next ch-3 sp, tr in next tr, 3 tr in next ch-3 sp, tr

Tablecloth Square

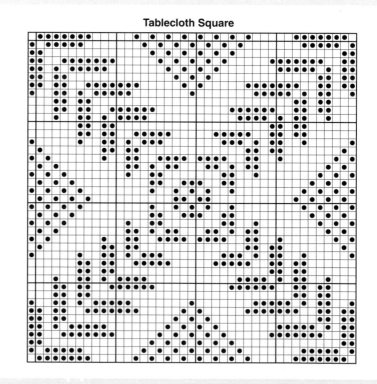

in each tr to next corner ch-7 sp, [4 tr, ch 7, 4 tr] in corner ch-7 sp, tr in each tr to next ch sp, 3 tr in next ch-3 sp **, tr in next tr, ch 3, rep from * around, ending last rep

Continued on page 50

Crochet Tidy

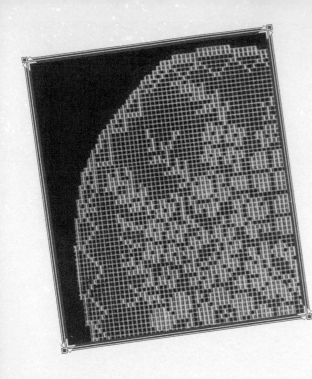

During the 1800s through the early 1900s, a "tidy" was a kind of antimacassar meant for wooden, or nonupholstered, chairs.

An unusual accessory by modern custom, this tidy will add charm to your kitchen or dining room, whether adorning a chair or a table.

SKILL LEVEL: INTERMEDIATE

SIZE:
16¼W inches x 22½H inches

MATERIALS
➤ DMC Cebelia crochet cotton size 20: 2 balls white
➤ Size 9 steel crochet hook or size needed to obtain gauge
➤ Plastic foam plate
➤ Acrylic paint: white, rose, yellow, lavender, and green
➤ Textile medium
➤ 2-inch stiff-bristle brush
GAUGE
13 dc and 5 rows = 1 inch
Check gauge to save time.

PATTERN NOTES
Weave in loose ends as work progresses.

Count the number of blocks in the extreme width and multiply by 3, with the addition of 1 for the length of the chain; and then select a cotton which will bring the tidy to the size you require; our sample is crocheted with size 20 cotton. In an oval tidy, you do not commence on a chain of the full length, but on one that will make the number of blocks at the

left side. In this tidy, as there are 12 blocks, ch 37, fasten off. In the next row, as there are 6 blocks extra on each side, ch 18, then work on the ch for the 12 closed blocks; then finish with ch 18, fasten off.

PATTERN STITCHES
BLOCK (BL): 3 dc.

SPACE (SP): Ch 2, sk 2 sts, dc in next st.

INC 1 BL AT BEG OF A ROW: Ch 5, dc in 4th ch from hook, dc in next ch.

INC 2 BLS AT BEG OF A ROW: Ch 8, dc in 4th ch from hook, dc in each of next 4 chs.

TIDY
FOUNDATION: Beg at left edge of tidy, ch 37, fasten off.

ROW 1: Ch 18, pick up ch 37, dc in each ch across (12 blocks), ch 18, fasten off, turn.

ROW 2: Ch 12, dc in each of next 18 chs (6 blocks), dc in each of next 4 dc, [ch 2, sk 2 sts, dc in next dc] 10 times, dc in each of next 3 dc, dc in each of next 18 chs, fasten off, turn.

ROW 3: Ch 12, dc in next 4 dc, [ch 2, sk 2 sts, dc in next st] 5 times, dc in each of next 6 sts, [ch 2, sk 2 sts, dc in next st] 8 times, dc in next 6 sts, [ch 2, sk 2 sts, dc in next st] 5 times, dc in each of

next 3 sts, ch 12, fasten off, turn.

ROWS 4–75: Continue to inc blocks by fastening off and ch number of chs required for blocks at beg and end of row until only 1 or 2 block incs are needed, then simply make number of required chs of blocks needed. Follow graph working sps and bls as indicated. Work over loose ends whenever possible.

PAINTING FILET DOILIES
On a plastic foam plate, mix a puddle of rose acrylic paint with an equal amount of textile medium. Mix a second puddle of white acrylic paint with textile medium, right next to first puddle. Drag white paint into rose paint and blend slightly to form streaks of color. Dip 2-inch stiff bristle into cup of water, then into blended paint, and back into water. Pounce brush on solid flower areas of filet crochet until color is desired depth. Mix more white into rose, blending slightly, then pounce another flower area of doily. Repeat with different colors such as rose, lavender, yellow and shades of green, to paint different flowers and leaves. Not mixing paint thoroughly will automatically produce shadows and shading on the painted doily. Let dry thoroughly before displaying. ✧

Continued on page 50

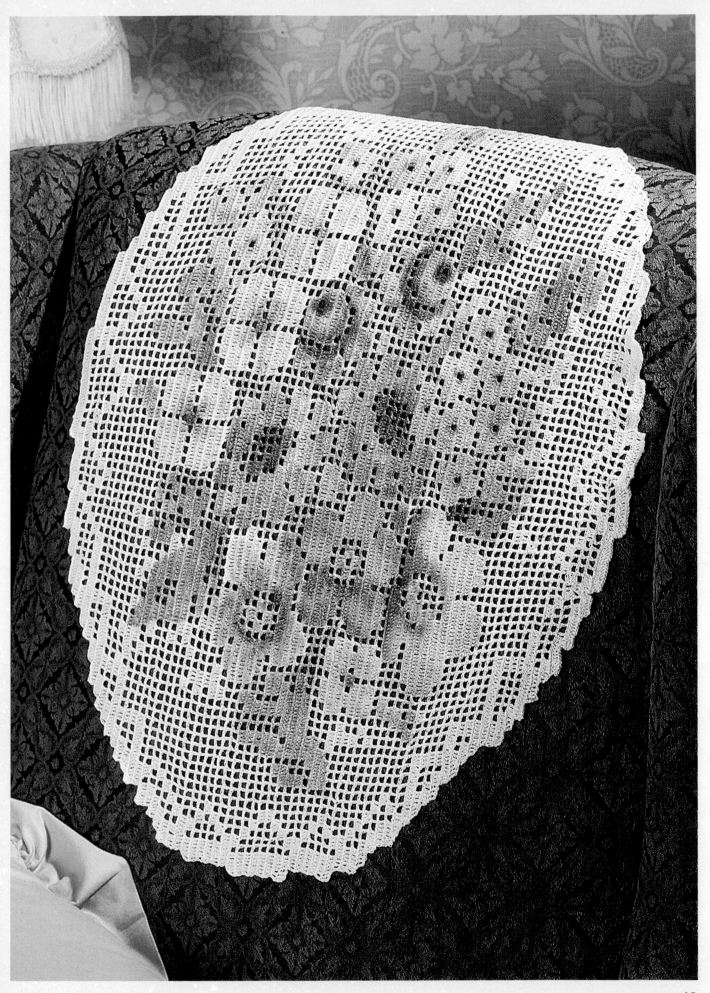

Crochet Tidy continued from page 48

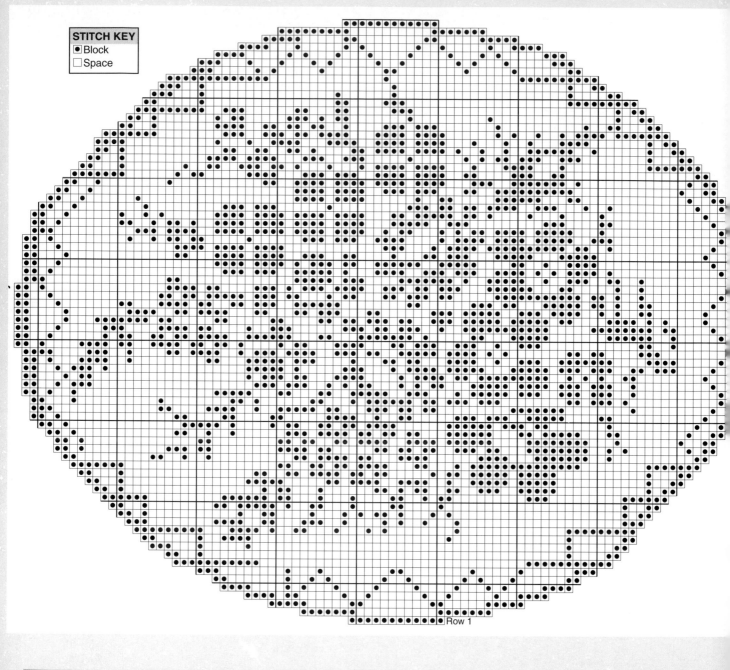

STITCH KEY
◉ Block
☐ Space

Row 1

Square-a-Day Tablecloth continued from page 46

at **, join in 4th ch of beg ch-7 sp.

RNDS 6–20: Work in this manner following graph, making ch-3 for sps and ch-7 for each corner sp, join each rnd in 4th ch of beg ch-7 or top of beg ch-4, depending how each rnd beg.

At the end of Rnd 20, fasten off. With WS facing, sew tog 5 rows of 3 blocks each.

EDGING

RND 1 (RS): Attach thread in any tr, ch 4, working around entire outer edge, tr in each tr, 3 tr in each ch-3 sp, 3 tr in each joining sp of blocks and [4 tr, ch 7, 4 tr] in each corner sp, join in top of beg ch-4.

RND 2: Ch 4, tr in each tr around, working [4 tr, ch 7, 4 tr] in each corner ch-7 sp, join in 4th ch of beg ch-4.

RND 3: Working evenly sp around entire outer edge, ch 1, [{sc, ch 3, sc}, in next st, sk 2 sts] rep around, working at each corner ch-7 sp [sk 1 ch, {sc, ch 3, sc} in next ch] 3 times, join in beg sc, fasten off.

NOTE: *Adjustments may be made by skipping only one st if edging puckers by using a tighter tension or smaller hook if edging ruffles.* Block and press, starch lightly if desired. ◇

A Trolley Conductor Who Makes Filet Lace

By Harriet Sisson Gillespie

To evolve intricate patterns of filet lace is the unusual occupation of Charles Wallace, a trolley conductor at Garden City, N.J. All his spare moments are devoted to turning out the most exquisite bits of needlework of this sort, which find a steady sale among the commuters who travel back and forth between New York and this suburban community. Mr. Wallace, a splendid type of Scotchman, plies his vocation on the shuttle line running between the main station at Garden City and the Garden City development, but the business of ringing up fares in no way interferes with his ability as a lace maker, in the exercise of which talent he far surpasses most women.

This needleman's fame has gone the length and breadth of Long Island, where he with his lace frame is a familiar figure. Between trips he works assiduously, and it is apparently as easy for Mr. Wallace to originate intricate patterns in filet lace as to ring up fares, help passengers on and off the car, or give city folk who come down the Island prospecting points on land values.

At the time this article was written, he was completing a beautiful table cover composed of 16 22-inch squares, put together with bands of insertion and a 12-inch border. Not only does he weave in the design, but he makes the net foundation, which in itself is a task of heroic proportions. It takes him from a month to 6 weeks, according to the amount of leisure he has, to do one square.

Not only is he deeply interested in the work, but is mighty proud of it as well, as indeed he may be, for no feminine fingers ever evolved more beautiful articles of household adornment. His patrons on the trolley evince as much interest in his lacemaking as in the war, and though naturally the feminine portion of the community take the lead in this respect, the men do not lag far behind. Some of the latter have learned more about the making of filet lace than they ever knew before and they appreciate it accordingly.

Naturally, the first question put to Mr. Wallace by the curious is, "How did you come to learn lacemaking?" "Because I wanted something to occupy my time," is his reply. This is true, too, only there is another and more interesting meaning lying hidden beneath it. It lies in the fact that Wallace had a thrifty Scotch mother who brought up her boys to despise no work so long as it was honorable.

She taught her sons to sew and darn the same as her daughters, and saw nothing contemptible in boys doing their share of the work. Then, too, the family lived near the sea and the boys just naturally learned to make and mend nets so that the making of filet lace was only another step in the art.

It happened one day that a Scandinavian woman, visiting on his line, was an expert in filet lacemaking. She showed Wallace her work and it revived his interest in netting. As time hung heavy on his hands between trips, he determined to learn the art and soon he outdistanced his instructor. He presented the fruit of his first effort to his wife with no thought of marketing his wares, but his women patrons saw the beautiful things he was doing and offered to buy them. Now he has orders far ahead for bits of lace for household adornment and is unable to supply the demand.

The Modern Priscilla, February 1919

Timeless Treasure Frame

This antique pattern will frame any photograph in simple elegance, from vintage snapshots of your ancestors to a portrait of the new baby. Use it under a glass frame, or arrange it over an oval frame covered with velvet fabric.

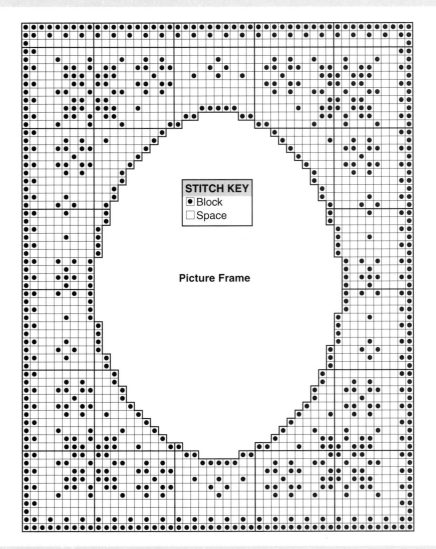

STITCH KEY
● Block
☐ Space

Picture Frame

SKILL LEVEL: INTERMEDIATE

SIZE:
10 inches x 11¼ inches

MATERIALS
➤ Crochet cotton size 20: 500 yds ivory
➤ Size 10 steel crochet hook or size needed to obtain gauge

GAUGE
5½ bls = 1 inch
Check gauge to save time.

PATTERN NOTES
Weave in loose ends as work progresses.

Ch 3 counts as first dc at beg of a row.

This pattern will can be crocheted in any size cotton, depending on size picture frame wanted. Check your gauge for number of sps and bls per inch in width and rows for larger or smaller frames.

PATTERN STITCHES
BLOCK (BL): Dc in each of next 3 dc.

SPACE (SP): Ch 2, sk next 2 sts, dc in next st.

INC 1 BL AT THE BEG OF ROW: Ch 5, dc in 4th ch from hook, dc in next ch.

INC 1 BL AT END OF ROW: Yo, draw up a lp in top of turning ch where last dc was worked, yo, draw through 1 lp on hook (base st), [yo, draw through 2 lps on hook] twice (dc), *yo, draw up lp in base st, yo, draw through 1 lp on hook for next base st, [yo, draw through 2 lps on hook] twice, rep from * once for 1 bl inc.

Frame

BOTTOM
ROW 1 (RS): Beg at bottom edge, ch 150, dc in 4th ch from hook, dc in each rem ch across, turn. (148 dc; 49 bls)

ROW 2 (WS): Ch 3, dc in each of next 6 sts, [ch 2, sk next 2 sts, dc in each of next 4 sts] 23 times, dc in each of next 3 sts, turn.

ROW 3 (RS): Ch 3, dc in each of next 3 dc, [ch 2, sk next 2 sts, dc in next st] 47 times, dc in each of next 3 sts, turn. (1 bl; 47 sps; 1 bl)

ROWS 4–10: Follow graph working bls and sps as indicated, turn at the end of each row.

RIGHT EDGE
ROW 11 (RS): Ch 3, dc in each of next 3 dc, [ch 2, sk next 2 sts, dc in next st] 4 times, dc in each of next 9 sts, ch 2, sk next 2 sts, dc

Continued on page 61

Family Heritage

In the past, family names and crests were valued and honored through various forms of reverent display. This filet sampler, adapted from an old-time pattern, will preserve this honorable tradition for your own family name for generations to come.

Design by Nancy Hearne

SKILL LEVEL: INTERMEDIATE

SIZE
10¾ x 25 inches, before blocking

MATERIALS
- DMC Cebelia cotton size 30 (50g per ball): 2 balls cream #712
- Size 12 steel crochet hook or size needed to obtain gauge

GAUGE
18 sts = 1 inch; 6 rows = 1 inch
Check gauge to save time.

PATTERN NOTE
Weave in loose ends as work progresses.

PATTERN STITCHES

BLOCK (BL): 3 dc.

SPACE (SP): Ch 2, dc.

POPCORN (PC): 5 dc in indicated st or sp, draw up a lp, remove hook, insert hook in top of first dc, pick up dropped lp, draw lp through st on hook to form pc with bump on RS of work, ch 1 to lock.

BEG BL: Ch 3, 3 dc.

BL OVER BL: Dc in next 3 dc.

BL OVER SP: 2 dc in sp, dc in next dc.

BL OVER PC: 2 dc in top of pc, dc in next dc.

BL INC AT BEG OF ROW: Ch 5 for first bl, ch 3 for each additional bl.

BL INC AT END OF ROW: Dc in top of turning ch-3 of previous row, [yo hook, insert hook in base of last st made, yo, draw up a lp, yo, draw through 1 lp on hook, {yo, draw through 2 lps on hook} twice] 3 times.

BL DEC AT BEG OF ROW: Sl st across first 4 sts.

BL DEC AT END OF ROW: Leave last bl of previous row unworked.

SP OVER BL: Ch 2, sk next 2 dc, dc in next dc.

SP OVER SP: Ch 2, dc in next dc.

SP OVER PC: Ch 2, sk pc, dc in next dc.

Sampler Alphabet

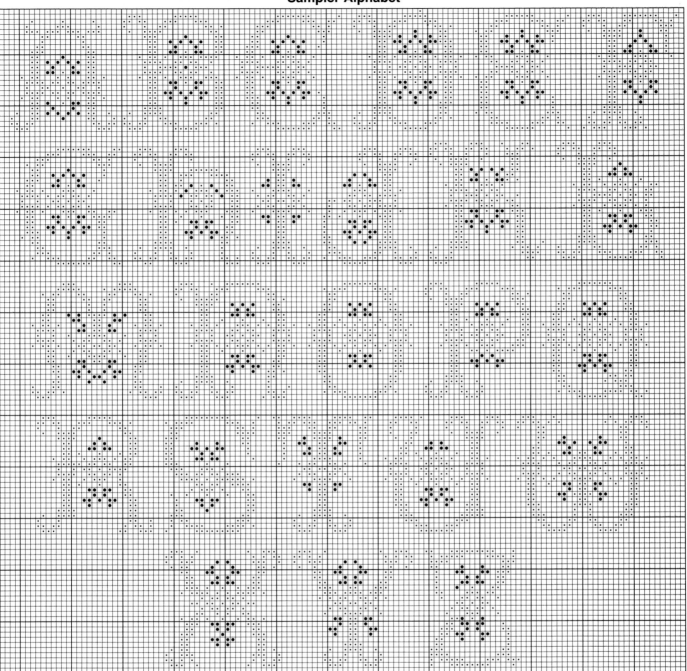

PC OVER A BL: Dc in next dc, sk 1 dc, pc in next dc, dc in next dc.

PC OVER A SP: Pc in ch-2 sp, dc in next dc.

PC OVER PC: Pc in top of pc, dc in next dc.

FILET
ROW 1 (RS): Ch 111, dc in 4th ch from hook, dc in each rem ch across, turn.

ROW 2: Bl inc at beg of row, [pc over bl, sp over bl] rep across, ending with sp over last bl, bl inc at end of row, turn.

ROWS 3–160: Follow graph, utilizing techniques. At the end of Row 160, fasten off.
Block lightly. ✧

STITCH KEY
◉ Block
☐ Space
⊡ Popcorn

Continued on page 60

Roses in Bloom

Roses bloom in many colors—choose your favorite
and bring grace and decorum to your home with
this exquisite filet centerpiece from 1912.

← Center Row

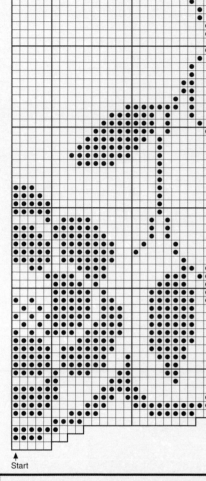

STITCH KEY
- ● Block
- □ Space

↑ Start

hook, [ch 2, sk 2 ch, dc in next ch] 12 times, ch 2, dc in top of next dc, make 4 bls, [ch 2, sk 2 dc, dc in next dc] 9 times (9 sps over 9 bls); make 3 bls, 2 dc in next sp, dc in 5th st of turning ch, ch 5, dc in same place as last dc; [ch 5, turn, dc in 3rd st of previous ch-5] 13 times (14 sps inc at both ends of row), turn.

ROW 5: Ch 10, inc 2 sps, make 6 bls, 6 sps, 4 bls, 3 sps, 7 bls, 3 sps, 4 bls, 6 sps 6 bls, inc 2 sps, turn.

ROW 6: Ch 7, dc in top of next dc, make 10 bls, 3 sps, 3 bls, 4 sps, 9 bls, 4 sps, 3 bls, 3 sps, 10 bls, ch 5, dc in same place as last dc, turn, sl st to 3rd st of last ch-5 (1 sp inc at both ends), turn.

Note: Chart shows one quarter of design. To make 2nd half of each row, omit the center sp or bl as the case may be and follow chart back to the beg of row. Starting with the 7th row (ch 7 to beg) and follow chart to top. Reverse chart and omitting last row, follow chart back until the 79th row has been completed.

ROW 80: Sl st across 2 ch, sl st in next dc, ch 5 and follow chart across to last sp, do not work over last sp (1 sp dec at both ends), ch 5, turn.

Now follow chart back to first row. Do not fasten off.

TRIM

RND 1: Ch 1, sc evenly sp around entire outer edge, sl st to join in beg sc, fasten off.

Starch lightly and block to measurements. ✧

Centerpiece

ROW 1: Starting at bottom of chart, ch 32, dc in 8th ch from hook, [ch 2, sk 2 ch, dc in next ch] 8 times, turn.

ROW 2: Ch 10, dc in 8th ch from hook, ch 2, dc in next dc (2 sps inc at beg of row); ch 2, dc in next dc (sp over sp); [2 dc in next sp, dc in next dc] 7 times (7 bls over 7 sps); ch 2, sk 2 sts of turning ch, dc in next ch, ch 5, dc in same place as last dc, ch 5, turn, dc in 3rd st of previous ch-5 (2 sps inc at end of row), turn.

ROW 3: Ch 10, dc in 8th ch from hook, ch 2, dc in top of next dc, ch 2, dc in base of same dc, make 2 bls, dc in next 21 dc (7 bls over 7 bls); make 2 bls, ch 2, sk 2 sts of turning ch, dc in next ch, ch 5, dc in same place as last dc, ch 5, turn, dc in 3rd st of previous ch-5 (2 sps inc at each end of row), turn.

ROW 4: Ch 46, dc in 8th ch from

SKILL LEVEL: INTERMEDIATE

SIZE
30¾ inches x 26 inches

MATERIALS
➤ Crochet cotton size 30 (175 yds per ball): 5 balls rose
➤ Size 10 or 11 crochet hook or size needed to obtain gauge

GAUGE
16 dc and 6 rows = inch
Check gauge to save time.

PATTERN NOTE
Weave in loose ends as work progresses.

"Sunday Best" Guest Towel & Washcloth

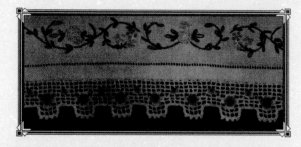

Long ago, the presentation of one's home to guests involved a great deal of ceremony. Add a bit of graciousness the next time you host a visitor by decorating your towels and washcloths with these beautiful edgings.

Designs revised by Agnes Russell

SKILL LEVEL: BEGINNER

SIZE:

TOWEL FILET:
Ends 5⅝ inches;
center 3½ x 15¾ inches

WASHCLOTH FILET:
3⅝ x 3⅝ inches

MATERIALS
➤ Coats Big Ball crochet cotton size 20 (400 yds per ball): 1 ball white #1
➤ Size 10 steel crochet hook or size needed to obtain gauge
➤ 16 x 24-inch hand towel
➤ 11½-inch washcloth
➤ Straight pins
➤ Tapestry needle

GAUGE
19 dc = 1 inch; 6 rows = 1 inch
Check gauge to save time.

PATTERN NOTES
Weave in loose ends as work progresses.

Filet piece for towel and washcloth are crocheted vertically.

Towel

TOWEL EDGING
ROW 1 (RS): Ch 95, dc in 8th ch from hook, dc in each of next 6 chs, [ch 2, sk next 2 chs, dc in next ch] 27 times, turn. (1 sp; 2 bls; 27 sps)

ROW 2: Ch 5 (counts as first dc, ch-2 throughout), dc in next dc, [ch 2, dc in next dc] 15 times, 2 dc in next ch-2 sp, [dc in next dc, ch 2] 10 times, dc in next 7 dc, ch 2, sk next 2 chs, dc in next ch, turn. (16 sps; 1 bl; 10 sps; 2 bls; 1 sp)

ROW 3: Ch 5, dc in next dc, ch 2, sk next 2 dc, dc in each of next 4 dc, [ch 2, dc in next dc] 8 times, [2 dc in next ch-2 sp, dc in next dc] twice, ch 2, sk next 2 dc, dc in next dc, [ch 2, dc in next dc] 16 times, turn.

ROWS 4–88: Following graph, ch 5 to beg each row, work blocks and sps as indicated by graph, turn at the end of each row.

At the end of Row 88, do not fasten off, turn.

Trim
ROW 89 (RS): Ch 3, dc evenly sp across Row 88, working in ends of rows, dc evenly sp across top edge and down opposite side across foundation ch, do not turn.

RND 90 (RS): Ch 1, [sc, ch 3] twice and sc in corner sp, working across bottom edge, [sc, ch 2, sc] over side edge of each dc row, [sc, ch 3] twice and sc in corner, [{sc, ch 3, sc} in next dc, sk 1 dc] rep evenly sp around rem outer edge,

rep corner in each rem corner, sl st to join in beg sc, fasten off.

Press and block piece to measurement.

TOWEL TRIM
ROW 1 (RS): Attach white in bottom edge of towel, working across short edge only, ch 1, [{sc, ch 3, sc}] in same sp] rep evenly sp across edge, fasten off.

Pin crocheted piece to towel, with length of crochet cotton, sew crocheted piece around entire outer edge to towel.

Washcloth

ROW 1: Ch 40, dc in 8th ch from hook, [ch 2, sk next 2 chs, dc in next ch] 11 times, turn. (12 sps)

ROW 2: Ch 7, dc in first dc (1 sp inc at beg of row), [ch 2, dc in next dc] 12 times, ch 2, tr in same st as last dc (1 sp inc at end of row), turn. (14 sps)

ROW 3: Ch 7, dc in tr, [ch 2, dc in next dc] 14 times, ch 2, tr in same st as last dc, turn. (16 sps)

ROW 4: Ch 7, dc in tr, [ch 2, dc in next dc] 11 times, [2 dc in next ch-2 sp, dc in next dc] twice, [ch 2, dc in next dc] 3 times, ch 2, tr in same st as last dc, turn. (12 sps; 2 bls; 4 sps)

ROWS 5–14: Following graph, ch 5 to beg each row, working bls and sps as indicated, turn at the end of each row.

Continued on next page

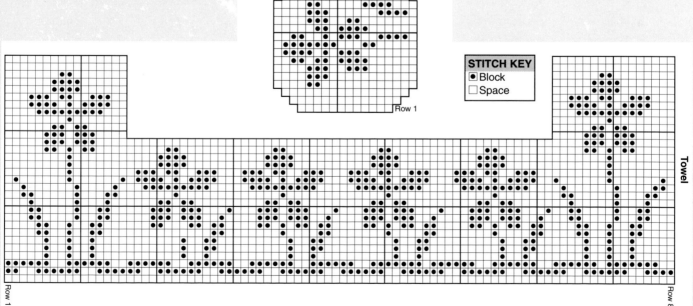

Washcloth

Row 17

Row 1

STITCH KEY
● Block
□ Space

Towel

Row 1

Row 88

"Sunday Best"
Guest Towel & Washcloth
continued from previous page

ROWS 15–17: Following graph, (dec a block at beg of row, sl st in first dc, each of next 2 chs and into next dc), ch 5, work across each row to within last sp, turn. At the end of Row 17, do not fasten off, turn.

Trim

RND 18: Ch 3, dc evenly sp around entire outer edge, sl st to join in top of beg ch-3.

RND 19: Ch 1, [{sc, ch 3, sc} in next dc, sk 1 dc] rep evenly sp around entire outer edge, sl st to join in beg sc, fasten off.

Press and block crocheted piece.

WASHCLOTH TRIM

RND 1: Attach cotton in edge of washcloth, ch 1, [sc, ch 3, sc] rep evenly sp around entire outer edge, sl st to join in beg sc, fasten off.

Pin crocheted piece centered at any corner of washcloth. Sew piece to washcloth. ✧

Family Heritage Doily continued from page 55

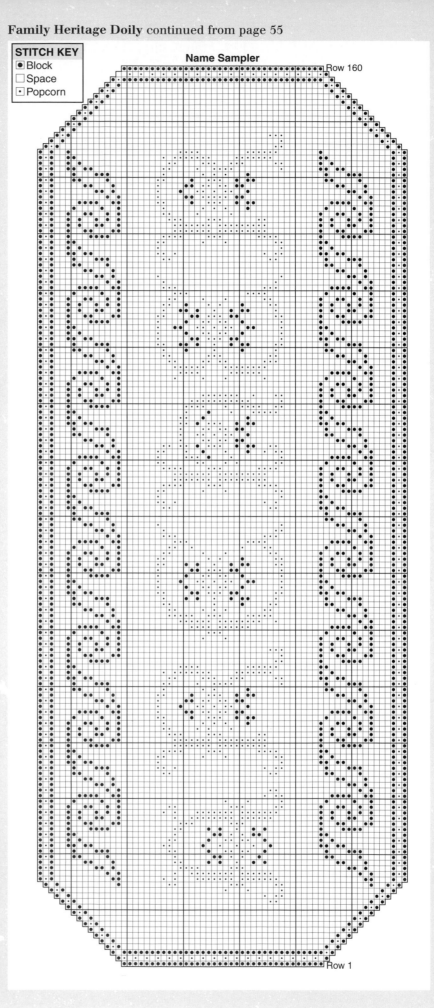

Name Sampler

Row 160

STITCH KEY
- ⬤ Block
- ☐ Space
- ⊡ Popcorn

Row 1

in each of next 10 sts, [ch 2, sk next 2 sts, dc in next st] twice, dc in each of next 3 sts, [ch 2, sk next 2 sts, dc in next st] 5 times, dc in each of next 6 sts, turn leaving rem of row unworked, sl st into 7th dc.

ROWS 12–53: Follow graph working bls and sps as indicated, turn at the end of each row.

At the end of Row 53, ch 14, fasten off.

LEFT EDGE
ROW 11 (RS): Sk 14 dc at center of Row 10, attach cotton in next dc, ch 3, follow graph across rem of row, turn.

ROWS 12–53: Follow graph working bls and sps as indicated, turn at the end of each row.

TOP
ROW 54 (WS): Ch 3, dc in each of next 6 sts, [ch 2, sk next 2 sts, dc in next st] 4 times, dc in each of next 6 sts, ch 2, sk next 2 sts, dc in each of next 7 sts, [ch 2, sk next 2 sts, dc in next st] 11 times, working across ch-14 from right edge, making sure ch and edge are not twisted, dc in each of next 14 ch, dc in next dc, [ch 2, sk next 2 sts, dc in next st] 11 times, dc in each of next 6 dc, ch 2, sk next 2 sts, dc in each of next 7 sts, [ch 2, sk next 2 sts, dc in next st] 4 times, dc in each of next 6 sts, turn.

ROWS 55–63: Follow graph working bls and sps as indicated, turn at the end of each row. At the end of Row 63, fasten off.

Block picture frame and press. ✧

Family Heirlooms Last for Decades

By Agnes Russell

Family heirlooms are designed to last for decades, to be passed from generation to generation with love as are little family trade secrets. Here's a little family secret I'll share with you that will restore that gift of love you make for many decades to come.

Many years ago my grandmother crocheted from wool a beautiful granny afghan for my 16th birthday which I treasure deeply. Well, through normal wear and tear the yarns are getting old and I found a few breaks at the joining of the squares, and of course, the border is black. I don't care what the color, you will never match it!

Well, around the edge on the wrong side of the border was a little knot, not very noticeable, but a knot and low and behold it was a strand of black yarn woven though the border of my afghan. With care I removed just enough yarn to do my repair and left the remaining black yarn in place with a little knot on the end for future repair.

Now, I find myself, adding strands of yarn through the back of every afghan I make. It's great because the woven yarn ages with the afghan through laundry and simple wear and tear. When a repair has to be made the yarns match perfectly.

I also now do this on tablecloths. When I work the border, I work over a single strand of my cotton around the entire outer edge and then knot the ends together on the wrong side of my tablecloth. If repairs are needed it's right at the border and has aged with my tablecloth and matches perfectly.

Think of all the items you have crocheted over the years and have had to repair and didn't have that scrap of yarn, or did and it no longer matched. Try this on all your crocheted heirlooms it really works wonderfully.

Chapter Three

Grandmother's Kitchen

Our grandmothers, who lived through the lean years of the early 1900s, often valued crocheted items that had a practical use as well as an attractive appearance. Take a peek inside those strong women's kitchen, with this sample of classic kitchen accessories.

Fans Across the Border Hostess Set

This breezy table setting and apron will keep your guests cheerful, whether indoors or outdoors. Pure white lace and bright, fruit-slice borders will make you quite the proper hostess!

Designs revised by Maggie Petsch Chasalow

SKILL LEVEL: INTERMEDIATE

SIZE
PLACE MAT: 12¼ x 17½ inches
APRON: 18½ inches long
GLASS MUFF: 2¾ inches in diameter x 3½ inches high

MATERIALS
➤ Crochet cotton size 10 (225 yards per ball): 2 balls white (A), 1 ball each blue (B), yellow (C), green (D) and pink (E)

➤ Size 7 steel crochet hook or size needed to obtain gauge

➤ 1½ yards blue denim or cotton for place mats and apron

➤ Snap fastener

➤ Safety pin

➤ Sewing needle and thread

GAUGE
Pocket trim = 5½ inches long x 2½ inches deep
Check gauge to save time.

PATTERN NOTES
Weave in loose ends as work progresses.

Sl st to join each rnd in top of beg st unless otherwise indicated.

Continued on page 66

PATTERN STITCHES

P: Ch 6, sc in 5th ch from hook.

SHELL: [2 dc, ch 2, 2 dc] in indicated st or sp.

SPLIT SHELL: 2 dc in next st, ch 2, 2 dc in next st.

BEG SHELL: [Ch 3, dc, ch 2, 2 dc] in indicated st or sp.

QUADRUPLE TR (QDTR): Yo hook 5 times, insert hook in indicated st, yo, draw up a lp, [yo, draw through 2 lps on hook] 6 times.

Apron

POCKET TRIM

ROW 1: With A, ch 50, sc in 2nd ch from hook, *p, ch 2, sk next 5 chs, shell in next ch, p, ch 2, sk next 5 chs, sc in next ch, rep from * across, turn. (4 shells)

ROW 2: Ch 3 (counts as first dc throughout), *p, ch 2, shell in next shell sp, p, ch 2, sk next p, dc in next sc, rep from * across, turn. (4 shells)

ROWS 3–6: Ch 3, *p, ch 2, shell in next shell sp, p, ch 2, sk next p, dc in next dc, rep from * across, ending with dc in 3rd ch of turning ch-3, turn; at the end of Row 6, do not fasten off, do not turn; remove hook from lp, place safety pin in lp.

First Fan

ROW 1: Attach B with a sl st in first shell sp at beg of last row, ch 1, sc in same sp, turn. (1 sc)

ROW 2: Ch 1, 3 sc in sc, turn. (3 sc)

ROW 3: Ch 1, 2 sc in first sc, sc in next sc, 2 sc in last sc, turn. (5 sc)

ROWS 4–7: Ch 1, 2 sc in first sc, sc in each sc across to last sc, 2 sc in last sc, turn; at end of Row 7, fasten off. (13 sc)

Rem Three Fans

ROWS 1–7: Rep Rows 1–7 of first fan in each of 3 rem shell sps in the following color sequence: C, D and E.

Edging

ROW 1 (WS): Pick up dropped lp at end of Row 6, turn, ch 7 (counts as first qdtr), sc in each of next 13 sc on first fan, [sk next p, qdtr in next dc, sc in each of next 13 sc on next fan] 3 times, qdtr in 3rd ch of turning ch-3, fasten off, turn.

ROW 2: With RS facing, attach A with a sl st in end sc of Row 1, ch 1, sc in same st, **[3 sc in end sp of next row] 5 times **, 6 sc over end sp of next row, sc in first sc of first fan, *[ch 3, sk next sc, sc in next sc] 6 times **, sc in first sc of next fan, rep from * across ending last rep at **, 6 sc over end sp of last row, rep from ** to **, sc in end sc of Row 1, fasten off.

APRON BORDER

ROW 1: With A, ch 254, sc in 2nd ch from hook, rep Row 1 of pocket trim from * across. (21 shells)

ROWS 2–6: Rep Rows 2–6 of pocket trim.

First Fan

ROWS 1–7: Rep Rows 1–7 of first fan for pocket trim.

Rem Twenty Fans

ROWS 1–7: Rep Rows 1–7 of first fan in each of 20 rem shell sps in the following color sequence: [C, D, E, B] 5 times.

Edging

ROWS 1 & 2: Rep Rows 1 and 2 of edging for pocket trim.

Place Mat Border

(make 2)

ROW 1: With A, ch 110, sc in 2nd ch from hook, rep Row 1 of pocket trim from * across. (9 shells)

ROWS 2–6: Rep Rows 2–6 of pocket trim.

FIRST FAN

ROWS 1–7: Rep Rows 1–7 of first fan for pocket trim.

REM EIGHT FANS

ROWS 1–7: Rep Rows 1–7 of first fan in each of 8 rem shell sps in the following color sequence: [C, D, E, B] twice.

EDGING

ROWS 1 & 2: Rep Rows 1 and 2 of edging for pocket trim.

Glass Muff

BASE

RND 1 (RS): With B, ch 7, join to form a ring, ch 3, 17 dc in ring, join in 3rd ch of beg ch-3, fasten off. (18 dc)

RND 2: With RS facing, attach C with a sl st in same st as joining, ch 3, dc in same st, 2 dc in each rem st around, join in 3rd ch of beg ch-3, fasten off. (36 dc)

RND 3: With RS facing, attach D with a sl st in same st as joining, ch 3, 2 dc in next st, [dc in next st, 2 dc in next st] rep around, join in 3rd ch of beg ch-3, fasten off. (54 dc)

RND 4: With RS facing, attach E with sl st in same st as joining, ch 3, dc in next st, 2 dc in next st, [dc in each of next 2 sts, 2 dc in next st] rep around, join in 3rd ch of beg ch-3, fasten off. (72 dc)

RND 5: With RS facing, attach A with sl st in same st as joining, ch 3, dc in each of next 2 sts, 2 dc in next st, [dc in each of next 3 sts, 2 dc in next st] rep around, join in 3rd ch of beg ch-3, do not fasten off. (90 dc)

TOP

RND 1 (RS): Working in back lps for this rnd only, beg shell in same st as joining, ch 1, sk 5 sts, shell in next st, [ch 1, sk 5 sts, split shell, ch 1, sk 5 sts, shell in next st] rep around to last 5 sts, ch 1, join in 3rd ch of beg ch-3.

RNDS 2–8: Sl st in next dc and in ch-2 sp, beg shell in same sp, ch 1, [shell in next ch-2 sp, ch 1] rep around, join in 3rd ch of beg ch-3. (14 shells)

RND 9: Sl st in next dc and in ch-2 sp, beg shell in same sp, *p, ch 2, sc in next shell sp, p, ch 2 **, shell in next shell sp, rep from * around, ending last rep at **, join in 3rd ch of beg ch-3. (7 shells)

RND 10: Sl st in next dc and in ch-2 sp, beg shell in same sp, *p, ch 2, sk next p, dc in next sc, p, ch 2 **, shell in next shell, rep from * around, ending last rep at **, join in 3rd ch of beg ch-3. (7 shells)

RND 11: Sl st in next dc and in ch-

2 sp, beg shell in same sp, *p, ch 2, sk next p, dc in next dc, p, ch 2 **, shell in next shell sp, rep from * around, ending last rep at **, join in 3rd ch of beg ch-3, fasten off. (7 shells)

FIRST FAN
ROW 1: With RS facing, attach B with a sl st in first shell sp, rep Row 1 of first fan for pocket trim.

ROWS 2–7: Rep Rows 2–7 of first fan for pocket trim.

REM SIX FANS
ROWS 1–7: Rep Rows 1–7 of first fan in each of 6 rem shell sps in the following color sequence: C, D, E, B, C and D.

EDGING
RND 1: With RS facing, attach A with a sl st in last dc of Rnd 11, ch 7 (counts as first qdtr), sc in each of next 13 sc on first fan, [sk next p, qdtr in next dc, sc in each of next 13 sc on next fan] rep around, join in 7th ch of beg ch-7.

RND 2: Sc in first sc of first fan, *[ch 3, sk next sc, sc in next sc] 6 times **, sc in first sc of next fan, rep from * around, ending last rep at **, join in beg sc, fasten off.

FINISHING
Cut piece of fabric 1 inch wider than length of apron border and 15 inches long for apron. Make a doubled ¼ inch hem on one long edge for bottom and 2 short edges for sides. Sew apron border to bottom of apron. Run basting sts ⅜ inch from top of apron and gather top of apron to fit waist.

Cut piece of fabric 4 inches wide and 3 inches longer than waist measurement for belt. Fold under ½ inch on each short edge and sew in place. Fold ½ inch to WS on each long edge. Fold belt in half so WS of long edges are tog. Center open edge of belt over gathering sts at top of apron and sew in place, sewing opening of belt on either side of apron top closed. Sew snap fastener to ends of belt.

Cut piece of fabric 1 inch wider than length of pocket trim and 4 inches long for pocket. Make a doubled ¼ inch hem on each side and on top and bottom of pocket and pin in place. Sew pocket trim across top of pocket. Pin pocket on apron and sew in place.

Cut piece of fabric 1 inch wider than length of place mat border and 13⅓ inches long. Make a doubled ¼ inch hem on each of four sides. Sew place mat border to edges of place mat. ✧

Mrs. Someone Else
By Constance Vivien Frazier

When I get tired of doing all my
endless household chores,
And long for fun and freedom,
and the great big out-o'-doors;
When I get sick of dusting,
and just hate to bake and brew,
And my very soul is weary
of the common tasks I do—
Well, I have no time to idle,
so I cannot sit me down
And mourn, and fuss, and grumble,
and fidget, wail and frown,
So I don a brand new house-frock,
just as gay as it can be,
And pretend I'm Mrs. Someone Else,
instead of only me;
And it does the trick like magic,
for I feel so fresh and gay,
That the next thing I know it's being
just one grand, successful day!

Granny's Bloomers Pot Holder

Bloomers are an item that people gave up wearing long ago, yet the notion of bloomers still carries a nostalgic charm for all, whether you can remember their heyday or not! Enjoy giving these old garments a new form and function by stitching this irresistible pot holder.

Design revised by
Maggie Petsch Chasalow

SKILL LEVEL: INTERMEDIATE

SIZE
8 x 7½ inches

MATERIALS
➤ Crochet cotton size 10: 225 yard ball white, small amount red

➤ Size 7 steel crochet hook or size needed to obtain gauge

➤ 1⅛-inch plastic ring

➤ 18 inches ¼-inch-wide red satin ribbon

➤ Tapestry needle

GAUGE
10 dc = 1 inch

Check gauge to save time.

PATTERN NOTES
Weave in loose ends as work progresses.

Join rnds with a sl st unless otherwise indicated.

PATTERN STITCHES

V-ST: [Dc, ch 1, dc] in indicated st or sp.

SHELL: [2 dc, ch 2, 2 dc] in indicated st or sp.

BEG SHELL: [Ch 3, dc, ch 2, 2 dc] in indicated st or sp.

Continued on page 70

Ear of Corn Pot-Handle Cover

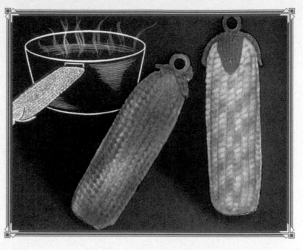

Add an old-time sense of humor to your stovetop and table with this peppy pot handle cover. Realistic "kernels" in slightly varied colors provide insulation while looking almost good enough to eat!

Design revised by Maggie Petsch Chasalow

SKILL LEVEL: INTERMEDIATE

SIZE
7 inches long x 2½ inches wide

MATERIALS
➤ Crochet cotton size 10 (150 yds per ball): 1 ball shaded yellows (A), small amount green (B)
➤ Size 7 steel crochet hook or size needed to obtain gauge
➤ 1⅛-inch plastic ring
➤ Tapestry needle

GAUGE
9 sc = 1 inch
Check gauge to save time.

PATTERN NOTES
Weave in loose ends as work progresses.

Join rnds with a sl st unless otherwise indicated.PATTERN STITCH

POPCORN (PC): 5 dc in indicated st, remove hook from lp, insert hook from RS to WS in top of first dc of 5-dc group, pick up dropped lp, draw tightly through st on hook.

TOP
ROW 1 (WS): With A, ch 46, sc in 2nd ch from hook, sc in each rem ch across, turn. (45 sc)

ROW 2: Ch 1, sc in each of first 2 sts, hdc in next st, dc in next st, [pc in next st, dc in next st] 19 times, hdc in next st, sc in each of next 2 sts, turn.

ROW 3: Ch 1, sc in each st across, turn.

ROWS 4–15: Rep Rows 2 and 3 alternately; at the end of Row 15, fasten off.

BOTTOM
ROWS 1–15: Rep Rows 1–15 of top.

JOINING TOP & BOTTOM
With WS tog and top facing, working through both thicknesses, attach A with a sl st in first dc after first pc on last row, sl st in each rem st across to last st, working over row ends, [sc, dec over end st of next 2 rows] rep across to first rem lp of foundation ch; working in rem lps across foundation ch, sl st in each rem lp across to last dc before last pc; working in top only, sl st in each rem st across to last st; sc over end st of each row across top, sl st in each of first 5 sts on last row of top, sl st in seam, sl st in last 5 unworked sts on last row of bottom, sc over end st of each row across bottom, sl st in each unworked rem lp of foundation ch of bottom, sl st in seam, fasten off.

LEAF *(make 4)*
ROW 1: With B, ch 4, dc in 4th ch

Continued on next page

from hook, ch 1, 8 sc over post of dc just worked, turn. (8 sc)

ROW 2: Ch 1, sc in each st across, turn. (8 sc)

ROWS 3–10: Rep Row 2.

ROW 11: Ch 1, sc dec, sc in each st across to last 2 sts, sc dec, turn. (6 sts)

ROWS 12 & 13: Rep Row 2. (6 sts)

ROW 14: Rep Row 11. (4 sts)

ROW 15: Rep Row 2. (4 sts)

ROW 16: Ch 1, [sc dec] twice, turn.

ROW 17: Ch 1, sc dec, fasten off.

FINISHING
Using photo as a guide, sew one leaf at top center of top and one at top center of bottom. Sew one leaf at each side.

With B, cover plastic ring with sc rnd, join in beg sc, leaving a length of cotton, fasten off. With tapestry needle, sew ring to center top of pot-handle cover. ✧

Granny's Bloomers Pot Holder continued from page *68*

Bloomers

RND 1 (RS): Beg at waist, with white, ch 74, sl st to join to form a ring, ch 3 (counts as first dc throughout), dc in each of next 17 chs, V-st in next ch, dc in each of next 36 chs, V-st in next ch, dc in each of next 18 chs, join in 3rd ch of beg ch-3, turn.

RNDS 2–12: Ch 3, [dc in each dc across to V-st sp, V-st in V-st sp] twice, dc in each rem dc around, join in 3rd ch of beg ch-3, turn.

FIRST LEG
RND 1: Ch 3, dc in each of next 29 dc, dc in next V-st sp, sk next 60 dc, dc in next V-st sp, dc in each of next 30 dc, join in 3rd ch of beg ch-3, turn. (62 dc)

RNDS 2–6: Ch 3, dc in each dc around, join in 3rd ch of beg ch-3, turn. (62 dc)

RND 7: Beg shell in same sp as joining, sk next 2 dc, shell in next dc, [sk next 3 dc, shell in next dc] 14 times, join in 3rd ch of beg ch-3, turn. (16 shells)

RNDS 8–10: Sl st into shell sp, beg shell in same sp, shell in each rem shell sp around, join in 3rd ch of beg ch-3, turn. At the end of Rnd 10, fasten off.

SECOND LEG
RND 1 (RS): Attach white with a sl st in first V-st sp of Rnd 12, ch 3, dc in each dc around to next V-st sp, dc in V-st sp, join in 3rd ch of beg ch-3, turn. (62 dc)

RNDS 2–10: Rep Rnds 2–10 of first leg.

WAISTBAND
RND 1 (RS): Attach white with sl st in opposite side of foundation ch at waist, ch 5 (counts as first tr, ch 1), working in rem free lps of foundation ch, sk next ch, tr in next ch, ch 1, [sk next ch, tr in next ch, ch 1] rep around, join in 4th ch of beg ch-5, fasten off.

RND 2 (RS): Attach red with a sl st in same st as joining, ch 1, sc in same st, sc in each rem sp and in each rem tr around, join in beg sc, fasten off.

PANT LEG TRIM
RND 1 (RS): Attach red with sl st in any shell sp of Rnd 10, ch 3, 4 dc in same sp, *ch 1, sc between same shell and next shell; working down toward Rnd 6 of pant leg, sl st in same sp as last sc made, [ch 2, sl st between 2 shells of next row] 3 times, ch 2, turn; working back in same sps to Rnd 10, [sl st between 2 shells of next row, ch 2] 3 times, sl st between 2 shells on working row, ch 1 **, 5 dc in next shell sp on working row, rep from * around, ending last rep at **, join in 3rd ch of beg ch-3, fasten off. Rep around bottom of rem pant leg.

Beg at center front, weave ribbon through ch-1 sps of Rnd 1 of waistband. Tie ends in a bow.

HANGER
With red, sc closely around plastic ring, join in beg sc, leaving a length of cotton, fasten off. Sew bottom of plastic ring to top corner at one side of bloomers. ✧

Open Mesh Shopping Bag

When you go to an open-air market or country fair, take this pretty bag with you! The open mesh pattern and deep pastel colors bring to mind the fragrances of long ago: lilacs, lavender, and garden roses. This bag has a special self-closure so you can fold it and tuck it away when not in use.

folds up fits purse!

Design revised by Maggie Petsch Chasalow

SKILL LEVEL: BEGINNER

SIZE
6¼ inches in diameter x 15 inches tall

MATERIALS
➤ South Maid crochet cotton size 10 (300 yds per ball): 2 balls pastels ombre #465
➤ Size 6 steel crochet hook or size needed to obtain gauge
➤ 2 snap fasteners
➤ Sewing needle and thread

GAUGE
Rnds 1–3 = 2 inches in diameter
Check gauge to save time.

PATTERN NOTES
Weave in loose ends as work progresses.

Join rnds with sl st unless otherwise stated.

PATTERN STITCH
SHELL: [Dc, ch 2, dc] in indicated sp or st.

CARRYING CASE (make 2)
RND 1 (RS): Ch 8, join to form a ring, ch 3 (counts as first dc throughout), 23 dc in ring, join in 3rd ch of beg ch-3. (24 dc)

RND 2: Ch 3, dc in each of next 2 dc, ch 2, [dc in each of next 3 dc, ch 2] rep around, join in 3rd ch of beg ch-3. (8 groups 3-dc)

RND 3: Ch 3, [dc in each dc across to next ch-2 sp, shell in ch-2 sp] rep around, ending with dc in last dc, join in 3rd ch of beg ch-3. (8 groups 5-dc)

RNDS 4–11: Ch 3, [dc in each dc across to next shell, shell in shell sp] rep around, ending with dc in each rem dc across to beg ch-3, join in 3rd ch of beg ch-3; at end of Rnd 11, fasten off. (8 groups 21-dc)

Joining carrying case pieces
Holding both pieces with RS tog and working through both

Continued on page 73

French Kitchen Dishcloth

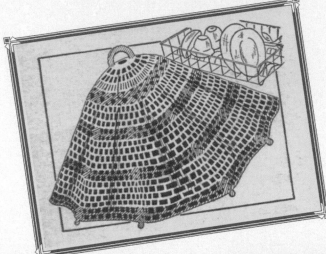

The next time you wash dishes the old-fashioned way—by hand!—try using this vintage dishcloth. It's pretty enough to make the task more pleasant, and sturdy enough to do it well. The yellow, blue, and white colors create the atmosphere of a provincial French kitchen.

Design revised by Maggie Petsch Chasalow

SKILL LEVEL: BEGINNER

SIZE
12½ inches in diameter

MATERIALS
➤ Crochet cotton size 10 (150 yards per ball): 1 ball yellow (A), small amounts each shaded blues (B) and white (C)
➤ Size 7 steel crochet hook or size needed to obtain gauge
➤ Tapestry needle

GAUGE
Rnds 1–3 = 2 inches in diameter
Check gauge to save time.

PATTERN NOTES
Weave in loose ends as work progresses.

Join rnds with sl st unless otherwise indicated.

PATTERN STITCHES
SHELL: [2 dc, ch 2, 2 dc] in indicated sp or st.

BEG SHELL: [Ch 3, dc, ch 2, 2 dc] in indicated sp or st.

V-ST: [Dc, ch 2, dc] in indicated sp or st.

BEG V-ST: [Ch 5, dc] in indicated st or sp.

P: Ch 4, sl st in top of last dc made.

P SHELL: [2 dc, p, 2 dc] in indicated st of sp.

DISHCLOTH
RND 1 (RS): With A, ch 12, sl st to join to form a ring, ch 3 (counts as first dc throughout), 23 dc in ring, join in 3rd ch of beg ch-3. (24 dc)

RND 2: Ch 6 (counts as first dc, ch 3 throughout), sk 1 dc, dc in next dc, ch 3, [sk next dc, dc in next dc, ch 3] rep around, join in 3rd ch of beg ch-6. (12 ch-3 sps)

RND 3: Ch 5 (counts as first dc, ch 2 throughout), dc in next sp, ch 2, [dc in next dc, ch 2, dc in next sp, ch 2] rep around, join in 3rd ch of beg ch-5. (24 ch-2 sps)

RND 4: Rep Rnd 3, fasten off. (48 ch-2 sps)

RND 5 (RS): Attach B with sl st in any sp, beg shell in same sp, ch 2, [sk next 2 sps, shell in next sp, ch 2] rep around, join in 3rd ch of beg ch-3. (16 shells)

RND 6: Sl st into ch sp of next shell, beg shell in same sp, ch 3, [shell in next shell sp, ch 3] rep around, join in 3rd ch of beg ch-3, fasten off. (16 shells)

RND 7 (RS): Attach A with sl st in any shell sp, beg V-st in same sp, *ch 2, dc in next sp, ch 2 **, V-st in next shell sp, rep from * around, ending last rep at **, join in 3rd ch of beg ch-5. (16 V-sts)

RND 8: Sl st into V-st sp, ch 5, dc in next sp, *ch 2, dc in next dc, ch 2, dc in next sp, ch 2 **, dc in next V-st sp, ch 2, dc in next sp, rep from * around, ending last rep at **, join in 3rd ch of beg ch-5. (64 sps)

RND 9: Sl st in first sp, ch 5, [dc in next sp, ch 2] rep around, join in 3rd ch of beg ch-5, fasten off. (64 sps)

RND 10 (RS): Attach C with sl st in any sp on last rnd directly above a Rnd 6 shell sp, beg shell in same sp, *[ch 2, dc in next sp] 3 times, ch 2 **, shell in next sp, rep from * around, ending last rep at **, join in 3rd ch of beg ch-3. (16 shells)

RND 11: Sl st into shell sp, beg shell in same sp, *ch 2, [dc in next sp, ch 2] 4 times **, shell in next shell sp, rep from * around, ending last rep at **, join in 3rd ch of beg ch-3, fasten off. (16 shells)

RND 12 (RS): Attach A with sl st in any shell sp, ch 5, *[dc in next sp, ch 2] 5 times **, dc in next shell sp, ch 2, rep from * around, ending last rep at **, join in 3rd ch of beg ch-5. (96 sps)

RNDS 13 & 14: Sl st in first sp, ch 5, [dc in next sp, ch 2] rep around, join in 3rd ch of beg ch-5. (96 sps)

RND 15: Sl st in first sp, ch 6, [dc in next sp, ch 3] rep around, join in 3rd ch of beg ch-6, fasten off. (96 sps)

RND 16 (RS): Attach B with sl st in any sp on last rnd directly above a Rnd 11 shell sp, beg shell in same sp, *[ch 2, dc in next sp] 5 times, ch 2 **, shell in next sp, rep from * around, ending last rep at **, join in 3rd ch of beg ch-3. (16 shells)

RND 17: Sl st into shell sp, beg shell in same sp, *[ch 2, dc in next sp] 6 times, ch 2 **, shell in next shell sp, rep from * around, ending last rep at **, join in 3rd ch of beg ch-3, fasten off. (16 shells)

RND 18 (RS): Attach A with sl st in any shell sp, beg V-st in same sp, *[ch 2, dc in next sp] 7 times, ch 2 **, V-st in next shell sp, rep from * around, ending last rep at **, join in 3rd ch of beg ch-5. (16 V-sts)

RND 19: Sl st into V-st sp, ch 5, *[dc in next sp, ch 2] 8 times **, dc in next V-st sp, ch 2, rep from * around, ending last rep at **, join in 3rd ch of beg ch-5. (144 sps)

RND 20: Rep Rnd 13. (144 sps)

RND 21: Rep Rnd 15. (144 sps)

RND 22 (RS): Attach C with sl st in any sp on last rnd directly above a Rnd 17 shell sp, beg shell in same sp, *[ch 2, dc in next sp] 8 times, ch 2 **, shell in next sp, rep from * around, ending last rep at **, join in 3rd ch of beg ch-3. (16 shells)

RND 23: Sl st into shell sp, beg p shell in same sp, *[ch 2, dc in next sp] 9 times, ch 2 **, p shell in next shell sp, rep from * around, ending last rep at **, join in 3rd ch of beg ch-3, fasten off. (16 p shells)

HANGER
ROW 1 (RS): Attach B with a sl st over post of any dc on Rnd 1, ch 14, sk next 11 dc, sl st over post of next dc, turn,

ROW 2: Ch 1, 25 sc over ch-14, sl st over post of same dc as beg sl st, fasten off. ✧

Open Mesh Shopping Bag continued from page 71

thicknesses, attach thread with sl st in first dc of any 21-dc group, ch 1, sc in same st, sc in each of next 20 dc, [sc in each of next 2 chs, sc in each of next 21 dc] 4 times, working in top piece only, sc in each rem ch and dc around, join in beg sc. (184 sc)

BAG
RND 1 (RS): Ch 1, sc in same st as joining, [ch 9, sk next 3 sc, sc in next sc] rep around, ending with ch 4, sk next 3 sc, dtr in beg sc to form last ch-9 sp. (46 ch-9 sps)

RNDS 2 & 3: Ch 1, sc in sp just formed, [ch 9, sc in next sp] rep around to last sp, ending with ch 4, dtr in beg sc to form last ch-9 sp.

RND 4: Ch 12 (counts as first dc, ch 9), dc in next sp, [ch 9, dc in next sp] rep around to last sp, ending with ch 4, dtr in 3rd ch of beg ch-12 to form last ch-9 sp.

RNDS 5–24: Ch 13 (counts as first dc, ch 10), dc in next sp, [ch 10, dc in next sp] rep around to last sp, ending with ch 5, dtr in 3rd ch of beg ch-13 to form last sp.

RND 25: Ch 13, dc in next sp, ch 10, [dc in next sp, ch 10] rep around, join in 3rd ch of beg ch-13.

RND 26: Ch 1, sc in same st as joining, 10 dc in next sp, [sc in next dc, 10 dc in next sp] rep around, join in beg sc, fasten off.

CORD (make 2)
With 2 strands held tog, make a ch 1 yard long, fasten off.

FINISHING
Beg at any point on bag, weave 1 cord through ch-10 sps of Rnd 25 around to starting point. Hold ends of cord tog and knot. Beg on opposite side of bag, weave rem cord through ch-10 sps around to starting point. Hold ends tog and knot.

Holding bag so that carrying case piece with partial unworked edge is on inside of bag bottom, turn inside out and tuck beg inside between case pieces

With sewing needle and thread, sew snaps evenly sp across carrying case opening, positioning each at center of a ch-9 sp on Rnd 1 of bag. ✧

Ruffled Pot Holder or Hot Mat

Give your meals a taste of fresh mint with this lovely green hot mat. The intricate three-dimensional ruffle effect, achieved with simple stitches, gives this mat extra thickness, making it practical and decorative at the same time.

Design revised by Maggie Petsch Chasalow

SKILL LEVEL: INTERMEDIATE

SIZE
7¼ inches square

MATERIALS
➤ Crochet cotton size 10 (350 yds per ball): 1 ball each shaded greens (A) and dark green (B)
➤ Size 7 steel crochet hook or size needed to obtain gauge
➤ 1⅛-inch plastic ring
➤ Tapestry needle

GAUGE
4 sps and 4 rows = 1¼ inches in filet mesh
Check gauge to save time.

PATTERN NOTES
Weave in loose ends as work progresses.

Join rnds with sl st unless otherwise indicated.

FRONT
ROW 1: With A, ch 69 (foundation ch), ch 5 more (turning ch-5), dc in 8th ch from hook, [ch 2, sk 2 chs, dc in next ch] rep across, turn. (23 ch-2 sps)

ROWS 2–23: Ch 5 (counts as first dc, ch 2 throughout), sk first ch-2 sp, [dc in next ch, ch 2] rep across to last dc, dc in 3rd ch of turning ch-5, turn; at the end of Row 23, fasten off. (23 ch-2 sps)

RUFFLES
RND 1: Attach B with sl st in ch-2 sp at top of center sp on Row 12 (point 1A on chart), ch 3 (counts as first dc throughout), [2 dc, ch 1] in same sp, [3 dc, ch 1] over end st of next sp on next row above (point 2 on chart), [3 dc, ch 1] in ch-2 sp at top of same sp (point 3 on chart), [3 dc, ch 1] over next end st on same sp (point 4 on chart), [3 dc, ch 1] in sp at bottom of same sp (point 5 on chart); continue to follow chart in numerical order through point 20, working [3 dc, ch 1] in each indicated sp, join in 3rd ch of beg ch-3, fasten off.

RND 2: Attach B with sl st in sp indicated at point 1B on chart; following chart in numerical order through point 28, work as for Rnd 1, join in

3rd ch of beg ch-3, fasten off.

RND 3: Attach A with sl st in sp indicated at point 1C on chart; following chart in numerical order through point 52, work as for Rnd 1, join in 3rd ch of beg ch-3, fasten off.

RND 4: Attach A with sl st in sp indicated at point 1D on chart; following chart in numerical order through point 60, work as for Rnd 1, join in 3rd ch of beg ch-3, fasten off.

RND 5: Attach B with sl st in sp indicated at point 1E on chart; following chart in numerical order through point 84, work as for Rnd 1, join in 3rd ch of beg ch-3, fasten off.

RND 6: Attach B with sl st in sp indicated at point 1F on chart; following chart in numerical order through point 92, work as for Rnd 1, join in 3rd ch of beg ch-3, fasten off.

RND 7: Attach A with sl st in sp indicated at point 1G on chart; following chart in numerical order through point 116, work as for Rnd 1, join in 3rd ch of beg ch-3, fasten off.

RND 8: Attach A with sl st in sp indicated at point 1H on chart; following chart in numerical order through point 124, work as for Rnd 1, join in 3rd ch of beg ch-3, fasten off.

RND 9: Attach B with sl st in sp indicated at point 1I on chart; following chart in numerical order through point 148, work as for Rnd 1, join in 3rd ch of beg ch-3, fasten off.

RND 10: Attach B with sl st in sp indicated at point 1J on chart; following chart in numerical order through point 156, work as for Rnd 1, join in 3rd ch of beg ch-3, fasten off.

RND 11: Attach A with sl st in sp indicated at point 1K on chart; following chart in numerical order through point 180, work as for Rnd 1, working [3 dc, ch 1] twice in each of 4 corners, join in 3rd ch of beg ch-3, fasten off.

BACK
ROW 1: With A, ch 69 (foundation ch), ch 3 more (turning ch-3), dc in 4th ch from hook, dc in each rem ch across, turn. (70 dc)

ROWS 2–23: Ch 3, dc in each dc across, turn.

JOINING FRONT & BACK
Holding front and back tog with front facing and working through both thicknesses behind ruffle, sc between two 3-dc groups at upper right corner on front and in first dc on back, [{sc in base of next dc on

Ruffled Pot Holder/Hot Mat

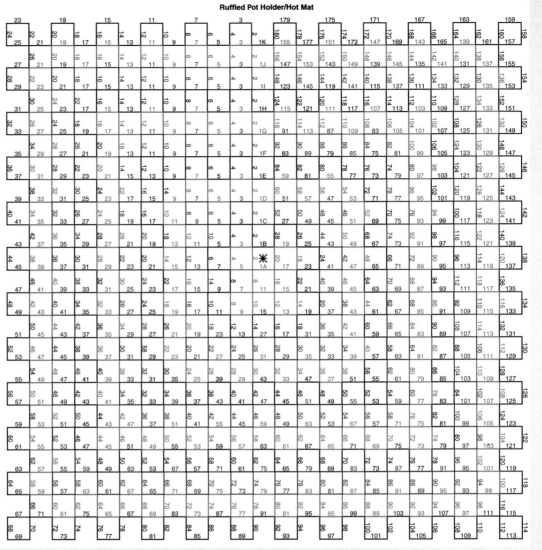

front and in top of next dc on back} 3 times, sc in next sp on front and next dc on back, {sc in same sp on front and next dc on back} twice] 11 times, sc in base of next dc on front and in top of next dc on back] 3 times, sc between same 3-dc group and in top of same dc as last sc made, [sc in base of next dc on front and over end st of last row on back] 3 times, *[sc in next sp on front and over end st of next row on back, {sc in same sp on front and over end st of same row on back} twice, sc in base of next dc on front and over end st of next row on back, {sc in base of next dc on front and over end st of same row on back} twice] 11 times *, sc between same 3-dc group and next 3-dc group and in first rem lp of foundation ch; working in rem lps of foundation ch across, [[sc in base of next dc on front and in next rem lp on back} 3 times, sc in next sp on

front and in next rem lp on back, {sc in same sp on front and in next rem lp on back} twice] 11 times, [sc in base of next dc on front and in next rem lp on back] 3 times, sc between same 3-dc group and next dc group and in same rem lp as last sc made, [sc in base of next dc on front and over end st of first row on back] 3 times, rep from * to *, join in beg sc, fasten off.

FINISHING
Cover plastic ring with sc, leaving a length of cotton, fasten off. Sew plastic ring to corner for hanging lp. ✧

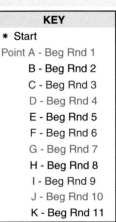

KEY	
✳	Start
	Point A - Beg Rnd 1
	B - Beg Rnd 2
	C - Beg Rnd 3
	D - Beg Rnd 4
	E - Beg Rnd 5
	F - Beg Rnd 6
	G - Beg Rnd 7
	H - Beg Rnd 8
	I - Beg Rnd 9
	J - Beg Rnd 10
	K - Beg Rnd 11

Seashell Place Mat Set

Take a trip to the beaches of old when you place these dainty shell mats and coasters on your patio or deck table. Don't forget to bring your picnic lunch and your knee-length swim suit!

Design revised by Maggie Chasalow

SKILL LEVEL: INTERMEDIATE

PLACE MAT: 13¾ x 14½ inches

COASTER: 4¼ inches at widest point

MATERIALS

➤ Worsted weight crochet cotton (2.5 ozs per ball): 2 balls cream (MC), 1 ball pink (CC)

➤ Size 0 steel crochet hook or size needed to obtain gauge

GAUGE

5 dc = 1 inch

Check gauge to save time.

Coaster

With CC, ch 2, [7 sc, hdc] in 2nd ch from hook, drop CC, attach MC with sl st in back lp only of first sc, ch 1, working in back lps only throughout coaster, 2 sc in same st, 2 hdc in next st, 3 dc in each of next 3 sts, 2 dc in each of next 2 sts, drop MC; pick up dropped lp of CC, 2 sc in first MC sc, 2 hdc in next st, 2 dc in each of next 14 sts, drop CC, pick up dropped lp of MC, 2 dc in each of next 10 sts, [dc in next st, 2 dc in next st] 7 times, fasten off MC; pick up dropped lp of CC, [dc in each of next 2 dc, 2 dc in next dc] 14 times, fasten off.

Place Mat

SCROLL

ROW 1 (RS): With MC, ch 23, [sc, hdc, 8 dc] in 2nd ch from hook, [dc in each of next 6 sts, 2 dc in next st] twice, dc in each of next 6 sts, [8 dc, hdc, sc] in last st, fasten off, turn.

ROW 2: With WS facing, attach CC with sl st in first rem lp of foundation ch after last sc of last row, sc in last sc made, 2 hdc in next st, 3 dc in each of next 4 sts, 2 dc in each of next 5 sts, [dc in each of next 6 sts, 2 dc in next st] twice, dc in each of next 6 sts, 2 dc in each of next 5 sts, 3 dc in each of next 4 sts, 2 hdc in next st, sc in next st, sl st in next unworked rem lp of foundation ch, fasten off, turn.

ROW 3: With RS facing, attach MC with sl st in next unworked rem lp of foundation ch, sk sl st, hdc in next sc, 2 dc in each of next 7 sts, [dc in next st, 2 dc in next st] 8 times, dc in each of next 13 sts, mark last 2 sts made with safety pin or other small marker, dc in each of next 11 sts, [2 dc in next st, dc in next st] 8 times, 2 dc in each of next 7 sts, hdc in next st, sl st in next unworked rem lp on foundation ch, fasten off.

UPPER SHELL

ROW 1: With RS facing, attach MC with sl st in back lp only of first marked st to the right, [ch 1, 2 dc, 3 tr] in same st, [4 tr, 2 dc, ch 1] in back lp only of next st, sk next st, sl st in each of next 4 sts, turn. (11 sts)

ROW 2: Ch 1, dc in first dc, [ch 1, dc in next st] 10 times, ch 1, sk next 2 unworked sts on Row 3 of scroll, sl st in front lp only of each of next 4 sts, turn. (11 dc)

ROW 3: Ch 1, [2 dc in next dc, ch 1] 11 times, sk next 2 unworked sts on Row 3 of scroll, sl st in back lp only of each of next 3 sts, turn. (11 groups 2-dc)

ROW 4: Ch 1, [2 dc in next dc, dc in next dc, ch 1] 11 times, sk next 2 unworked sts on Row 3 of scroll, sl st in front lp only of each of next 3 sts, turn. (11 groups 3-dc)

ROW 5: Ch 1, [dc in next dc, 2 dc in next dc, dc in next dc, ch 1] 11 times, sk next unworked st on Row 3 of scroll, sl st in back lp only of each of next 3 sts, turn. (11 groups 4-dc)

ROW 6: Ch 1, [dc in each dc of next dc group, inc 1 dc at center of dc group, ch 1] rep across, sk next unworked st on Row 3 of scroll, sl st in front lp only of each of next 3 sts, turn. (11 groups 5-dc)

ROW 7: [Dc in each dc of next dc group, inc 1 dc at center dc group, ch 1] rep across, sk next unworked st of Row 3 of scroll, sl st in back lp only of each of next 3 sts, turn. (11 group 6-dc)

ROWS 8–11: Rep Rows 6 and 7 alternately. (11 groups 10-dc)

ROW 12: *[Dc in each dc of next dc group, inc 2 dc evenly sp, ch 1] twice *, [dc in each dc of next dc group, inc 1 dc at center of dc group, ch 1] 7 times, rep from * to *, sk next unworked st on Row 3 of scroll, sl st in front lp only of

Continued on page 80

Grandmother's Kitchen   ✧ 77

Floral Kitchen Set

This cheery kitchen set combines old-time techniques with bold modern colors, giving you the best of both worlds as you stitch and display its delicate flowers.

Designs revised by
Maggie Petsch Chasalow

SKILL LEVEL: INTERMEDIATE

SIZE
COASTER: 4½ inches in diameter
POT HOLDER: 6½ inches in diameter
PLACE MAT: 15 inches in diameter

MATERIALS
➤ Crochet cotton size 10 (350 yds per ball): 1 ball each pink green, yellow and white
➤ Crochet cotton size 3: 100 yards white
➤ Sizes 3 and 7 steel crochet hooks or sizes needed to obtain gauge
➤ 1-inch plastic ring
➤ Sewing needle and thread
➤ Tapestry needle

GAUGE
With crochet cotton size 10 and smaller hook, Rnds 1 and 2 of flower = 1¼ inches in diameter

With crochet cotton size 3 and larger hook, Rnds 1–4 of pot holder = 1¾ inches in diameter

Check gauge to save time.

PATTERN NOTES
Weave in loose ends as work progresses.

Join rnds with sl st unless otherwise indicated.

PATTERN STITCHES
CH-4 P: Ch 4, sl st in top of last tr made.

CH-3 P: Ch 3, sl st in top of last sc made.

CH-7 P: [Sc, ch 7, sc] in indicated sp or st.

Coaster

FLOWER
RND 1 (RS): With yellow and smaller hook, ch 7, sl st to join to form a ring, ch 4 (counts as first dc, ch 1), [dc, ch 1] 11 times in ring, join in 3rd ch of beg ch-4. (12 ch-1 sps)

RND 2: Ch 3 (counts as first dc), 2 dc in next sp, [dc in next dc, 2 dc in next sp] rep around, join in 3rd ch of beg ch-3, fasten off. (36 dc)

RND 3: With RS facing, using smaller hook, attach pink with sl st in same st as joining, ch 1, sc in same st, sc in each of next 2 sts, *[sc, ch 9, sc] in next st **, sc in each of next 5 sts, rep from * around, ending last rep at **, sc in each of last 2 sts, join in beg sc. (6 ch-9 sps)

RND 4: Ch 1, sc in same st as joining, *[2 dc, {2 tr, ch 4 p} 7 times, 2 tr, 2 dc] in ch-9 sp **, sc in center sc of next 7-sc group, rep from * around, ending last rep at **, join in beg sc, fasten off. (6 petals)

LEAF *(make 6)*
With green and smaller hook, ch 13, 2 sc in 2nd ch from hook, hdc in next ch, dc in each of next 2 chs, tr in each of next 4 chs, dc in each of next 2 chs, hdc in next ch, [2 sc, ch-3 p, sc] in last ch; working on opposite side of foundation ch, hdc in next ch, dc in each of next 2 chs, tr in each of next 4 chs, dc in each of next 2 chs, hdc in next ch, sc in same ch as beg sc, join in beg sc, leaving a length of cotton, fasten off.

FINISHING
With tapestry needle and green, using photo as a guide, tack leaves between and behind petals of flower. Tack first 2 ch-4 picots on each side of each petal to leaf between each pair of petals. Starch lightly.

Pot Holder

RND 1 (RS): With larger hook and white size 3 cotton, ch 4, sl st to join to form a ring, ch 1, 8 sc in ring, join in beg sc. (8 sc)

RND 2: Ch 1, 2 sc in same st as joining, 2 sc in each rem sc around, join in beg sc. (16 sc)

RND 3: Ch 1, sc in same st as joining, 2 sc in next sc, [sc in next sc, 2 sc in next sc] rep around, join in beg sc. (24 sc)

RND 4: Ch 1, 2 sc in same st as joining, sc in each of next 2 sc, [2 sc in next sc, sc in each of next 2 sc] rep around, join in beg sc. (32 sc)

RNDS 5–16: Ch 1, beg in same st as joining, sc in each sc around, inc 8 sc evenly sp each rnd, join in beg sc; at the end of Rnd 16, fasten off. (128 sc)

RND 17: With RS facing, using larger hook, attach 2 strands of pink held tog with a sl st in same st as joining, ch 1, sc in same st, *sk next st, 5 dc in next st, sk next st **, sc in next st, rep from *

around, ending last rep at **, join in beg sc, fasten off.

FLOWER *(make 1)*
RNDS 1–4: Rep Rnds 1–4 of flower for coaster.

LEAF *(make 6)*
Rep instructions for leaf of coaster.

With tapestry needle and green, using photo as a guide, tack leaves between and behind petals of flower. Tack first 2 ch-4 picots on each side of each petal to leaf between each pair of petals.

HANGER
With smaller hook, sl st over plastic ring, ch 1, sc closely around plastic ring, join in beg sc, leaving a length of cotton, fasten off. Sew ring to center 3 dc of any 5-dc group on Rnd 17.

FINISHING
With sewing needle and thread, sew flower with leaves to center of pot holder. Steam press pot holder lightly.

Place Mat

FLOWERS *(make 7)*
RNDS 1–4: Rep Rnds 1–4 of flower for coaster.

LEAF *(make 42)*
Rep instructions for leaf for coaster.

With tapestry needle and green, using photo as a guide, tack leaves between and behind petals of flowers. Tack first 2 ch-4 picots on each side of each petal to leaf between each pair of petals.

Using photo as a guide, arrange 6 flowers around 1 center flower. With tapestry needle and green,

tack ch-3 picots at adjoining tips of leaves tog.

BORDER
RND 1: With smaller hook and RS facing, attach white size 10 cotton with a sl st in ch-3 p at tip of first free leaf to the right on any flower, ch 1, ch-7 p in same st, *ch 7, sc halfway down side of same leaf, ch 7, sc in center ch-4 p of next petal, sc halfway up side of next leaf, ch 7, ch-7 p in ch-3 p at tip of same leaf, ch 7, sc halfway down side of same leaf, ch 7, sc in center ch-4 p of next petal, ch 7, sc halfway up side of next leaf, ch 7, sc between next 2 ch-3 picots, ch 7, sc halfway up side of next leaf, ch 7, sc in center ch-4 p of next petal, ch 7, sc halfway up side of next leaf, ch 7

Continued on next page

**, ch-7 p in ch-3 p at tip of same leaf, rep from * around, ending last rep at **, join in sc at base of ch-7 p.

RND 2: Sl st in each of first 3 chs of same ch-7 p, ch 1, sc in same ch-7 p, *ch 10, dtr in 2nd sc at base of same ch-7 p, [ch 5, dtr in next ch-7 sp] twice, dtr in next ch-7 sp, ch 5, dtr in next ch-7 sp, turn, ch 10, sk last 3 dtr made, sc in top of next dtr, sl st in each of next 5 chs, sc in top of next dtr, turn, ch 10, sc in last ch-10 sp made, ch 10, dtr in top of dtr at base of same ch-10, dtr in sc at base of next ch-7 p, ch 10, sc in center ch of same ch-7 p, ch 10,

dtr in 2nd sc at base of same ch-7 p, [ch 5, dtr in next ch-7 sp] 4 times, dtr in next ch-7 sp, ch 5, dtr in next ch-7 sp, turn, ch 10, sk last 3 dtr made, sc in top of next dtr, sl st in each of next 5 chs, sc in top of next dtr, turn, ch 10, sc in last ch-10 sp made, ch 10, dtr in top of dtr at base of same ch-10 sp, dtr in next ch-7 sp, ch 5, dtr in next ch-7 sp, turn, ch 10, [sc in next ch-10 sp, ch 10] twice, sk next ch-5 sp, sc in top of next dtr, sl st in each of next 5 chs, sc in top of next dtr, turn, [ch 10, sc in next ch-10 sp] 3 times, ch 10, dtr in top of next dtr, dtr in sc at base of next ch-7 p, ch 10 **, sc in center ch of

same ch-7 p, rep from * around, ending last rep at **, join in beg sc, fasten off.

RND 3: With RS facing, using smaller hook, attach pink with a sl st in first ch-10 sp after joining st, ch 1, sc in same st, *[7 dtr in sc between same ch-10 sp and next ch-10 sp, sc in next ch-10 sp] 3 times, 5 dtr in sc between same ch-10 sp and next ch-10 sp, sc in next ch-10 sp, [7 dtr in sc between same ch-10 sp and next ch-10 sp, sc in next ch-10 sp] 5 times, 5 dtr in sc between same ch-10 sp and next ch-10 sp **, sc in next ch-10 sp, rep from * around, ending last rep at **, join in beg sc, fasten off. ✧

Seashell Place Mat continued from page 76

next st, fasten off, turn.

ROW 13: With RS facing, sk first dc group, attach MC with sl st in next st, ch 1, sc in same st and in next st, hdc in each of next 2 sts, dc in each of next 2 sts, 2 dc in next st, dc in each of next 5 sts, ch 1, [dc in each dc of next dc group, inc 1 dc at center of dc group, ch 1] 7 times, dc in each of next 5 sts of next dc group, 2 dc in next dc, dc in each of next 2 sts, hdc in each of next 2 sts, sc in each of next 2 sts, fasten off, turn.

ROW 14: With WS facing, attach MC with sl st in first dc of first 12-dc group, ch 1, sc in same st, sc in next st, hdc in each of next 2 sts, dc in next st, 2 dc in next st, dc in each of next 6 sts, ch 1, [dc in each dc of next dc group, inc 1 dc at center of dc group, ch 1] 5 times, dc in each of next 6 dc, 2 dc in next dc, dc in each of next 2 sts, hdc in each of next 2 sts, sc in each of next 2 sts, fasten off, turn.

ROW 15: With RS facing, attach MC with sl st in first dc of first 13-dc group, ch 1, sc in same st, sc in next st, hdc in each of next 2 sts, dc in each of next 2 sts, 2 dc in next st, dc in each of next 6 sts, ch 1, [dc in each dc of next dc group, inc 1 dc at center of dc

group, ch 1] 3 times, dc in each of next 6 dc, 2 dc in next st, dc in each of next 2 sts, hdc in each of next 2 sts, sc in each of next 2 sts, fasten off, turn.

ROW 16: With WS facing, attach MC with sl st in first dc of first 14-dc group, ch 1, sc in same st, sc in next st, hdc in each of next 2 sts, dc in each of next 3 sts, 2 dc in next st, dc in each of next 6 sts, ch 1, dc in each dc of next dc group, inc 1 dc at center of dc group, ch 1, dc in each of next 6 dc, 2 dc in next st, dc in each of next 3 sts, hdc in each of next 2 sts, sc in each of next 2 sts, fasten off, turn.

ROW 17: With RS facing, attach MC with sl st in first dc of 15-dc group, ch 1, sc in same st, sc in next st, hdc in each of next 2 sts, dc in each of next 3 sts, 2 dc in next st, dc in each of next 3 sts, hdc in each of next 2 sts, sc in each of next 2 sts, fasten off.

UPPER SHELL EDGING
With RS facing, attach CC with a sl st in last sl st of Row 12 of upper shell, sl st in next ch-1 sp, ch 1, [{sl st, ch 1} in each st across to next ch-1 sp; working down to

corner of upper shell, {sl st in next ch-1 sp, ch 1} in each ch-1 sp to Row 2, turn, {sl st, ch 1} in each ch-1 sp back to outer edge of upper shell] 10 times, [sl st, ch 1] in each st across to last ch-1 sp, sl st in ch-1 sp, sl st in next sl st, sl st in each st of Row 3 of scroll to foundation ch, sl st in each rem lp across foundation ch, working [sk next st, sl st in next st] twice at center of foundation ch, [sl st, ch 1] in each of next 5 sts on Row 3 of scroll, sl st in next st on Row 3, sl st in corresponding sl st directly across on scroll, [sl st, ch 1] in each rem st on Row 3 of scroll across to first rem lp of Row 3 of scroll at bottom of upper shell, [sl st, ch 1] in each rem lp across to last rem lp, sl st in last rem lp, fasten off.

With RS facing, attach CC with a sl st in first ch-1 sp of Row 2 of upper shell, ch 1, [sl st, ch 1] in each rem ch-1 sp across Row 2 to last sp, turn. [Sl st, ch 1] in each ch-1 sp back across Row 2 to last sp, fasten off. ✧

A Look At Crochet Hooks

By Maggie Petsch Chasalow

Most of us give little thought to our crochet hooks other than to check the instructions for the suggested size for the project at hand and then go with the hook that duplicates the stated gauge. If we don't have the appropriate size at home we can always run out to the nearest craft or yarn store and pick up something made of steel, aluminum, or plastic.

The earliest crocheters, however, didn't have chain stores or mail-order catalogs to fulfill their needs for crochet implements. They fashioned their own implements, usually of wood, bone, or metal.

Looking back into crochet history, I can't fail but to be amazed that these crocheters could turn out such lovely pieces of needlework with the crude tools with which they had to work. I have, for instance, a wooden hook fashioned out of a chair leg by a gentleman in Texas for his wife.

In Ireland, exquisite Irish crochet laces were worked with hooks made from stiff wire inserted into a piece of wood or cork. The end of the wire was filed down and a hook turned at the end.

At the other end of the spectrum, I have a beautiful and fine-tipped antique sterling silver hook with a mother-of-pearl handle that reads "Savannah." Every time I use it, it conjures up an image of a lovely Southern belle sitting on her wisteria-covered veranda on a sunny afternoon leisurely crocheting yards of lovely lace to edge her petticoats or trim her pillowcases. On the whimsical side, I have an ivory hook with a pelican carved at the top, and another hook fashioned out of a material which looks suspiciously like an old-fashioned peppermint candy. This hook has been accordingly relegated to the "look-but-don't-use" category.

Since many crochet historians feel that thread crochet at least may have evolved from tambour work, an ancient chain-stitch form of oriental embroidery—we can assume tambour hooks were the first tools used in Europe for thread crochet. Tambour hooks had sharp pointed hooks to pierce the fabric on which the embroidery was worked; later crochet hooks had more rounded hooks.

As crochet grew in popularity and technology flourished, crocheters enjoyed a Renaissance in the production of crochet hooks. Crocheters of the upper classes could take their pick of beautiful hooks hand-carved of wood, bone, or ivory, or made of mother-of-pearl, tortoiseshell, horn, agate, or sterling silver, and sometimes inlaid with gemstones.

For those more concerned with the quality of their work than the appearance of their hook, all sorts of shapes and styles of hooks designed to facilitate the crocheting process, most notably those hooks with enlarged section on the shank on which to rest the thumb while working.

In the early 1920s, sets of interchangeable crochet hooks became popular. Each set consisted of a single handle, perhaps of bone or amber, with an assortment of short steel hooks generally ranging in size from 1 to 14. The crocheter simply selected the size hook she needed for her project and screwed it into the tip of the handle.

In this country, Boye Needle Company produced the first complete line of American-made steel crochet hooks in 1917. Each hook sold for a nickel. World War II forced the government to order the cessation of nickel plating for crochet hooks in 1942, and Boye began a special black plating process known as hoto black process. Nickel plating was not reinstated until the latter part of May 1945. Aluminum crochet hooks appeared in 1923 and crochet forks for hairpin crochet in 1935. ✧

Chapter Four

Elegant Edgings

*N*othing adds a simple touch of old-time elegance like a simple edging gracing a piece of antique linen or favorite handkerchief. With this collection of more than 20 enchanting edgings, you'll be able to dress up pillowcases, valances, napkins, handkerchiefs and more with pretty strips of ruffles, flowers, shells, scallops and filet.

Fanciful Flowers

These friendly, floral edgings will warm your heart and your kitchen with their bright, cheery colors and sweet white and rose petals! Use them to adorn crisp, white linen from your Grandmother's hope chest!

Designs revised by Ruth Shepherd

Daisies in the Dell

SKILL LEVEL: BEGINNER

SIZE
1½ inches wide

MATERIALS
➤ DMC embroidery floss: white, green and yellow
➤ Size 8 steel crochet hook or size needed to obtain gauge
➤ Sewing needle and thread

GAUGE
Each flower section is approximately ⅞ inch long

Check gauge to save time.

PATTERN NOTES
Weave in loose ends as work progresses.

Do not separate plies of floss. Floss amounts will vary depending on length of edging.

BASE
RND 1: With green, [ch 6, trtr in 5th ch from hook] rep for desired length, working along long side edge, [{3 sc, ch 3, 3 sc} in next ch lp, ch 1] rep across, working on opposite long edge, [{3 sc, ch 3, 3 sc} across bar of trtr, ch 1] rep across, join in beg sc, fasten off.

DAISY
ROW 1: With RS facing, attach yellow in first sc, ch 1, sc in same sc, *ch 3, [sc, ch 3, sc] in ch-3 sp, ch 3, sc in next ch-1 sp, rep from * across, ending last rep with ch 3, sc in last sc, fasten off.

ROW 2: With RS facing, attach white in first sc, ch 1, sc in same sc, *[ch 3, dc] in same sc, sk next ch-3 sp, [sl st, ch 3, dc, ch 3] 4 times in next ch-3 sp, sk next ch-3 sp, sc in next sc, rep from * across, fasten off.

FINISHING
Press edging lightly and sew in place. ✧

Roses in a Row

SKILL LEVEL: BEGINNER

SIZE
1¼ inches wide

MATERIALS
➤ DMC embroidery floss: medium dusty rose #962, ultra very light dusty rose #963 and medium parrot green #906
➤ Size 8 steel crochet hook or size needed to obtain gauge
➤ Sewing needle and thread

GAUGE
Each rose section is approximately ⅞ inch

Check gauge to save time.

PATTERN NOTES
Weave in loose ends as work progresses.

Do not separate plies of floss.

Floss amounts will vary depending on length of edging.

Edging

BASE
RND 1: With medium parrot green, [ch 6, trtr in 5th ch from hook] rep for desired length; working along long side edge, [{3 sc, ch 3, 3 sc} over ch lp] rep across edge; working on opposite long edge [{3 sc, ch 3, 3 sc} over bar of trtr, ch 1] rep across edge, sl st to join in beg sc, fasten off.

ROSES
ROW 1: With RS facing, attach medium dusty rose in first sc at either end, ch 1, sc in same sc, sc in each of next 2 sc, [{sc, ch 5, 3 sc in 2nd ch from hook, 3 sc in each of next 3 chs} in ch-3 sp, ch 3, sc in next ch-1 sp, ch 3] rep across, ending with sc in last sc, fasten off.

ROW 2: With RS facing, attach ultra very light dusty rose in first sc of previous row, ch 1, beg in same sc as beg ch-1, [sc, ch 5, 3 sc in 2nd ch from hook, 3 sc in each of next 3 chs] all in same sc, [ch 3, holding medium dusty rose forward and working behind, {sc, ch 5, 3 sc in 2nd ch from hook, 3 sc in each of next 3 chs} in next ch-3 sp] rep across, fasten off.

FINISHING
Press Rnd 1 of edging lightly; do not press roses. Sew edging in place. ✧

Delicate Edgings

Unique stitch combinations make each of these enchanting edgings rich with texture and elegance.

Designs revised by
Nancy Hearne

SKILL LEVEL: BEGINNER

SIZE

No. 1: Approximately 1 inch wide

No. 2: Approximately 1 inch wide

No. 3: Approximately 1 inch wide

MATERIALS

➤ Crochet cotton size 10

➤ Size 7 steel crochet hook or size needed to obtain gauge

GAUGE

No. 1: Each scallop = 1 inch wide

No. 2: 5 dc and 5 ch-1 sps = 1 inch

No. 3: 9 sc = 1 inch

Check gauge to save time.

PATTERN NOTE
Edging may be crocheted to length desired.

PATTERN STITCH
DTR: Yo hook 3 times, insert hook in indicated st, yo, draw up a lp, [yo, draw through 2 lps on hook] 4 times.

No. 1

ROW 1: Ch 14, sl st in 8th ch from hook, [ch 18, sl st in 8th ch from hook] rep for desired length.

ROW 2: Sl st to center of lp, ch 9, sl st in 4th st from hook (for p), ch 1, dtr in same st, *ch 4, sl st in 4th ch from hook (for p), ch 1, dtr in same st, rep from * 5 times, [sk 5 sts of ch, dc in next st, 8 dtr with p and ch 1 between each dtr in center st of next lp] rep across, ending with dc in last st of ch, fasten off.

No. 2

ROW 1: Ch for desired length, dc in 6th st from hook, [ch 1, sk 1 st, dc in next st] rep across, turn.

ROW 2: [Ch 7, sk next dc, sc in next dc] rep across, turn.

ROW 3: Sl st to lp, ch 1, 3 sc over lp, [ch 5, 3 sc over next lp] rep across, turn.

ROW 4: Sl st to center of lp, **ch 5, dc in next ch-5 lp, *ch 5, sl st in 5th st from hook (for p), rep from * twice, dc in top of last dc, dc in same sp with first dc, ch 5, sl st in next lp, rep from ** across.

No. 3

ROW 1: Ch for desired length, sc in 2nd ch from hook, sc in each rem ch across, turn.

ROW 2: [Ch 7, sk 3 sc, sc in next sc] rep across, turn.

ROW 3: Sl st to center of lp, *[ch 7, sl st in 5th st from hook (for p)] twice, ch 2, sc in next lp, ch 12, sl st in 9th st from hook to form a ring, ch 3, sc in next lp, rep from * across, turn.

ROW 4: Sl st to center of double p lp, *ch 3, work 5 dc in ch-9 ring, ch 5, sl st in last dc for p, ch 5, [dc, ch 3, sc] between next 2 picots, rep from * across. ✧

Photo: Top pillow is pattern No. 3, middle pillow is pattern No. 1, and bottom pillow is pattern No. 2.

SKILL LEVEL: BEGINNER

SIZE

PRETTY FANS: ¾ inch wide (yellow)

FLOWERS IN A ROW: 1¼ inches wide (pink)

DAINTY RUFFLES: 1 inch wide (white)

ROYAL CROWN: ⅞ inch wide (green)

BUTTERFLY: 1¾ inches wide (ecru)

MATERIALS

➤ DMC Cebelia crochet cotton size 30 (50 grams per ball): 1 ball each yellow #745, pink #818, white, green #955 and ecru

➤ Size 12 steel crochet hook or size needed to obtain gauge

➤ 10½-inch Irish linen hem-stitched hankie for each edging

GAUGE

15 sts = 1 inch

Check gauge to save time.

Pretty Pastel Edgings

Turn an ordinary handkerchief into a one-of-a-kind crocheter's treasure with any one of these charming edgings! They're just like those Grandmother used to carry in her handbag to church and other special occasions!

PATTERN NOTES

Weave in loose ends as work progresses.

Ch 3 counts as first dc throughout.

Pretty Fans

ROW 1: Starting at narrow edge with yellow, ch 6, dc in 6th ch from hook, turn.

ROW 2: Ch 3, 7 dc in sp, turn.

ROW 3: Ch 4 (counts as first dc, ch-1), [dc in next dc, ch 1] 6 times, dc in top of turning ch, turn.

ROW 4: Ch 5 (counts as first dc, ch-2), dc in first dc, turn.

ROW 5: Ch 5, dc in next dc, turn.

Rep Rows 2–5 for length desired, ending with Row 3.

HEADING

ROW 1: Attach yellow to first free

ch-5 sp, ch 1, sc in same ch-5 sp, [ch 10, sc in next ch-5 sp] rep across, fasten off.

SCALLOPED EDGE

ROW 1: Attach yellow to first ch-1 sp, *ch 3, sc in same sp, [{sc, ch 3, sc} in next ch-1 sp] 6 times, ch 8, sc in first ch-1 sp in next scallop, rep from * across, fasten off.

Flowers in a Row

FIRST MOTIF

RND 1: Starting at center with pink, ch 10, sl st to join in first ch to from a ring, ch 5 (counts as first dc, ch-2), [dc in ring, ch 2] 11 times, join in 3rd ch of beg ch-5.

RND 2: [{Sc, 3 dc, sc (for scallop)} in next ch-2 sp] rep around, join in beg sc, fasten off.

SECOND MOTIF

RND 1: Rep Rnd 1 of first motif.

RND 2: Sc in next ch-2 sp, 2 dc in same ch sp, sl st in center dc of any scallop on previous motif, dc and sc in same ch-2 sp of working motif, in next sp make sc, 2 dc, sl st in corresponding dc on previous motif, dc and sc on working motif, complete motif as for first motif.

Make necessary number of motifs, joining two scallops of each motif to two scallops of previous motif, leaving 4 free scallops on each side of joining on each motif.

HEADING

ROW 1: Attach pink to 3rd free scallop preceding center of next

scallop, *ch 5 holding back on hook the last lp of each tr, make tr in center of next 2 free scallops, yo and draw through all lps on hook (joint tr), ch 5, dc in center of next scallop, ch 2, dc in center of next scallop, rep from * across, ending with dc, ch 2, dc, turn.

ROW 2: Ch 5 (counts as first dc, ch-2), dc in next dc, *ch 2, dc in next sp, ch 2, dc in next joint tr, ch 2, dc in next sp, [ch 2, dc in next dc] twice, rep from * across, fasten off.

Dainty Ruffles

ROW 1: Starting at narrow edge with white, ch 6, dc in 6th ch from hook, turn.

ROW 2: Ch 5, dc in next dc, turn.

Rep Row 2 for length desired, fasten off.

HEADING

ROW 1: Attach white to first free lp on long side, ch 4, tr in same lp, *ch 5, holding back on hook the last lp of each tr, make 2 tr in next lp, yo and draw through all lps on hook (cl), rep from * across, turn.

ROW 2: Ch 8 (counts as first dc, ch-5), sk first cl, [dc in top of next cl, ch 5] rep across, fasten off.

SCALLOPED EDGE

ROW 1: Attach white to first free lp on opposite side of heading, sc in same place, *ch 3, [{dc, ch 1} in next ch lp] 4 times and dc, ch 3, sc in next ch lp, ch 5, sc in next ch lp, rep from * across, ending with ch 3, sc in last lp, turn.

Continued on page 90

ROW 2: Ch 1, sc in first sc, *3 sc in next lp, sc in next dc, [ch 4, sc in next dc] 4 times, 3 sc in next lp, sc in next sc, ch 8, sc in next sc, rep from * across, turn.

ROW 3: Sl st in next 3 sc and in next lp, ch 4, tr in same lp, *[ch 5, make a 2-tr cl in next lp] 3 times, ch 5, sc in next lp, ch 5, 2-tr cl in next lp, rep from * across, ending with 2-tr cl in last lp, turn.

ROW 4: Sl st in next lp, 3 sc in same lp, *[ch 7, 3 sc in next lp] twice, ch 7, sc in next lp, sc in next sc, sc in next lp, ch 7, 3 sc in next lp, rep from * across, fasten off.

Royal Crown

HEADING

ROW 1: Starting at narrow edge with green, ch 5, tr in 5th ch from hook, turn.

ROW 2: Ch 4, tr in previous tr, tr at base of same tr, turn.

ROW 3: Ch 4, tr in previous tr, tr at base of next tr, turn.

Rep Row 3 for length desired.

SCALLOPED EDGE

ROW 1: Sc in first side tr, *ch 4, sc in tip of next tr along side, ch 7, sc in tip of next tr, rep from *

across, being sure to have an uneven number of ch-7 lps and ending with ch 4, sc in base of last tr on side, turn.

ROW 2: Ch 1, sc in first lp, [ch 3, 10 dc in next lp, ch 3, sc in next lp] rep across, turn.

ROW 3: Ch 1, sc in first lp, *ch 5, holding back on hook the last lp of each tr, make tr in first 3 dc of next 10-dc group, yo and draw through all lps on hook (cl), ch 5, dc in each of next 4 dc, ch 5, cl over next 3 dc, ch 5, sk 4 dc, sc in next 2 dc, rep from * across, ending with ch 5, sc in last lp, turn.

ROW 4: Sl st to center of next lp, sc in same lp, *ch 5, sc in next lp, ch 7, make a 4-tr cl over next 4 dc, ch 7, sc in next lp, ch 5, 2 sc in next lp, sc in next 2 sc, 2 sc in next lp, rep from * across, fasten off.

Butterfly

ROW 1: Starting at narrow edge with ecru, ch 6, [dc, ch 1, dc] in 6th ch from hook, turn.

ROW 2: Ch 5, [dc, ch 1, dc] in next ch-1 sp, turn.

ROWS 3–9: Rep Row 2.

ROW 10: Ch 5, [dc, ch 1, dc] in next ch-1 sp, ch 5, dc in next 5 lps

along side, ch 1, turn, sl st in 3rd ch of ch-5, ch 2.

ROW 11: [Dc, ch 1, dc] in next ch-1 sp, turn.

Rep Rows 3–11 for length desired, ending with Row 11.

HEADING

ROW 1: *Holding back on hook last lp of each tr, make 3 tr in center of next dc group, yo and draw through all lps on hook (cl), [ch 5, sc in next lp] 3 times, ch 5, rep from * across, ending with [ch 5, sc in next lp] 3 times, turn.

ROW 2: Ch 5, *[dc in next sp, ch 5] twice, cl in next ch-2 sp, ch 5, rep from * across, fasten off.

SCALLOPED EDGE

ROW 1: Attach ecru to sp in center of first dc group on opposite side of heading, sc in same sp, *[ch 8, cl in next free lp] 3 times **, ch 8, sc in next sp in center of dc group, rep from * across, ending at ** on last rep, turn.

ROW 2: Ch 8, sc in first sp, ch 12, sc in next sp, *ch 12, 4 sc in next sp, sc in next sc, 4 sc in next sp, [ch 12, sc in next sp] twice, rep from * across, fasten off. ✧

And She Did It all Herself

Doesn't your heart just naturally warm to a sweet little girl of 11 whose skill with the needle and the crochet hook makes a lovely display possible?

Miss La Pearl Weeter, that's the young lady's name, lives in Thistle, Utah. I have before me, as I write, a letter from one who is evidently proud of her, either as a relative or merely as a fellow citizen.

When little Miss Weeter was 8 years old, so this letter says, she could copy anything presented to her, either from the work itself or from a paper pattern.

Today, at 11, the old ladies of her acquaintance, as well as the young ones, turn to her for help when their crochet goes wrong.

This smiling little lady has taken eleven prizes at state fairs—"first prizes and eight special first prizes", our correspondent tells us.

Not every little girl has the natural aptitude for needlework that you see evidenced here. But even so, needle skill and the love of the work can be cultivated, and better so in early years.

The thing that most impresses us was not the remarkable display, worthy of admiration though it is, but the fact that all through her lifetime this little girl will reap the reward of early acquired house wifely skill— a source of pleasure and profit to herself and others. Is your little girl being taught to love needlework?

Published in *The Modern Priscilla*, June 1923

Dainty Scallops

Freshen up your bedroom or bathroom with this charming scallop edging accenting the bottom of a pretty valance. Stitch it in any color to coordinate with your room's decor, and weave in a coordinating satin ribbon for a finishing touch!

Design revised by Nancy Hearne

SKILL LEVEL: BEGINNER

SIZE
Approximately 1 inch wide

MATERIALS
- ➤ Crochet cotton size 10: dark red
- ➤ Size 7 steel crochet hook or size needed to obtain gauge

GAUGE
4 dc and 3 ch-2 sps = 1 inch
Check gauge to save time.

EDGING

ROW 1: Ch 11, dc in 8th ch from hook, ch 2, sk next 2 chs, dc in next ch, turn.

ROW 2: Ch 5 (counts as first dc, ch-2 throughout), dc in next dc, ch 2, sk next 2 sts, dc in next dc, turn.

ROW 3: Ch 5, dc in next dc, ch 2, dc in next ch-2 sp, [ch 2, dc] 4 times in same ch-2 sp, turn.

ROW 4: Ch 4, sc in first ch-2 sp, [ch 4, sc in next ch-2 sp] 3 times, ch 3, dc in next dc, [ch 2, dc in next dc] twice, turn.

ROW 5: Ch 5, dc in next dc, ch 2, dc in next dc, turn.

ROW 6: Ch 5, dc in next dc, ch 2, dc in next dc, turn.

Rep Rows 3–6 to desired length, fasten off. ✧

Irish Lace Edging

Give your bedroom a soft, romantic touch with this beautiful Irish lace edging gracing a piece of crisp white linen. It makes a lovely dresser cloth.

Design revised by Nancy Hearne

SKILL LEVEL: INTERMEDIATE

MATERIALS
➢ Crochet cotton size 20 (400 yds per ball): 1 ball white

➢ Size 10 or 11 steel crochet hook or size needed to obtain gauge

GAUGE
Rnds 1–4 = 1¾ inches
Check gauge to save time.

PATTERN NOTE
Join rnds with a sl st unless otherwise indicated.

Edging

MOTIF
RND 1: Ch 6, dc in first ch of ch-6, [ch 2, dc in same sp] 4 times, ch 2, join in 4th ch of beg ch-6. (6 ch-2 sps)

RND 2: Sl st into ch-2 sp, [sc, 3 dc, sc] in each ch-2 sp around, join in beg sc. (6 petals)

RND 3: *Ch 5, sc in back of work between the sc of next 2 petals, rep from * 5 times.

RND 4: [Sc, hdc, 5 dc, hdc, sc] over each ch-5 sp around, join in beg sc. (6 petals)

RND 5: Sl st to first dc, sc in same dc, ch 7, sc in last dc of same petal, ch 7, *sc in first dc of next petal, ch 7, sc in last dc of same petal, ch 7, rep from * around, join in beg sc. (12 lps)

RND 6: Sl st into lp, ch 3, [yo, insert hook in lp, yo, draw up a lp, yo, work off 2 lps] twice, yo and work off all lps on hook, ch 3, [yo, insert hook in lp, yo, draw up a lp, yo, draw through 2 lps on hook] 3 times, yo, draw through 2 lps, yo, draw through rem 3 lps on hook (cl), ch 3, work another cl in same sp, *ch 5, sc in next lp, ch 3, sc in top of last sc (for p), sc in same lp, ch 7, sc in next lp, ch 3, sc in top of last sc (for p), sc in same lp, ch 5, 3 cls with ch 3 between each cl in next lp, rep from * twice, ch 5, sc in next lp, ch 3, sl st in top of last sc (for p), sc in same lp, ch 7, sc in next lp, ch 3, sl st in top of last sc (for p), sc in same lp, ch 5, join in top of first cl.

RND 7: Sl st in next ch-3 lp, *ch 9, sc in next lp, [ch 7, sc in next lp] 4 times, rep from * around, join in beg st, fasten off.

Work next motif, joining to previous motif in the last rnd as follows: Ch 4, sc in corner lp of previous motif, ch 4, sc in next lp of working motif, *ch 3, sc in next lp of previous motif, ch 3, sc in next lp of working motif, rep from * 3 times, ch 4, sc in corner lp of previous motif, ch 4, sc in next lp of working motif and complete motif same as previous motif.

Work as many motifs as required joining each in the same manner.

HEADING
ROW 1: Attach thread to corner lp, ch 5, sc in next lp, *[ch 5, sc in next lp] 3 times, ch 3, insert hook in next lp, yo, draw up a lp, yo, draw through 2 lps on hook, yo, insert hook in next lp, yo, draw up a lp, yo, draw through 2 lps on hook, then work off rem lps 2 at a time, ch 3, sc in last lp, rep from * across, fasten off.

SCALLOP EDGE
ROW 1 (WS): Attach thread in corner lp, ch 5, sc in next lp, [ch 7, sc in next lp] 3 times, ch 5, sc in next lp, ch 3, sc in next lp, rep pattern across, turn.

ROW 2 (RS): Ch 1, 5 sc in next lp, [4 sc, ch 5, sl st in first ch of ch-5 (for p), 4 sc] in each of next 3 lps, 5 sc in next lp, 3 sc in next lp, rep pattern across, fasten off. ❖

Irish Crochet
By Nancy Hearne

Just like filet crochet is considered an imitation of net darning, Irish crochet is believed to come from another traditional form of lace making called Venetian point.

The 17th-century Italian and Spanish raised-needlepoint laces also served as models, but the crocheted version had its own characteristics.

Irish crochet, also known as "guipure lace" (in the mid-1800s) was considered one of the best examples of crochet artistry and was more readily accepted in the traditional lace-making industry. The great Irish potato famine between 1845 and 1859 brought more popularity to Irish crochet.

During this time, cottage industries sprang up as a means of income for many. Those who had earlier learned to crochet and were already supplementing their husband's incomes selling lace, taught others. Soon groups of crocheters were working together. Since Irish crochet is worked in parts and the parts then crocheted together, different women could make different pieces and hand them over to others to connect. Thus an assembly line was created which would produce more lace than single crocheters would by themselves.

Nuns and others with experience, began teaching crochet in the state elementary schools and in packed barns or public rooms. Upper-class ladies helped by organizing lessons, locating designs and finding agents to sell the finished laces. It was the income from Irish Crochet sales that helped many peasant families to emigrate and start new lives abroad.

By the 1860s, cottage industries began to decline, yet the market for their crochet items remained. Convents continued to broker buyers with crochet workers, but the market dwindled away due to the lack of designs and a diminishing lace quality.

The demand for Irish crochet grew again in the 1880s. Art teachers began teaching their students how to draw designs. Cooperatives and training schools were formed.

Between the 1880s and around 1910, Irish crochet won international recognition through exhibitions in Great Britain, France and the United States. Buyers from the United States and Canada went to Ireland for articles in Irish crochet including parasols and blouses. San Francisco was one of the major distribution centers until the earthquake of 1906.

By 1904, Irish crochet returned to Italy from where its origins in that country's needle lace had been forged.

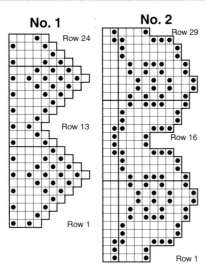
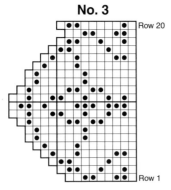

Filet Edgings

Because these edgings are wider than many, they are the perfect accent for large pieces such as bath towels and sheets.

Designs revised by
Nancy Hearne

SKILL LEVEL: BEGINNER

MATERIALS
➤ Crochet cotton size 10
➤ Size 7 steel crochet hook or size needed to obtain gauge

GAUGE
NO. 1: 3 inches wide at widest point
NO. 2: 3½ inches wide at widest point
NO. 3: 5 inches wide at widest point
Check gauge to save time.

No. 1
Row 24
Row 13
Row 1

No. 2
Row 29
Row 16
Row 1

No. 3
Row 20
Row 1

PATTERN STITCH
DTR: Yo hook 3 times, insert hook in indicated at, yo, draw up a lp, [yo, draw through 2 lps on hook] 4 times.

No. 1 *(Cream)*
ROW 1: Ch 17, dc in 8th ch from hook, dc in each of next 3 chs, ch 2, sk 2 chs, dc in each of next 4 chs, turn.

ROW 2: Ch 5 (counts as first dc, ch-2 throughout), sk 2 dc, dc in next dc, ch 2, dc in next dc, ch 2, sk next 2 dc, dc in next dc, dc in each of next 3 chs, ch 2, dtr in same ch as last dc (inc 1 sp at end of row), turn.

ROW 3: Ch 8, dc in dtr (inc 1 sp at beg of row), 2 dc in ch-2 sp, dc in next dc, ch 2, sk 2 dc, dc in next dc, [ch 2, dc in next dc] twice, 2 dc in next ch-2 sp, dc in next dc, turn.

ROW 4: Ch 5, sk next 2 dc, dc in next dc, [ch 2, dc in next dc] 3 times, ch 2, sk next 2 dc, dc in next dc, dc in each of next 3 chs, ch 2, dtr in same ch as last dc (inc at end of row), turn.

ROWS 5–13: Follow graph, working sps and bls, inc and dec as indicated.

ROWS 14–24: Rep Rows 2–13.

Rep Rows 14–24 to desired length, ending with Row 24 of pattern if edging is to be joined to form a circle, and with Row 13 if using on a straight edge.

No. 2 *(Mocha)*
ROW 1: Ch 21, dc in 4th ch from hook, dc in each of next 2 chs, [ch 2, sk next 2 chs, dc in next ch] 3 times, dc in each of next 3 chs, ch 2, sk next 2 chs, dc in next ch, turn.

ROW 2: Ch 5, dc in each of next 4 dc, [ch 2, dc in next dc] 3 times, dc in each of next 3 dc, turn.

ROW 3: Ch 11, dc in 4th ch from hook, dc in each of next 7 chs (3-bl inc at beg of row), dc in next dc, ch 2, sk next 2 dc, dc in next dc, [ch 2, dc in next dc] twice, 2 dc in next ch-2 sp, dc in each of next 4 dc, ch 2, dc in next dc, turn.

ROWS 4–29: Follow graph, working bls and sps, inc and dec as indicated.

Rep Rows 16–29 for pattern to desired length, ending with Row 28 if joining to form a circle, and with Row 16 if using on a straight edge.

No. 3 *(Green)*
ROW 1: Ch 32, dc in 8th ch from hook, dc in each of next 6 chs, ch 2, sk next 2 chs, dc in next ch, ch 2, sk next 2 chs, dc in each of next 7 chs, [ch 2, sk next 2 chs, dc in next ch] twice, turn.

ROW 2: Ch 8, dc in first dc (sp inc at beg of row), 2 dc in ch-2 sp, dc in next dc, 2 dc in next ch-2 sp, dc in next dc, [ch 2, sk next 2 dc, dc in next dc] twice, 2 dc in next ch-2 sp, dc in next dc, ch 2, dc in next dc, ch 2, sk next 2 dc, dc in each of next 4 dc, ch 2, sk 2 chs, dc in next ch, turn.

ROWS 3–20: Follow graph, working bls and sps, inc and dec as indicated.

Rep Rows 3–20 for pattern for desired length, ending with Row 18 if joining to form a circle, and with Row 19 if using on a straight edge.

Edging
Working along scalloped edge (inc edge of edging), [2 sc in next ch sp, {ch 3, sl st in last sc} twice, 2 sc in same sp] rep in each ch-2 sp across, except the ch-2 sp of pattern Row 19, work 2 sc in ch-2 sp of Row 19, fasten off. ✧

Photos: Top left is pattern No. 2, Top right is pattern No.3, Bottom photo is pattern No. 1

Hairpin Lace Edged Hankies

Hairpin crochet creates a uniquely lovely look for a pair of simple white handkerchiefs. In earlier times, women used to crochet trims onto handkerchiefs to give to their beaux. Crochet a pair for someone you love, too!

Designs revised by Nancy Hearne

SKILL LEVEL: INTERMEDIATE

SIZE
LAVENDER HANKIE EDGING: 1⅜ inches wide

BLUE HANKIE EDGING: 1⅝ inches wide

MATERIALS
➤ DMC Cebelia crochet cotton size 30 (50 grams per ball): 1 ball each white, lavender #210 and blue #800

➤ Size 12 steel crochet hook or size needed to obtain gauge

➤ Hairpin lace loom

➤ 2 Irish linen 10½-inch-square hankies with hem-stitched edge

GAUGE
On hankie edging, 11 sc = 1 inch
Check gauge to save time.

PATTERN NOTES
Weave in loose ends as work progresses.

Join rnds with a sl st unless otherwise stated.

PATTERN STITCH
HAIRPIN LACE: Adjust loom to 1 inch. With crochet hook, make a slip knot, slide lp off hook and onto right-hand prong of loom. Holding thread in your left hand, turn loom from right to left so that the thread passes behind both prongs and slip knot is on opposite prong. Insert crochet hook under front and over back of slip knot, yo, draw lp through, yo, draw through lp on hook. *Turn loom from right to left and sc in new lp in the same manner; rep from * until you have desired number of lps on each side. Slide strip off loom, do not fasten off. If loom becomes too full, slide all lps off, then thread last 3 or 4 back onto loom and continue working.

Lavender Hankie

HAIRPIN LACE
Adjust loom to 1 inch, with white, make lace slightly longer than outer edges of hankie, fasten off.

Attaching hairpin lace to hankie
With lavender, work sc in each hankie hole (hemstitched edging), catching one untwisted hairpin lp as follows: Insert hook in hole, yo and draw up a lp, insert hook in lp, yo and draw through all lps on hook, reach around hairpin lp just attached and ch 1. Continue as established, attaching hairpin lace along hankie side, work the following in each corner: [Sc attaching 2 hairpin lps held tog, ch 1] twice. (This means that each corner will have 5 sc total), work as established attaching hairpin lace, join in beg sc, fasten off.

SCALLOPED EDGING
Keeping all lps straight, make a sc in first 2 lps held tog, *holding back on hook the last lp of each tr, make 2 tr in next 2 lps held tog, yo and draw through all lps on hook (cl), [ch 4, hdc in tip of cl, make cl in same place as last cl] twice, sc in next 2 lps held tog, rep from * around, join in beg st, fasten off.

Blue Hankie

HAIRPIN LACE
Adjust loom to 1 inch, with white, make lace slightly longer than outer edges of hankie, fasten off.

Attaching hairpin lace to hankie
RND 1: With blue, work [sc, ch 1] in each hankie hole (hemstitch edging) around entire outer edge, with [sc, ch 1] 3 times in each corner hole, join in beg sc.

RND 2: Ch 4, catching a twisted hairpin lp in 3rd ch and reaching around its side, completing the 4th ch (counts as first dc, ch-1), *in next dc, dc, catching a twisted hairpin lace lp, ch 1, rep from * around working [dc, ch 1] 3 times in each corner sc, join in 3rd ch of beg ch-4, fasten off.

SCALLOPED EDGING
RND 1: Keeping the twist in lps, attach blue to first 3 lps, sc in same place, *keeping next lp straight, make 7 dc in lp, keeping the twist in lps make a sc in next 3 lps, ch 5, keeping twist in lps, make a sc in next 3 lps, rep from * around, join in beg sc, fasten off.

RND 2: Attach white to first dc of scallop, sc in same place, *[ch 3, sc in next dc] 6 times, ch 5, sc in next dc, rep from * around, join in beg sc, fasten off. ✧

Linens & Lace Edgings

Nothing dresses up a piece of ordinary linen as much as a rich tan or creamy-colored lace edging. Use this set of three exquisite edgings to accent pillowcases, handkerchiefs, hand towels or table runners.

Antique Age Lace Hanky Edging

Design revised by Ruth Shepherd

SKILL LEVEL: BEGINNER

SIZE
1 inch wide

MATERIALS
➤ DMC Cebelia size 30: ecru
➤ Size 9 steel crochet hook or size needed to obtain gauge
➤ White linen hanky

GAUGE
Rnd 1, 8 sc = 1 inch
Check gauge to save time.

PATTERN NOTES
Weave in loose ends as work progresses.

EDGING
RND 1 (RS): Attach cotton in any corner, ch 1, 3 sc in corner, working 8 sc to the inch, sc around entire outer edge, working 3 sc in each corner, join in beg sc.

RND 2: Ch 1, sc in same sc as beg ch, ch 5, sk next 2 sc, [sc in next sc, ch 5, sk next 2 sc] rep around, join in beg sc.

RND 3: Sl st into ch-5 sp, ch 1, sc, ch 1 in same ch-5 sp, [2 sc, ch 3, 2 sc] in next ch-5 sp, ch 1, [sc, ch 1 in next ch-5 sp, {2 sc, ch 3, 2 sc} in next ch-5 sp, ch 1] rep around, join in beg sc.

RND 4: Sl st into next ch-3 sp, ch 1, sc in same ch-3 sp, ch 5, [sc in next ch-3 sp, ch 5] rep around, join in beg sc.

RND 5: Sl st into ch-5 sp, ch 1, [3 sc, ch 3, 3 sc in same ch-5 sp, ch 1, [{3 sc, ch 3, 3 sc} in next ch-5 sp, ch 1] rep around, join in beg sc.

RND 6: Ch 1, sc in same ch-1 sp, ch 3, [sc, ch 3, sc] in next ch-1 sp, ch 3, [sc in next ch-1 sp, ch 3, {sc, ch 3, sc} in next ch-3 sp, ch 3] rep around, join in beg sc, fasten off.

Press edging lightly. ✧

Edging in an Evening

Design revised by Sharon Valiant

SKILL LEVEL: BEGINNER

SIZE
2½ inches at widest point

MATERIALS
➤ DMC Celelia crochet cotton size 5: 1 ball ecru
➤ Size 00 steel crochet hook or size needed to obtain gauge
➤ Tapestry needle

GAUGE
4 dc, ch 2, sk 2 ch, dc in next ch = 1 inch

Check gauge to save time.

PATTERN NOTES
Weave in loose ends as work progresses.

Edging may be made to any length; project shown is on 13 = inch towel. Each rep is approximately 2¼ inches.

EDGING
ROW 1: Beg at narrow edge, ch 8, [dc, ch 2, 2 dc] in 8th ch from hook, turn.

ROW 2: Ch 3 (counts as first dc throughout), dc in next dc, ch 2, [dc, ch 2] twice in next dc, sk next 2 chs, dc in next ch, turn.

ROW 3: Ch 5 (counts as first dc, ch 2), [dc, ch 2, dc] in next dc, 2 dc in ch-2 sp, dc in next dc, ch 2, dc in next dc, dc in top of beg ch-3, turn.

ROW 4: Ch 3, dc in next dc, ch 2, dc in next dc, ch 2, sk next 2 dc, [dc in next dc, ch 2] twice, sk next 2 chs, dc in next ch, turn.

ROW 5: Ch 5, [dc, ch 2, 2 dc] in next dc, turn.

Rep Rows 2–5 to desired length, ending last rep with Row 4. At the end of last rep, turn to work across bottom edge.

BOTTOM BORDER
ROW 1 (RS): Work 2 sc in first sp, [ch 3, 2 sc in next row end] 6 times, *ch 3, [sc in next row end] twice, [ch 3, 2 sc in next row end] 5 times, rep from * across, ending with ch 3, 2 sc in last row end, ch 2, turn to work across top straight edge.

TOP BORDER
ROW 1: Ch 3, dc in first sp, [ch 3, sl st in last dc for p, 2 dc in next sp] rep across, ending with dc in last st, fasten off. ✧

Spider Lace Towel Edging

Design revised by Sharon Valiant

SKILL LEVEL: BEGINNER

SIZE
4½ inches wide

MATERIALS
➤ DMC Cebelia crochet cotton size 10: 1 ball ecru
➤ Size 7 steel crochet hook or size needed to obtain gauge
➤ 16-inch-wide hand towel

GAUGE
[Dc, ch 2] 4 times and dc = 1 inch

Check gauge to save time.

PATTERN NOTES
Weave in loose ends as work progresses.

Edging shown is 16 inches long; edging may be made to any length. Each rep is approximately 2¼ inches wide.

EDGING
ROW 1: Beg at narrow edge, ch 24, dc in 4th ch from hook, dc in each of next 2 chs, [ch 2, sk next 2 chs, dc in next ch] 5 times, dc in next 2 chs, [dc, ch 2, tr] in last ch, turn.

ROW 2: Ch 6, 3 dc in first ch-2 sp, dc in next dc, ch 2, sk next 2 dc, dc in next dc, 2 dc in next ch-2 sp, dc in next dc, [ch 2, dc in next dc] 4 times, dc in each of next 3 dc, turn.

ROW 3: Sl st in first dc, ch 3 (counts as first dc throughout), dc in each of next 3 dc, [ch 2, dc in next dc] 3 times, 2 dc in ch-2 sp, dc in next dc, ch 3, sk next 3 dc, tr in ch-2 sp, ch 3, sk next 3 dc, dc in next dc, [3 dc, ch 2, tr] in last sp, turn.

ROW 4: Ch 6, 3 dc in first ch-2 sp, dc in next dc, ch 3, sc in next ch-3 sp, sc in next tr, sc in next ch-3 sp, ch 3, sk next 3 dc, dc in next dc, 2 dc in next ch-2 sp, dc in next dc, [ch 2, dc in next dc] twice, dc in last 3 sts, turn.

ROW 5: Sl st in first dc, ch 3, dc in each of next 3 dc, ch 2, dc in next dc, 2 dc in ch-2 sp, dc in next dc, ch 4, sc in next ch-3 sp, sc in each of next 3 sc, sc in next ch-3 sp, ch 4, sk next 3 dc, dc in next dc, [3 dc, ch 2, tr] in last sp, turn.

ROW 6: Ch 4, dc in each of next 4 dc, ch 5, sc in each of next 5 sc, ch 5, dc in each of next 4 dc, ch 2, sk next ch-2 sp, dc in last 4 sts, turn.

ROW 7: Sl st in first dc, ch 3, dc in each of next 3 dc, ch 2, dc in next dc, ch 2, sk next 2 dc, dc in next dc, 3 dc in next ch-5 sp, ch 4, sk next sc, sc in each of next 3 sc, ch 4, 3 dc in next ch-5 sp, dc in next dc, sk next 2 dc, tr in last dc, turn.

ROW 8: Ch 3, sk tr and next 3 dc, dc in next dc, 3 dc in next ch-4 sp, ch 3, sk next sc, tr in next sc, ch 3, 3 dc in next ch-4 sp, dc in next dc, ch 2, sk next 2 dc, dc in next dc, [ch 2, dc in next dc] twice, dc in last 3 sts, turn.

ROW 9: Sl st in next dc, ch 3, dc in each of next 3 dc, [ch 2, dc in next dc] 3 times, ch 2, sk next 2 dc, dc in next dc, 3 dc in ch-3 sp, ch 2, 3 dc in next ch-3 sp, dc in next dc, sk next 2 dc, tr in last dc, turn.

ROW 10: Ch 3, sk tr and next 3 dc, dc in next dc, 2 dc in next ch-2 sp, dc in next dc, ch 2, sk next 2 dc, dc in next dc, [ch 2, dc in next dc] 4 times, dc in next 3 sts, turn.

ROW 11: Sl st in next dc, ch 3, dc in each of next 3 dc, [ch 2, dc in next dc] 5 times, dc in next 3 dc, ch 2, tr in last sp, turn.

Rep Rows 2–11 to desired length, end last rep at Row 10. At end of last row, turn to work across top edge.

TOP BORDER
ROW 1: Ch 5 (counts as first dc, ch 2 throughout), [dc in base of next dc (or ch-3), ch 2] rep across, ending with dc in last st, turn.

ROW 2: Ch 5, [dc in next dc, ch 2] 3 times, *[dc in next dc, 2 dc in next ch-2 sp] twice (2 blocks) **, [dc in next dc, ch 2] 8 times (8 open sps), rep from * across, ending last rep at **, [dc in next dc, ch 2] 4 times, sk next 2 chs, dc in next ch, turn.

ROW 3: Ch 5, [dc in next dc, ch 2] twice, *work 1 block, 2 open sps, 1 block, 6 open sps, rep from * across, ending with 3 blocks, turn.

ROW 4: Ch 5, [dc in next dc, ch 2] 3 times, *work 2 blocks, 8 open sps, rep from * across, ending with 4 open sps, turn.

ROW 5: Ch 5, work open sps across, turn.

ROW 6 (RS): Sl st in next ch-2 sp, [ch 2, sl st in next ch-2 sp] rep across, fasten off.

BOTTOM BORDER
With RS facing, with crochet turned to work across bottom edge, attach thread with sl st in first row end, [ch 3, sl st in next row] rep across, fasten off.

FINISHING
Starch lightly and pin to width. Allow to dry completely. Sew in place on towel. ✧

Chapter Five

Vintage Toys & Dolls

*N*ot long ago Christmas and birthdays were the two occasions during the year when children received gifts. Many women spent the quiet evening hours after the children had gone to bed creating special toys such as these to delight their young ones.

Victorian Children Vintage Dolls

Little Gwynneth pouts in her pretty pink dress, while big sister Kendra concentrates on being the model Victorian child. Both girls are dressed in all the finery of the Victorian era, from ribbons and lace to feathers and pearls. Each of these beauties will make an elegant gift for a proper young lady.

Gwynneth
Design by
Carol Alexander for Crochet Trends & Traditions

SKILL LEVEL: BEGINNER

SIZE
15 inches tall

MATERIALS
- Caron Wintuk 4-ply acrylic yarn: 7 oz tea rose #3257
- Size G/6 crochet hook or size needed to obtain gauge
- 14-inch porcelain-look soft-body doll
- 1¼ yards 1¾-inch-wide white double-edge lace ruffle
- 3 yards ¾-inch-wide matching or similar white single-edge lace ruffle
- 3 yards ¼-inch-wide white satin ribbon
- 1¼ yards ¼-inch-wide pink/gold metallic trim
- 10 (½-inch) medium pink ribbon roses
- Hot-glue gun
- Sewing needle and thread
- 3 size 4/0 snap fasteners
- Tapestry needle

GAUGE
9 sts = 2 inches; 4 sc rows = 1 inch; 2 dc rows = 1 inch
Check gauge to save time.

PATTERN NOTES
Weave in loose ends as work progresses.

Sl st to join each rnd in top of beg st unless otherwise indicated.

Dress

BODICE

ROW 1: Beg at neck, ch 27, sc in 2nd ch from hook, [sc in each of next 2 chs, 2 sc in next ch] 4 times, [2 sc in next ch, sc in each of next 2 chs] 4 times, sc in last ch, turn. (34 sc)

ROW 2: Ch 1, [sc in each of next 11 sts, 2 sc in next st] twice, sc in each of next 10 sts, turn. (36 sc)

ROW 3: Ch 1, sc in each st across, turn.

ROW 4: Ch 1, [sc in each of next 11 sts, 2 sc in next st] twice, sc in each of next 12 sts, turn. (38 sc)

ROW 5: Ch 1, [sc in each of next 12 sts, 2 sc in next st] twice, sc in each of next 12 sts, turn. (40 sc)

ROW 6: Ch 1, sc in each of next 4 sts, 2 sc in next st, sc in each of next 14 sts, 2 sc in next st, sc in each of next 15 sts, 2 sc in next st, sc in each of next 4 sts, turn. (43 sc)

ROW 7: Ch 1, sc in each of next 3

Continued on page 106

sts, 2 sc in next st, sc in each of next 4 sts, ch 7 loosely, sk next 6 sts (armhole), 2 sc in next st, [sc in each of next 4 sts, 2 sc in next st] twice, sc in each of next 3 sts, 2 sc in next st, ch 9 loosely, sk next 6 sts (armhole), sc in each of next 4 sts, 2 sc in next st, sc in each of next 3 sts, turn. (55 sts)

ROW 8: Ch 2 (counts as first hdc throughout), hdc in each of next 7 sts, dec 1 hdc over next 2 sts, sc in each of next 9 ch sts, sc in each of next 2 sts, [sc in each of next 4 sts, 2 sc in next st] 3 times, sc in each of next 2 sts, sc in each of next 9 chs, dec 1 hdc over next 2 sts, hdc in each of next 7 sts, turn. (56 sts)

ROW 9: Ch 2, hdc in each of next 7 sts, dec 1 hdc over next 2 sts, sc in each of next 8 sts, dec 1 sc over next 2 sts, [sc in each of next 2 sts, dec 1 sc over next 2 sts] 5 times, sc in each of next 8 sts, dec 1 hdc over next 2 sts, hdc in each of next 7 sts, turn. (48 sts)

ROW 10: Ch 1, sc in each of next 4 sts, dec 1 sc over next 2 sts, sc in each of next 3 sts, dec 1 sc over next 2 sts, [sc in each of next 5 sts, dec 1 sc over next 2 sts] 4 times, sc in each of next 3 sts, dec 1 sc over next 2 sts, sc in each of next 4 sts, turn. (41 sc)

ROW 11: Ch 2, hdc in each of next 4 sts, dec 1 hdc over next 2 sts, hdc in each of next 2 sts, sc in next st, [sc in each of next 3 sts, dec 1 sc over next 2 sts] 4 times, sc in each of next 4 sts, hdc in each of next 2 sts, dec 1 hdc over next 2 sts, hdc in each of last 4 sts, turn. (35 sts)

ROWS 12 & 13: Rep Row 3.

ROW 14: Ch 1, sc in each st across, sl st in back lp of 2nd sc of first st of Row 14 to join.

SKIRT

RND 1: Working in back lps for this rnd only, ch 3, dc in same st as beg ch-3, 2 dc in each rem st around, join in 3rd ch of beg ch-3. (68 dc)

RND 2: Ch 3, dc in each st around, join in 3rd ch of beg ch-3.

RND 3: Ch 3, dc in each of next 32 sts, 2 dc in next st, dc in each of next 33 sts, 2 dc in next st, join in 3rd ch of beg ch-3. (70 dc)

RND 4: Ch 3, dc in each of next 5 sts, 2 dc in next st, [dc in each of next 6 sts, 2 dc in next st] rep around, join in 3rd ch of beg ch-3. (80 dc)

RNDS 5–10: Rep Rnd 2.

RND 11: Ch 3, dc in each of next 7 sts, dec 1 dc over next 2 sts, [dc in each of next 8 sts, dec 1 dc over next 2 sts] rep around, join in back lp of 3rd ch of beg ch-3. (72 dc)

RND 12: Working in back lps for this rnd only, ch 3, dc in each of next 7 sts, 2 dc in next st, [dc in each of next 8 sts, 2 dc in next st] rep around, join in 3rd ch of beg ch-3. (80 dc)

RND 13: Ch 3, dc in each of next 8 sts, 2 dc in next st, [dc in each of next 9 sts, 2 dc in next st] rep around, join in 3rd ch of beg ch-3. (88 dc)

RND 14: Rep Rnd 2.

RND 15: Ch 3, dc in each of next 9 sts, 2 dc in next st, [dc in each of next 10 sts, 2 dc in next st] rep around, join in 3rd ch of beg ch-3. (96 dc)

RND 16: Ch 3, dc in each of next 10 sts, 2 dc in next st, [dc in each of next 11 sts, 2 dc in next st] rep around, join in 3rd ch of beg ch-3. (104 dc)

RND 17: Ch 3, dc in each of next 2 sts, 2 dc in next st, [dc in each of next 3 sts, 2 dc in next st] rep around, join in 3rd ch of beg ch-3, fasten off. (130 dc)

RUFFLE

RND 1: Attach yarn in rem free lp at seam of Rnd 11 of skirt, ch 1, 2 sc in same st, 2 sc in each rem st around, join in beg sc. (144 sc)

RND 2: Ch 7 (counts as first dc, ch 4), sk next 3 sts, [sc, ch 4] in next st, sk next 3 sts, [{dc, ch 4} in next st, sk next 3 sts, {sc, ch 4} in next st, sk next 3 sts] rep around, join in 3rd ch of beg ch-7. (36 ch-4 lps)

RND 3: Ch 4, [sc, ch 4] in 2nd ch of sp, [sc, ch 2] in 2nd ch of next sp, [{dc, ch 1} in next dc, {sc, ch 4} in 2nd ch of sp, {sc, ch 2} in 2nd ch of next sp] rep around, join in 3rd ch of beg ch-4.

RND 4: Ch 3, 7 dc in ch-4 sp, [dc in next dc, 7 dc in next ch-4 sp] rep around, join in 3rd ch of beg ch-3.

RND 5: Ch 7, sc in center dc of 7-dc group, ch 4, [dc in next dc, ch 4, sc in center dc of next 7-dc group, ch 4] rep around, join in 3rd ch of beg ch-7.

RNDS 6 & 7: Rep Rnds 3 and 4. At the end of Rnd 7, fasten off.

SLEEVE (make 2)

RND 1: Attach yarn at center underarm, working evenly sp around armhole opening, ch 1, sc in each of next 5 sts, [hdc in next st, 2 hdc in next st] 5 times, sc in each of next 5 sts, do not join. (25 sts)

RND 2: [Sc in each of next 3 sts, dec 1 sc over next 2 sts] rep around, join in beg sc. (20 sc)

RNDS 3 & 4: Sc in each of next 4 sts, hdc in each of next 12 sts, sc in each of next 4 sts, do not join. (20 sts)

RND 5: [Sc in each of next 8 sts, dec 1 sc over next 2 sts] twice, do not join. (18 sc)

RND 6: Sc in each st around, join in front lp only of beg sc.

RND 7: Working in front lps for this rnd only, ch 3, 2 dc in next st, [dc in next st, 2 dc in next st] rep around, join in 3rd ch of beg ch-3. (27 dc)

RND 8: Ch 3, dc in each st around, join in 3rd ch of beg ch-3.

RND 9: Ch 3, dc in each of next 6 sts, dec 1 dc over next 2 sts, [dc in each of next 7 sts, dec 1 dc over next 2 sts] twice, join in 3rd ch of beg ch-3. (24 dc)

RND 10: Ch 3, dec 1 dc over next 2 sts, [dc in next st, dec 1 dc over next 2 sts] rep around, join in 3rd ch of beg ch-3. (16 dc)

RND 11: Ch 1, [dec 1 sc over next 2 sts] rep around, join in beg sc, fasten off. (8 sc)

Continued on page 120

Kendra
Design by
Carol Alexander for Crochet Trends & Traditions

SKILL LEVEL: BEGINNER

SIZE
15–16 inches tall

MATERIALS
- Patons Decor acrylic worsted weight yarn: 7 oz each sage green #1636 and Aran #1602
- Size G/6 crochet hook or size needed to obtain gauge
- 14–15-inch soft body porcelain-look doll
- 3 yards 1½-inch-wide gathered ecru lace ruffle
- 3½ yards ½-inch-wide flat ecru lace trim with center pearl bead string
- 3½ yards ¼-inch-wide ecru satin ribbon
- 2 ecru ½-inch satin ribbon roses with leaves
- 5–6 medium size feathers
- Hot–glue gun
- Sewing needle and thread
- 3 size 4/0 snap fasteners
- 3 map pins
- Tapestry needle

GAUGE
9 sts = 2 inches; 4 sc rows = 1 inch; 2 dc rows = 1 inch
Check gauge to save time.

PATTERN NOTES
Weave in loose ends as work progresses.

Sl st to join each rnd unless otherwise indicated.

Beg ch 3 counts as first dc unless otherwise indicated.

Dress

BODICE

ROW 1: Beg at neck with sage green, ch 27, sc in 2nd ch from hook, [sc in each of next 2 chs, 2 sc in next ch] 4 times, [2 sc in next ch, sc in each of next 2 chs] 4 times, sc in last ch, turn. (34 sc)

ROW 2: Ch 1, [sc in each of next 11 sts, 2 sc in next st] twice, sc in each of next 10 sts, turn. (36 sc)

ROW 3: Ch 1, sc in each st across, turn.

ROW 4: Ch 1, [sc in each of next 11 sts, 2 sc in next st] twice, sc in each of next 12 sts, turn. (38 sc)

ROW 5: Ch 1, [sc in each of next 12 sts, 2 sc in next st] twice, sc in each of last 12 sts, turn. (40 sc)

ROW 6: Ch 1, sc in each of next 4 sts, 2 sc in next st, sc in each of next 14 sts, 2 sc in next st, sc in each of next 15 sts, 2 sc in next st, sc in each of last 4 sts, fasten off sage green, attach Aran, turn.

ROW 7: Ch 1, sc in each of next 3 sts, 2 sc in next st, sc in each of next 4 sts, ch 9 loosely, sk next 6 sts (armhole), 2 sc in next st, [sc in each of next 4 sts, 2 sc in next st] twice, sc in each of next 3 sts, 2 sc in next st, ch 9 loosely, sk next 6 sts (armhole), sc in each of next 4 sts, 2 sc in next st, sc in each of last 3 sts, turn. (55 sts)

ROW 8: Ch 2, hdc in each of next 7 sts, hdc in next 2 sts, sc in each of next 9 chs, sc in each of next 2 sts, [sc in each of next 4 sts, 2 sc in next st] 3 times, sc in each of next 2 sts, sc in each of next 9 chs, hdc in next 2 sts, hdc in each of next 7 sts, turn. (56 sts)

ROW 9: Ch 2, hdc in each of next 7 sts, dec 1 hdc over next 2 sts, sc in each of next 8 sts, dec 1 sc over next 2 sts, [sc in each of next 2 sts, dec 1 sc over next 2 sts] 5 times, sc in each of next 8 sts, dec 1 hdc over next 2 sts, hdc in each of next 7 sts, turn. (48 sts)

ROW 10: Ch 1, sc in each of next 4 sts, dec 1 sc over next 2 sts, sc in each of next 3 sts, dec 1 sc over next 2 sts, [sc in each of next 5 sts, dec 1 sc over next 2 sts] 4 times, sc in each of next 3 sts, dec 1 sc over next 2 sts, sc in each of next 4 sts, turn. (41 sc)

ROW 11: Ch 2, hdc in each of next 4 sts, dec 1 hdc over next 2 sts, hdc in each of next 2 sts, sc in next st, [sc in each of next 3 sts, dec 1 sc over next 2 sts] 4 times, sc in each of next 4 sts, hdc in each of next 2 sts, dec 1 hdc over next 2 sts, hdc in each of next 4 sts, turn. (35 sts)

ROWS 12 & 13: Ch 1, sc in each st across, turn.

ROW 14: Ch 1, sc in each st across, sl st to join in back lp of 2nd sc of row, drawing sage green through, dropping Aran.

SKIRT

RND 1: Working in back lps for this rnd only, ch 3, dc in same st, 2 dc in each rem st around, join in 3rd ch of beg ch-3. (68 dc)

RND 2: Ch 3, dc in each st around, join in 3rd ch of beg ch-3.

RND 3: Rep Rnd 2.

RND 4: Ch 3, dc in each of next 2 sts, 2 dc in next st, [dc in each of next 3 sts, 2 dc in next st] rep around, join in 3rd ch of beg ch-3. (85 dc)

RNDS 5–7: Rep Rnd 2.

RND 8: Ch 3, dc in each of next 3 sts, 2 dc in next st, [dc in each of next 4 sts, 2 dc in next st] rep around, join in 3rd ch of beg ch-3. (102 dc)

RNDS 9–12: Rep Rnd 2.

RND 13: Ch 3, dc in next st, 2 dc in next st, [dc in each of next 2 sts, 2 dc in next st] rep around, join in 3rd ch of beg ch-3. (136 dc)

RND 14: Ch 3, 2 dc in next st, [dc in next st, 2 dc in next st] rep around, join in 3rd ch of beg ch-3. (204 dc)

RNDS 15 & 16: Rep Rnd 2.

RND 17: Rep Rnd 13, fasten off. (272 dc)

OVERSKIRT

RND 1: Working in rem free lps of
Continued on page 121

Lovable Puppy

You can almost hear this little puppy barking in excitement as he hears the school bus bringing his children home! His loopy fur and floppy ears give him a ragamuffin charm that is simply irresistible.

SKILL LEVEL: BEGINNER

SIZE
PUPPY: 9 inches tall

BALL: 3½ inches in diameter

MATERIALS
➤ Sport weight pompadour yarn: 5 oz white
➤ Worsted weight yarn: Small amount each red, white and blue
➤ Size F/5 crochet hook or size needed to obtain gauge
➤ 1 skein black 6-strand embroidery floss
➤ 2 (8mm) black round shank buttons
➤ 20 inches ½-inch-wide ribbon
➤ Fiberfill
➤ Tapestry needle

GAUGE
4 sts and 3 rows= 1 inch in lp st

Check gauge to save time.

PATTERN NOTES
Weave in loose ends as work progresses.

Do not join rnds unless otherwise stated. Use a scrap of yarn to mark rnds.

Join rnds with sl st in beg st.

Work puppy with 2 strands of yarn held tog throughout.

PATTERN STITCH
Lp st: Wind yarn over index finger twice, insert hook in st, draw yarn through, pulling yarn from under finger, drop lps from finger, letting them fall to RS of work, yo, draw through all lps on hook to complete sc.

Puppy

BODY
RND 1 (RS): Starting at bottom, ch 2, 6 sc in 2nd ch from hook. (6 sc)

RND 2: 2 sc in each sc around. (12 sc)

RND 3: [2 sc in next sc, sc in next sc] 6 times. (18 sc)

RND 4: [2 sc in next sc, sc in each of next 2 sc] 6 times. (24 sc)

RND 5: [2 sc in next sc, sc in each of next 3 sc] 6 times, join, turn. (30 sc)

RND 6 (WS): Lp st in each st around. (30 lp sts)

Rep Rnd 6 until lp st section measures 3 inches.

RNDS 7 & 8: Lp st around, sk 3 sts evenly sp around. (24 lp sts)

RND 9: Lp st in each st around, sl st in next st, fasten off. (24 lp sts)

HEAD
RND 1: Ch 2, work 6 lp sts in 2nd ch from hook. (6 lp sts)

RND 2: 2 lp sts in each st around. (12 lp sts)

RND 3: [Lp st in next st, 2 lp sts in next st] 6 times. (18 lp sts)

RND 4: Lp st around, inc 7 lp sts evenly sp around. (25 lp sts)

RND 5: Lp st in each st around.

Rep Rnd 5 until piece measures 3 inches from beg. At the end of last rep, sl st in next st, fasten off.

LEG *(make 4)*
RND 1: Starting at tip of paw, ch 2, 6 sc in 2nd ch from hook. (6 sc)

RND 2: 2 sc in each st around. (12 sc)

RND 3: Sc in each sc around, join, turn.

RND 4–7: Lp st in each st around. At the end of Rnd 7, sl st in next st, fasten off.

TAIL
RND 1: Starting at tip of tail, ch 2, 6 lp sts in 2nd ch from hook. (6 lp sts)

RND 2: 2 lp sts in each st around. (12 lp sts)

RND 3–8: Lp st in each st around. At the end of Rnd 8, fasten off.

EAR *(make 4)*
ROW 1: Ch 10, sc in 2nd ch from hook, sc in each rem ch across, turn. (9 sc)

ROW 2: Ch 1, lp st in each sc across, turn. (9 lp sts)

ROW 3: Ch 1, sc in each st across, turn.

Rep Rows 2 and 3 until there are 7 lp-st rows, fasten off.

SNOUT
RND 1: Starting at tip of nose, ch 2, 6 sc in 2nd ch from hook. (6 sc)

RNDS 2–5: Sc in each sc around. At the end of Rnd 5, sl st in next st, fasten off.

NOSE
RND 1: With black embroidery

floss, ch 2, 5 sc in 2nd ch from hook. (5 sc)

RND 2: 2 sc in each sc around, sl st in next sc, leaving a length of floss, fasten off. (10 sc)

ASSEMBLY
Stuff body, head, nose, legs and tail firmly with fiberfill. Sew head to body. Sew snout, legs and tail to body. Turn under both long edges of ear ¼ inch and sew. Sew ear in place. Rep with 2nd ear. Sew nose to tip of snout. Tie ribbon around neckline in a bow.

Patriotic Ball
Note: While working ball, do not fasten off yarn not in use, drop to WS unless otherwise indicated.

FIRST HALF
RND 1: With white, ch 4, 9 dc in 4th ch from hook, insert hook in 4th ch of beg ch-4, drop white, draw through a lp of red. (10 dc)

RND 2: Ch 1, sc in same st as beg ch, 2 sc in next dc, [sc in next dc, 2 sc in next dc] 4 times, insert hook in first sc, drop red, draw through a lp of white. (15 sc)

RND 3: Ch 1, sc in same st as beg ch, sc in next sc, 2 sc in next sc, [sc in each of next 2 sc, 2 sc in next sc] 4 times, insert hook in first sc, drop white, draw up a lp of blue. (20 sc)

RND 4: Ch 1, sc in each sc around, insert hook in first sc, drop blue, draw up a lp of white.

RND 5: Ch 3 (counts as first dc throughout), 2 dc in next sc, [dc in next sc, 2 dc in next sc] 9 times, insert hook in top of beg ch-3, drop white, draw up a lp of red. (30 dc)

RND 6: Ch 1, sc in each dc around, join.

RND 7: Ch 1, [sc in each of next 2 sc, 2 sc in next sc] 10 times, insert hook in first sc, drop red, draw up a lp of blue. (40 sc)

RND 8: Ch 1, sc in each sc around, insert hook in first sc, draw up a lp of white, fasten off blue.

RND 9: Ch 3, dc in each sc around, insert hook in top of beg ch-3, draw through a lp of red, fasten off white.

RND 10: Ch 1, sc in each dc around, join, fasten off.

SECOND HALF
Work 2nd half of ball in same manner as first half, using blue where red was used and red where blue was used. With double strand of white, sew the two halves tog stuffing with fiberfill before closing. ✦

Playful Lamb

From his perky ears to his lifelike hooves, this little lamb is covered in fluffy fleece. Stitched in a flecked ecru yarn, he looks as natural as can be, ready to play in the field or skip across the meadow.

Design revised by Agnes Russell

SKILL LEVEL: BEGINNER

SIZE
LAMB: 17 inches tall

MATERIALS
- Coats & Clark Red Heart Super Saver 4-ply yarn: 13 oz Aran fleck #4313, small amount black
- Size F/5 crochet hook or size needed to obtain gauge
- 2 (15mm) sew-on wiggle eyes
- 1 yard 1-inch-wide burgundy satin ribbon
- Fiberfill
- Tapestry needle

GAUGE
4 sc = 1 inch; 4 sc rows = 1 inch
Check gauge to save time.

PATTERN NOTES
Weave in loose ends as work progresses.

Use Aran fleck yarn unless otherwise indicated.

For the safety of little ones, do not use sew-on eyes; crochet black circles for eyes and sew in place.

Using same pattern, a variety of different sizes of the lamb can be made, using sport weight yarn with size D/3 crochet hook; crochet cotton size 10 and size 8 steel crochet hook; 4-ply cotton and size G/6 crochet hook.

PATTERN STITCH
LP ST: Wind yarn over index finger twice, insert hook in next st, draw yarn through, pulling yarn from under finger, drop lps from finger, letting them fall to RS of work, yo, draw through all 3 lps on hook.

LEFT SIDE
ROW 1: Starting at left hind leg, ch 7, sc in 2nd ch from hook, sc in each rem ch across, turn. (6 sc)

ROW 2: Ch 1, sc in each st across, turn.

ROW 3: Rep Row 2.

ROW 4: Ch 1, lp st in each st across, turn.

ROW 5: Ch 1, 2 sc in first st, sc across to last 2 sts, dec 1 sc over next 2 sts, turn.

ROWS 6–9: Rep Rows 4 and 5.

ROW 10: Rep Row 4.

ROW 11: Ch 1, 2 sc in first st, sc in each rem st across, turn. (7 sc)
ROW 12: Rep Row 4.

ROWS 13–24: Rep Rows 11 and 12. (13 sc)

ROW 25: Ch 1, 2 sc in first st, sc in each rem st across, ch 28 (for body), turn. (14 sc)

ROW 26: Beg in 2nd ch from hook, work 27 lp sts across ch, lp st in each st across leg, turn. (41 lp sts)

ROW 27: Rep Row 11. (42 sc)

ROW 28: Rep Row 4.

ROW 29: Rep Row 2.

ROW 30: Rep Row 4.

ROW 31: Ch 1, dec 1 sc over next 2 sts, sc in each st across to last 2 sts, dec 1 sc over next 2 sts, turn. (40 sc)

ROW 32: Rep Row 4.

ROWS 33–44: Rep Rows 2 and 4.

ROW 45: Ch 1, sc in each st across, ch 10 (for head), turn.

ROW 46: Sc in 2nd ch from hook, sc in each of next 8 chs, lp st in each rem st across, turn. (49 sts)

ROW 47: Ch 1, sc in each of next 39 sts, dec 1 sc over next 2 sts, sc in each of next 8 sts, turn. (48 sc)

ROW 48: Ch 1, lp st in each of next 47 sts, leaving last st unworked, turn. (47 lp sts)

ROW 49: Ch 1, dec 1 sc over next 2 sts, sc in each rem st across, turn. (46 sc)

ROW 50: Ch 1, lp st in each of next 18 sts for head, leaving rem sts unworked, turn. (18 lp sts)

ROW 51: Rep Row 49. (17 sc)

ROWS 52–57: Rep Row 4 and Row 2 alternately.

ROW 58: Ch 1, sk first st, lp st in each rem st across, turn. (16 lp sts)

ROW 59: Ch 1, dec 1 sc over next 2 sts, sc in each rem st across, turn. (15 sc)

ROWS 60–63: Rep Rows 58 and 59. (11 sts)

ROW 64: Rep Row 58, fasten off. (10 lp sts)

Face

ROW 1: Attach yarn in first st of the 46th row, ch 1, work 1 sc in each of next 18 rows of head, turn. (18 sc)

ROW 2: Ch 1, dec 1 sc over next 2 sc, sc in each sc across to last 2 sc, dec 1 sc over next 2 sc, turn. (16 sc)

Rep Row 2 until 2 sc remain, then dec 1 sc over next 2 sc, fasten off.

Back Trim

With WS facing, attach yarn at back of neck, ch 1, lp st in each sc across back, turn.

Tail

ROW 1: Ch 1, 2 sc in first st, sc in each of next 5 sts, 2 sc in next st, turn. (9 sc)

ROW 2: Ch 1, lp st in each st across tail, turn.

ROW 3: Ch 1, dec 1 sc over next 2 sts, sc in each rem st across, turn. (8 sc)

ROW 4: Ch 1, lp st in each st across tail, turn.

ROWS 5–12: Rep Rows 3 and 4. At the end of Row 12, fasten off.

Front Leg

ROWS 1–4: Rep Rows 1–4 of left side. (6 sts)

ROW 5: Ch 1, sc in each st across, turn.

ROW 6: Ch 1, lp st in each st across, turn.

ROWS 7–10: Rep Rows 5 and 6.

ROW 11: Ch 1, sc in each st across to last st, 2 sc in last st, turn. (7 sc)

ROW 12: Rep Row 6.

ROWS 13–16: Rep Rows 11 and 12. (9 sts)

ROW 17: Ch 1, 2 sc in first st, sc across to last 2 sts, dec 1 sc over next 2 sts, turn.

ROW 18: Rep Row 6.

ROWS 19 & 20: Rep Rows 17 and 18.

ROWS 21–24: Rep Rows 5 and 6. At the end of Row 24, fasten off.

Sew to body starting at the first sc of 26th row of body with the point at knee facing forward.

RIGHT SIDE

ROWS 1–24: Starting at the hind leg, work the first 24 rows the same as left side reversing all inc and dec sts. *Example:* In Row 5 of left side of lamb it indicates inc at beg and dec at end of row, simply work Row 5 of right side of lamb in reverse by dec at beg of row and inc at end of row. At the end of Row 24, ch 28 (for body), turn.

ROW 25: Sc in 2nd ch from hook, sc in each of next 26 chs, sc st in each st of leg to last st, 2 sc in last st, turn.

ROW 26: Ch 1, lp st in each st across, turn.

ROW 27: Ch 1, sc in each st across to last st, 2 sc in last st, turn.

ROWS 28–43: Rep Rows 28–43 of left side.

ROW 44: Ch 1, lp st in each st across, ch 10 (for head), turn.

ROW 45: Sc in 2nd ch from hook, sc in each of next 8 chs, sc in each rem st across, turn.

Continued on next page

ROW 46: Ch 1, lp st in each of next 39 sts, dec 1 st by working next 2 sts tog, lp st in each rem st of head, turn.

ROW 47: Ch 1, sc in each st across, turn.

ROW 48: Ch 1, dec 1 st at beg of row, lp st in each rem st across, turn.

ROW 49: Ch 1, sc across to last 2 sts, dec 1 sc over next 2 sts, turn.

ROW 50: Ch 1, lp st in each st across, turn.

ROW 51: Ch 1, sc in each of next 16 sts, dec 1 sc over next 2 sts, turn.

ROWS 52–64: Rep Rows 52–64 of left side.

Face

Rep face of left side.

Tail

Attach yarn in 7th st from the end of the Row 50 of right side, ch 1, 2 sc in same st as joining, sc in each of next 5 sts, 2 sc in next st, turn.

Rep Rows 2–12 of tail for left side.

Front Leg

Work as for front leg for left side, reversing all incs and decs.

CENTER HEAD & FACE SECTION
ROW 1: Ch 2, 2 sc in 2nd ch from hook, turn. (2 sc)

ROW 2: Ch 1, 2 sc in first sc, sc in next sc, turn. (3 sc)

ROWS 3–7: Ch 1, 2 sc in first sc, sc in each rem sc across, turn. (8 sc)

ROWS 8–10: Ch 1, sc in each sc across, turn.

ROW 11: Ch 1, lp st in each st across, turn.

ROW 12: Ch 1, sc in each st across, turn.

ROWS 13–24: Rep Rows 11 and 12.

ROW 25: Ch 1, lp st in each st across, turn.

ROW 26: Ch 1, dec 1 sc over next 2 sts, sc in each rem st across, turn. (7 sc)

ROW 27: Rep Row 25.

ROW 28: Ch 1, sc in each st across to last 2 sts, dec 1 sc over next 2 sts, turn. (6 sc)

ROWS 29–36: Rep Rows 25–28. (2 sts)

ROW 37: Rep Row 25.

ROW 38: Ch 1, dec 1 sc over next 2 sts, fasten off. (1 sc)

NECK SECTION
ROW 1: Ch 9, sc in 2nd ch from hook, sc in each rem ch across, turn. (8 sc)

ROW 2: Ch 1, lp st in each st across, turn.

ROW 3: Ch 1, sc in each st across, turn.

ROWS 4–15: Rep Rows 2 and 3.

ROW 16: Rep Row 2.

ROW 17: Ch 1, dec 1 sc over next 2 sts, sc in each rem st across, turn. (7 sc)

ROW 18: Rep Row 2.

ROW 19: Ch 1, sc in each st across to last 2 sts, dec 1 sc over next 2 sts, turn. (6 sc)

ROWS 20–27: Rep Rows 16–19. (2 sts)

ROW 28: Rep Row 2.

ROW 29: Ch 1, dec 1 sc over next 2 sts, fasten off. (1 sc)

UNDER SECTION
Work one section, rep Rows 1–30 of left side and left front leg. Work another section, rep Rows 1–30 of right side and right front leg.

FEET
RND 1: With black, ch 2, 6 sc in 2nd ch from hook, do not join. (6 sc)

RND 2: 2 sc in each sc around, sl st in next st, leaving a length of yarn, fasten off. (12 sc)

EAR *(make 2)*
ROW 1: Ch 15, sc in 2nd ch from hook, sc in each rem ch across, turn. (14 sc)

ROW 2: Ch 1, lp st in each st across, turn.

ROW 3: Ch 1, 2 sc in first sc, sc in each rem sc across, turn. (15 sc)

ROW 4: Rep Row 2.

ROWS 5 & 6: Rep Rows 3 and 4.

ROW 7: Ch 1, dec 1 sc over next 2 sc, sc in each rem sc across, turn. (14 sc)

ROW 8: Rep Row 2.

ROWS 9 & 10: Rep Rows 7 and 8. At the end of Row 10, fasten off. (13 sc)

ASSEMBLY
Match under section to body section. Starting at inside of leg, sew up leg, across under part of body and down opposite leg. Sew outside of front leg tog, leaving end of leg open for foot. Sew outside of hind leg tog, leaving end of leg open for foot. Sew other section in same manner.

Match body sections. Starting at the lower back, sew up back around tail and across back to neck. Sew in center head piece, starting at nose and working to back of neck. Sew the opposite side in same manner.

Sew the remainder of mouth down as far as the lp st row. Sew neck section in position, placing the narrow part to first row of lp st at mouth and sew to front of body. Sew opposite side in same manner.

Sew the 4 rows of under section to the neck section. Stuff lamb with fiberfill, sew across under side of under section. Sew feet to legs, and with length of black, embroider 3 lazy-daisy sts on lower edge of leg for toes. Sew ears in position. With black, embroider mouth and nose as illustrated. Sew eyes to each side of head as illustrated. Place satin ribbon around neckline, tie ends in a bow. ✧

Old-Style Teddy Bear

This old-fashioned teddy bear is just the right size for a young child's hug. Loopy and lovable, he's sure to be a treasured friend.

Design revised by Agnes Russell

SKILL LEVEL: BEGINNER

SIZE
18 inches tall, sitting

MATERIALS
➤ Coats & Clark Red Heart Super Saver 4-ply yarn: 9 oz warm brown #336 and 1 oz cornmeal #320

➤ Size F/5 crochet hook or size needed to obtain gauge

➤ 2 (15mm) sew-on wiggle eyes

➤ 1 yard 1½-inch-wide decorative satin ribbon

➤ Fiberfill

➤ 2 (3-inch) plastic canvas circles

➤ Tapestry needle

GAUGE
4 sc = 1 inch; 4 sc rows = 1 inch
Check gauge to save time.

PATTERN NOTES
Weave in loose ends as work progresses.

Do not join rnds unless otherwise indicated; use a scrap of CC yarn to mark rnds.

For the safety of children under age six, do not use sew-on eyes; crochet circles for eyes and sew in place.

Using same pattern, a variety of different sizes of teddy bear can be made, using baby yarn with size B/1 crochet hook; sport weight yarn and size D/3 crochet hook; 4-ply cotton and size G/6 crochet hook.

PATTERN STITCH
LP ST: Wind yarn over index finger twice, insert hook in next st, draw yarn through, pulling yarn from under finger, drop lps from finger, letting them fall to RS of work, yo, draw through all 3 lps on hook.

Continued on next page

BACK

Body

ROW 1: With warm brown, ch 26, sc in 2nd ch from hook, sc in each rem ch across, turn. (25 sc)

ROW 2: Ch 1, lp st in each st across, turn.

ROW 3: Ch 1, sc in each st across, turn.

ROWS 4–39: Rep Rows 2 and 3.

ROW 40: Rep Row 2.

Head

ROW 41: Sl st in each of next 4 sts, sl st in next st, ch 1, sc in same st as beg ch-1, sc in each of next 16 sts, leaving rem sts unworked, turn. (17 sc)

ROW 42: Rep Row 2.

ROW 43: Ch 1, 2 sc in first st, sc in each st across to last st, 2 sc in last st, turn. (19 sc)

ROW 44: Rep Row 2.

ROWS 45–54: Rep Rows 42 and 43. (29 sts)

ROW 55: Ch 1, dec 1 sc over next 2 sc, sc in each st across to last 2 sts, dec 1 sc over next 2 sts, turn. (27 sts)

ROW 56: Rep Row 2.

ROWS 57–66: Rep Rows 55 and 56. At the end of Row 66, fasten off. (17 sts)

LEFT FRONT

Body

ROW 1: With warm brown, ch 20, sc in 2nd ch from hook, sc in each rem ch across, turn. (19 sc)

ROWS 2–32: Rep Rows 2 and 3 of body for back. (19 sts)

Head

ROW 33: Sl st in each of next 4 sts, sl st in next st, ch 1, sc in same st as beg ch-1, sc in each of next 14 sts, turn. (15 sc)

ROW 34: Ch 1, lp st in each st across, turn.

ROW 35: Ch 1, 2 sc in first st, sc in each rem st across to last sc, 2 sc in last sc, turn. (17 sc)

ROW 36: Rep Row 34.

ROW 37: Rep Row 35, ch 8, turn.

ROW 38: Sc in 2nd ch from hook, sc in each of next 6 chs, work 1 lp st in each rem st across, turn. (26 sts)

ROW 39: Ch 1, sc in each st across, turn.

ROW 40: Ch 1, sc in each of next 7 sc, lp st in each rem st across, turn.

ROWS 41–46: Rep Rows 39 and 40.

ROW 47: Ch 1, dec 1 sc over next 2 sts, sc in each of next 15 sts, turn.

ROW 48: Ch 1, lp st in each st across, turn.

ROW 49: Ch 1, dec 1 sc over next 2 sts, sc in each st across to last 2 sts, dec 1 sc over next 2 sts, turn.

ROWS 50 & 51: Rep Rows 48 and 49.

ROW 52: Rep Row 48, fasten off.

RIGHT FRONT

Body

ROWS 1–32: Rep Rows 1–32 of body for left front. (19 sts)

Head

ROW 33: Ch 1, sc in each of next 15 sts, leaving rem 4 sts free for shoulder, turn. (15 sts)

ROW 34: Ch 1, lp st in each st across, turn.

ROW 35: Ch 1, 2 sc in first sc, sc in each sc across to last sc, 2 sc in last sc, turn. (17 sts)

ROW 36: Ch 1, lp st in each of next 17 sts, ch 8, turn.

ROW 37: Sc in 2nd ch from hook, sc in each of next 6 chs, 2 sc in next st, sc in each st across to last st, 2 sc in last st, turn. (26 sts)

ROW 38: Ch 1, lp st in each of next 19 sts, sc in each of next 7 sc, turn.

ROW 39: Ch 1, sc in each st across, turn.

ROW 40: Rep Row 38.

ROWS 41–44: Rep Rows 39 and 40.

ROW 45: Rep Row 39.

ROW 46: Ch 1, lp st in each of next 19 sts, turn. (19 lp sts)

ROW 47: Ch 1, sc across to last 2 sts, dec 1 sc over next 2 sts, turn. (18 sc)

ROWS 48–52: Rep Rows 48–52 of head for left front.

CENTER HEAD PIECE

ROW 1: With warm brown, ch 2, sc in 2nd ch from hook, turn. (1 sc)

ROW 2: Ch 1, 2 sc in sc, turn. (2 sc)

ROWS 3 & 4: Ch 1, sc in each sc across, turn.

ROW 5: Ch 1, 2 sc in first sc, sc in next sc, turn. (3 sc)

ROWS 6 & 7: Rep Rows 3 and 4.

ROW 8: Ch 1, 2 sc in first sc, sc in each rem sc across, turn. (4 sc)

ROWS 9 & 10: Rep Rows 3 and 4.

ROWS 11–25: Rep Rows 8–10. (9 sc)

ROW 26: Ch 1, lp st in each st across, turn.

ROW 27: Ch 1, 2 sc in first st, sc in each st across to last st, 2 sc in last st, turn. (11 sc)

ROWS 28–33: Rep Rows 26 and 27. (17 sts)

ROW 34: Rep Row 26.

ROW 35: Ch 1, sc in each st across, turn.

ROWS 36–43: Rep Rows 34 and 35.

ROW 44: Rep Row 34, fasten off.

ARM (make 2)

RND 1: With cornmeal, ch 2, 6 sc in 2nd ch from hook, do not join. (6 sc)

Note: Work in back lps only for Rnds 2–7.

RND 2: 2 sc in each st around. (12 sc)

RND 3: [Sc in next st, 2 sc in next st] rep around. (18 sc)

RND 4: [Sc in each of next 2 sts, 2 sc in next st] rep around. (24 sc)

RND 5: [Sc in each of next 3 sts, 2 sc in next st] rep around. (30 sc)

RND 6: Sc in each st around, fasten off.

RND 7: Attach warm brown, sc in each st around.

RNDS 8–22: Working in both lps of each st, sc in each sc around. At the end of Rnd 22, sl st in next st, fasten off.

LEG (make 2)

RND 1: With cornmeal, ch 2, 8

sc in 2nd ch from hook, do not join. (8 sc)

Note: Work in back lps only for Rnds 2–7.

RND 2: 2 sc in each st around. (16 sc)

RND 3: [Sc in next st, 2 sc in next st] rep around. (24 sc)

RND 4: [Sc in each of next 2 sts, 2 sc in next st] rep around. (32 sc)

RND 5: [Sc in each of next 3 sts, 2 sc in next st] rep around. (40 sc)

RND 6: Sc in each sc around, fasten off.

RND 7: Attach warm brown, sc in each st around.

RNDS 8–29: Sc in each sc around.

RND 30: [Sc in each of next 3 sc, dec 1 sc over next 2 sc] rep around. (32 sc)

RNDS 31–34: Sc in each sc around. At the end of Row 34, sl st in next st, fasten off.

EAR *(make 2)*

ROW 1: With warm brown, ch 20, sc in 2nd ch from hook, sc in each rem ch across, turn. (19 sc)

ROW 2: Ch 1, dec 1 sc over next 2 sc, sc in each of next 7 sc, 3 sc in next sc, sc in each of next 7 sc, dec 1 sc over next 2 sc, turn. (19 sc)

ROWS 3–8: Rep Row 2. At the end of Row 8, fasten off.

ROW 9: Attach warm brown in side edge of Row 1, ch 1, sc evenly sp up side edge of ear, across top edge and down opposite side edge, ending with last sc in side edge of Row 1, do not work across opposite side of foundation ch, fasten off.

ASSEMBLY

Sew last row of center head piece to top of last row of back body section. (The plain sc section of center head piece is for the nose.)

Sew left front section in position, starting at last st of last row of left front section and seam of last section just completed. Sew across top of head and center head piece down to nose matching the lps above nose.

Sew the plain part of center head piece around the nose piece of left front section, having the point at throat. Sew right front section to opposite side in same manner.

Sew the two front sections tog at front. Sew the back body section to front body section, fitting the side of head to center head piece, matching shoulders and leaving last rows of back body section free for sitting down. Sew opposite side in same manner. Stuff with fiberfill and sew lower part of back section to lower part of front section. Cut inner soles for legs from plastic canvas circles and insert. Stuff legs and arms with fiberfill; fold top edge flat across and sew opening closed. Sew arms to body, starting at shoulders. Sew legs to body at first row of front section.

Sew ears in position. Sew eyes in position, as shown. With cornmeal, embroider nose, using satin stitch. Shear all lps if desired. Place ribbon around neckline and tie ends in a bow. ✧

Humpty Dumpty

Jump into your childhood storybook and bring out a real-life incarnation of this treasured fairy-tale character. This Humpty is soft and cuddly, so he won't mind falling off the wall over and over again!

Design revised by Agnes Russell

SKILL LEVEL: BEGINNER

SIZE
12 inches tall, sitting

MATERIALS
- Coats & Clark Super Saver 4-ply yarn: 4 oz each light periwinkle #347 and white #311, small amounts each red and black
- Size F/5 crochet hook or size needed to obtain gauge
- Size D/3 crochet hook
- 2 (15mm) sew-on wiggle eyes
- 46 inches ⅜-inch-wide ribbon
- Fiberfill
- Tapestry needle

GAUGE
4 sc = 1 inch; 4 sc rnds = 1 inch
Check gauge to save time.

PATTERN NOTES
Weave in loose ends as work progresses.

Do not join rnds unless otherwise indicated; use a scrap of CC yarn to mark rnds.

Sl st to join each rnd in top of beg st.

Use crochet hook size F unless otherwise indicated

For the safety of children under age six, do not use sew-on eyes; crochet black circles or embroider eyes.

Using the same pattern a variety of different sizes of Humpty Dumpty can be made, using sport weight yarn with size D/3 crochet hook; crochet cotton size 10 and size 7 steel crochet hook; 2 strands of crochet cotton size 5 held tog and size 6 steel hook; 4-ply cotton and size G/6 crochet hook.

BODY
RND 1 (RS): With light periwinkle, ch 2, 8 sc in 2nd ch from hook. (8 sc)

RND 2: 2 sc in each sc around. (16 sc)

RND 3: [Sc in next sc, 2 sc in next sc] rep around. (24 sc)

RND 4: [Sc in each of next 2 sc, 2 sc in next sc] rep around. (32 sc)

RND 5: [Sc in each of next 3 sc, 2 sc in next sc] rep round. (40 sc)

RND 6: [Sc in each of next 4 sc, 2 sc in next sc] rep around. (48 sc)

RND 7: [Sc in each of next 5 sc, 2 sc in next sc] rep around. (56 sc)

RND 8: [Sc in each of next 6 sc, 2 sc in next sc] rep around. (64 sc)

RND 9: [Sc in next sc, dc in next sc] rep around, join, turn.

RND 10: Ch 1, [sc in next dc, dc in next sc] rep around, join, turn.

RNDS 11–14: Rep Rnd 10.

RND 15: Ch 1, sc in each st around, inc 6 sc evenly sp around, join, turn. (70 sc)

RND 16: Rep Rnd 9.

RNDS 17 & 18: Rep Rnd 10.

RNDS 19–26: Rep Rnds 15–18. (82 sts)

RND 27: Ch 1, sc in each st around, inc 10 sc evenly sp around, join, turn. (92 sc)

RND 28: Rep Rnd 9.

RNDS 29 & 30: Rep Rnd 10.

RND 31: Ch 1, sc in each st around, join, fasten off.

HEAD

RNDS 1–7: With white, rep Rnds 1–7 of body. (56 sc)

RND 8: Ch 1, sc in each sc around.

RNDS 9 & 10: Rep Rnd 8.

RND 11: [Sc in each of next 6 sc, 2 sc in next sc] rep around. (64 sc)

RNDS 12–14: Rep Rnd 8.

RND 15: [Sc in each of next 7 sc, 2 sc in next sc] rep around. (72 sc)

RNDS 16–18: Rep Rnd 8.

RND 19: [Sc in each of next 8 sc, 2 sc in next sc] rep around. (80 sc)

RNDS 20–22: Rep Rnd 8.

RND 23: [Sc in each of next 9 sc, 2 sc in next sc] rep around. (88 sc)

RNDS 24–26: Rep Rnd 8.

RND 27: Sc around, inc 4 sc evenly sp around. (92 sc)

RND 28: [Sc in next sc, dc in next sc] rep around, join in beg sc, fasten off.

FOOT & LEG *(make 2)*

RND 1 (RS): With light periwinkle, ch 9, 3 sc in 2nd ch from hook (toe), sc in each of next 6 chs, 3 sc in next ch (heel), working on opposite side of foundation ch, sc in each of next 6 chs, do not join. (18 sc)

RND 2: [2 sc in next sc] 3 times, sc in each of next 7 sc, 2 sc in next sc, sc in each of next 7 sc. (22 sc)

RND 3: Sc around, inc 3 sc across center 3 sc at toe end of foot. (25 sc)

RND 4: Sc around, dec 3 sc evenly sp across to toe end of foot. (22 sc)

RND 5: Sc around, dec 2 sc evenly sp across toe end of foot. (20 sc)

RNDS 6–10: Sc in each sc around.

RND 11: Working in back lps for this rnd only, [sc in next st, dc in next st] rep around, join, turn.

RNDS 12–17: Ch 1, [sc in dc, dc in sc] rep around, join, turn. At the end of Rnd 17, fasten off.

ARM *(make 2)*

RND 1 (RS): With light periwinkle, ch 14, sl st to join in first ch to form a ring, ch 1, [sc in next ch, dc in next ch] rep around, join, turn.

RNDS 2–9: Ch 1, [sc in dc, dc in sc] rep around, join, turn. At the end of Rnd 9, fasten off.

RND 10 (RS): Working in back lps for this rnd only, attach soft white, sc in each st around, do not join. (14 sc)

RNDS 11 & 12: Sc in each sc around.

RND 13: Sc in each sc around, join.

ROW 14: Fold Rnd 13 flat across, ch 1, working through both thickness, 7 sc across, turn. (7 sc)

ROW 15: Ch 1, sk 1 st, sc in each of next 6 sts, turn. (6 sc)

ROWS 16–18: Ch 1, sk 1 st, sc in each rem st across, turn. (3 sc) At the end of Row 18, fasten off.

COLLAR

RND 1 (RS): With white, ch 90, sl st to join to form a ring, ch 1, sc in each ch around, join. (90 sc)

RND 2: Ch 1, [sc in next sc, sk next 2 sc, 5 dc in next sc, sk 2 sc] rep around, join, fasten off.

EYELIDS *(make 2)*

ROW 1: With crochet hook size D and white, ch 5, sc in 2nd ch from hook, sc in each of next 3 chs, turn. (4 sc)

ROW 2: Ch 1, 2 sc in first sc, sc in each of next 2 sc, 2 sc in next sc, turn. (6 sc)

ROW 3: Ch 1, sc in each sc across, leaving a length of yarn, fasten off.

ASSEMBLY

Sew head to body, stuff with fiberfill before closing. Stuff arms and legs with fiberfill and sew to body. Sew collar over joining of body and head, positioning a sc of Rnd 2 at center front.

Starting at center front, weave ribbon through Rnd 2 of collar over sc sts and under 5-dc shell groups. Tie ends in a bow at center front.

Sew eyes to head between Rnds 15 and 16 approximately 1¾ inches apart. With black, sew eyebrows as shown. With red yarn, sew mouth as shown. For nose, make 1½-inch red pompom and sew into place. ✧

Dapper Frog

Do you remember catching frogs as a child, down by the creek? Here's one froggy friend who won't hop away too fast. Larger than life and full of personality, this frog makes a great pillow too!

Design revised by Agnes Russell

SKILL LEVEL: BEGINNER

SIZE

17 inches long

MATERIALS

➤ Coats & Clark Red Heart Super Saver 4-ply yarn: 9 oz dark spruce #361, 6 oz light celery #615

➤ Size F/5 crochet hook or size needed to obtain gauge

➤ Fiberfill

➤ 2 (13mm) decorative buttons

➤ Tapestry needle

GAUGE

4 sc = 1 inch; 4 sc rows = 1 inch

Check gauge to save time.

PATTERN NOTES

Weave in loose ends as work progresses.

Using same pattern, a variety of different sizes of the frog can be made, using sport weight yarn with size D/3 hook; crochet cotton size 10 and size 7 steel crochet hook; 4-ply cotton and size G/6 crochet hook.

HEAD & BODY

Note: Make 1 each from dark spruce and light celery.

ROW 1: Ch 17, sc in 2nd ch from hook, dc in next ch, [sc in next ch, dc in next ch] rep across, turn. (16 sts)

ROW 2: Ch 1, [sc, dc, sc] in first dc, [dc in next st, sc in next st] rep across to last st, [dc, sc, dc] in last sc, turn. (20 sts)

ROW 3: Ch 1, sc in first dc, dc in next sc, [sc in next dc, dc in next sc] rep across, turn.

ROW 4: Ch 1, [sc, dc, sc] in first dc, [dc in next sc, sc in next dc] rep across to last st, [dc, sc, dc] in last sc, turn. (24 sts)

ROWS 5–8: Rep Rows 3 and 4. (32 sts)

ROWS 9–21: Rep Row 3.

ROW 22: Rep Row 4. (36 sts)

ROWS 23 & 24: Rep Row 3.

ROW 25: Rep Row 4. (40 sts)

ROW 26: Rep Row 3.

ROW 27: Rep Row 3, ch 7, turn.

ROW 28: Sc in 2nd ch from hook, dc in next ch, [sc in next ch, dc in next ch] twice, [sc in next dc, dc in next sc] rep across, ch 7, turn.

ROW 29: Sc in 2nd ch from hook, dc in next ch, [sc in next ch, dc in next ch] twice, [sc in next dc, dc in next sc] rep across, turn. (52 sts)

ROWS 30–34: Rep Row 3.

ROW 35: Ch 1, sk first 2 sts, [sc in next dc, dc in next sc] rep across row, turn. (50 sts)

ROWS 36–49: Rep Row 35. At the end of Row 49, fasten off. (22 sts)

HIND LEG *(make 4)*

ROW 1: With dark spruce, ch 12, sc in 2nd ch from hook, sc in each rem ch across, turn. (11 sc)

ROWS 2–12: Ch 1, sc in each sc across, turn.

Foot

ROW 13: Ch 1, 2 sc in first sc, sc across to last sc, 2 sc in last sc, turn. (13 sc)

ROWS 14 & 15: Rep Row 13. (17 sc)

ROW 16: Ch 1, sc in each of next 4 sc, 2 sc in next sc, sc in each of next 3 sc, 3 sc in next sc, sc in each of next 3 sc, 2 sc in next sc, sc in each of next 4 sc, turn. (21 sc)

ROW 17: Ch 1, sc in each of next 4 sc, 2 sc in next sc, sc in each of next 5 sc, 3 sc in next sc, sc in each of next 5 sc, 2 sc in next sc, sc in each of next 4 sc, turn. (25 sc)

ROW 18: Ch 1, 2 sc in first sc, sc in each sc to center sc of 3-sc group, 3 sc in next sc, sc in each to last sc, 2 sc in next sc, turn. (29 sc)

ROW 19: Ch 1, 2 sc in first sc, sc across to center, 2 sc in center st, sc across to last sc, 2 sc in last sc, fasten off.

FRONT LEG *(make 4)*

ROW 1: With dark spruce, ch 10, sc in 2nd ch from hook, sc in each rem ch across, turn. (9 sc)

ROWS 2–22: Ch 1, sc in each sc across, turn.

ROWS 23–25: Ch 1, 2 sc in first sc, sc in each sc across to last sc, 2 sc in last sc, turn. (15 sc)

ROW 26: Ch 1, sc in each of next 4 sc, 2 sc in next sc, sc in each of next 2 sc, 3 sc in next sc, sc in each of next 2 sc, 2 sc in next sc, sc in each of next 4 sc, turn. (19 sc)

ROW 27: Ch 1, sc in each of next 4 sc, 2 sc in next sc, sc in each of next 4 sc, 3 sc in next sc, sc in each of next 4 sc, 2 sc in next sc, sc in each of next 4 sc, turn. (23 sc)

ROW 28: Ch 1, 2 sc in first sc, sc in each of next 10 sc, 3 sc in next sc, sc in each of next 10 sc, 2 sc in next sc, turn. (27 sc)

ROW 29: Ch 1, 2 sc in first sc, sc in each of next 12 sc, 2 sc in next sc, sc in each of next 12 sc, 2 sc in next sc, fasten off. (30 sc)

EYE *(make 4)*
RND 1: With light celery, ch 9, sc in 2nd ch from hook, sc in each of next 6 chs, 3 sc in next ch, working on opposite side of foundation ch, sc in each of next 6 chs, 2 sc in same ch as beg sc, do not join. (18 sc)

RND 2: Sc in each sc around.

RNDS 3 & 4: Sc around, inc 2 sc at each inc end of eye. (26 sc)

RND 5: Rep Rnd 2.

RND 6: Working in back lps only, sc in each st around.

RNDS 7–9: Rep Rnd 2. At the end of Rnd 9, fasten off.

EYE CENTER
ROW 1: With dark spruce, ch 9, sc in 2nd ch from hook, sc in each rem ch across, turn. (8 sc)
ROW 2: Ch 1, dec 1 sc over next 2 sc, sc in each rem sc across, turn. (7 sc)
ROWS 3–6: Rep Row 2. At the end of Row 6, fasten off. (3 sc)

ASSEMBLY
Sew one of the front leg pieces to

each side of dark spruce sections, starting at about Row 21 and sewing towards back.

Sew one of the hind leg sections to each side of dark spruce, starting at about Row 40, ending at last row.

Sew the other 4 leg sections to light celery section in same manner. Matching pieces, sew tog all around leaving opening at side to allow for stuffing. Stuff legs and feet slightly; stuff body and sew opening closed. Tack feet down to indicate toes.

Sew buttons to top center of back body, spacing evenly.

Sew eye center to eye. Stuff eye with fiberfill and sew as shown to body. With light celery embroider mouth as shown. ✧

BACK DRESS OPENING

Attach yarn at bottom left edge of back dress opening, ch 1, sc evenly sp in ends of row to neckline, fasten off.

Attach yarn at top right neckline edge of back dress opening, ch 1, sc evenly sp in ends of rows to waist, fasten off.

COLLAR

Attach yarn at end of neckline on left side of dress, with RS facing, ch 3, 6 dc in next st, [sk next 2 sts, dc in next st, sk next 2 sts, 7 dc in next st] 4 times, fasten off.

NECKLINE RUFFLE

ROW 1: Ch 30, sc in 2nd ch from hook, 2 sc in each rem ch across, turn. (57 sc)

ROW 2: Ch 2, [{dc, ch 4} in next st, sk next 3 sts, {sc, ch 4} in next st, sk next 3 sts] rep across, ending with dc in last st, turn. (14 ch-4 lps)

ROW 3: Ch 2, [{dc, ch 1} in next dc, {sc, ch 4} in 2nd ch of sp, {sc, ch 2} in 2nd ch of next sp] rep across, ending with dc in last dc, turn.

ROW 4: Ch 2, [dc in next dc, 7 dc in next ch-4 sp] rep across, ending with dc in last dc, fasten off.

DRESS FINISHING

Attach snap fasteners evenly sp down back opening of dress.

Following shape of scallops, sew single-edge lace around bottom of skirt ruffle. Sew lace around bottom of neck ruffle and around top of collar in same manner. Sew lace around bottom of each sleeve.

Beg at back dress opening, sew neck ruffle to neckline of dress at base of collar.

Using the rem free lps of Row 14 of bodice as a guide, cut double-edge lace to fit around waist and sew in place. Glue pink/gold trim around center of lace.

Cut double-edge lace to fit around skirt at top edge of ruffle and sew in place as illustrated. Glue pink/gold metallic trim around center of double-edge lace. Place dress on doll from bottom and fasten snaps. Fold lace collar down.

Cut 6 lengths of ribbon 9 inches each and tie each into a bow. Glue bows evenly sp around metallic trim on double-edge lace on skirt. Glue a ribbon rose to center of each bow. Make a ribbon bow and glue to front center of lace collar. Glue a ribbon rose to center of bow same as those on skirt.

Push sleeve up on arm to create puffy sleeve above Rnd 7. Cut 2 (12-inch) lengths of ribbon, tie length tightly around sleeve between Rnds 6 and 7, tie ends in a bow on outer edge.

Hat

CROWN

RND 1: Ch 24 loosely, sl st to join in beg ch to form a ring, sl st to join in front lp of beg sc. (24 sc)

BRIM

RND 2: Working in front lps for this rnd only, ch 1, 2 sc in same st, 2 sc in each rem st around, join in beg sc. (48 sc)

RND 3: Ch 4, sk next 2 sts, [sc, ch 4] in next st, sk next 2 sts, [sc, ch 2] in next st, sk next st, [{dc, ch 1} in next st, sk next 2 sts, {sc, ch 4} in next st, sk next 2 sts, {sc, ch 2} in next st, sk next st] rep around, join in 3rd ch of beg ch-4.

RND 4: Ch 3, 8 dc in ch-4 sp, [dc in next dc, 8 dc in next ch-4 sp] rep around, join in 3rd ch of beg ch-3, fasten off.

FINISHING

Cut a length of double-edge lace ruffle to fit around crown of hat, allowing slight overlap. Sew in place, stitch ends tog. Glue pink/gold metallic trim around center of ruffle. Sew single-edge lace around edge of brim in same manner as on skirt and neck ruffles.

Make 2 ribbon bows same as on skirt and glue to sides of hat on double-edge ruffle. Glue ribbon rose to center of each bow. Place hat on doll's head, secure in place with map pins pushed into doll's head to hold. Arrange brim evenly.

Purse

Note: *Do not join rnds unless otherwise indicated; use a scrap of CC yarn to mark rnds.*

RND 1: Beg at center bottom, ch 2, 5 sc in 2nd ch from hook. (5 sc)

RND 2: 2 sc in each st around. (10 sc)

RND 3: [Sc in next st, 2 sc in next st] rep around. (15 sc)

RND 4: [Sc in each of next 2 sts, 2 sc in next st] rep around. (20 sc)

RNDS 5–8: Sc in each st around. At the end of Rnd 8, sl st in next st to join.

RND 9: Ch 3, 4 dc in same st, sk next st, dc in next st, sk next st, [5 dc in next st, sk next st, dc in next st, sk next st] rep around, join in 3rd ch of beg ch-3, fasten off.

STRAP (*make 2*)

Ch 23, fasten off.

FINISHING

Sew single-edge lace around top edge of purse, following shape of scallops.

Place ends of each strap tog and sew inside purse at Rnd 8 on opposite sides. Beg on inside of purse, weave yarn through Rnd 8. Lightly stuff purse with fiberfill to shape, draw yarn ends to gather purse closed and tie off securely. Glue a ribbon bow to front of purse. Glue ribbon rose to center of bow. Hang purse over doll's wrist. ✧

Row 13 of bodice, attach Aran at seam, ch 3, dc in same st, 3 dc in next st, [2 dc in next st, 3 dc in next st] rep around, join in 3rd ch of beg ch-3. (85 dc)

RND 2: Ch 3, dc in each st around, join in 3rd ch of beg ch-3.

RND 3: Rep Rnd 8 of skirt. (102 dc)

RND 4: Rep Rnd 2, fasten off.

ROW 5: Attach Aran in 48th st of Rnd 4, ch 3, dc in each of next 96 sts, leaving rem 6 sts unworked, turn. (96 dc)

ROW 6: Ch 3, dec 1 dc over next 2 sts, dc in next st, [dc in each of next 5 sts, 2 dc in next st] 14 times, dc in each of next 8 sts, turn. (109 dc)

ROW 7: Ch 3, dec 1 dc over next 2 sts, dc in each rem st across, turn. (108 dc)

ROWS 8–10: Rep Row 7. (105 dc)

ROW 11: [Ch 3, sk next st, sc in next st] rep across, fasten off.

Arrange top section of front split of overskirt into a circular ruffle as shown, tack to overskirt to hold.

SLEEVE (*make 2*)
RND 1: Attach sage green at center underarm, working evenly sp around armhole opening, ch 1, work 7 sc, 2 hdc in each of next 9 sts, work 7 sc, do not join. (32 sts)

RNDS 2–4: Sc in each sc hdc in each hdc around, do not join.

RNDS 5 & 6: Sc in each st around, do not join.

RND 7: [Dec 1 sc over next 2 sts] rep around. (16 sc)

RND 8: [Sc in each of next 2 sts, dec 1 sc over next 2 sc] 4 times, sl st in next sc, fasten off. (12 sc)

BACK DRESS OPENING
Attach Aran at bottom left edge of back dress opening, ch 1, sc evenly in ends of rows to beg of dark sage section of bodice, drop Aran, pick up dark sage, sc in ends of rows to neckline, fasten off.

Beg at end of neckline on right edge of dress opening, rep edge finishing instruction in reverse to those on left edge.

NECKLINE FINISHING
With back of dress facing, attach sage green at right end of neckline, sl st in each st of foundation ch of neckline to other end, fasten off.

DRESS FINISHING
Sew ecru lace ruffle around bottom of skirt and each sleeve. Sew flat lace pearl trim over top edge of lace ruffle. Sew lace pearl trim to front and back of bodice over joining area of sage green and Aran sections.

NECKLINE TRIM
Sew flat ecru lace pearl trim around neckline for stand-up style collar. Attach snap fasteners along back opening of dress. Place dress on doll from bottom and fasten snaps.

OVERSKIRT FINISHING
Cut a yard of ribbon, beg at top of front split on overskirt and leaving approximately 12-inch length of ribbon on outside at beg and end, weave ribbon through turning ch-3 lps on ends of rows down one side of split, through ch-3 sps around bottom of overskirt and through turning ch-3 lps on ends of rows up other side of split. Tie ribbon ends into bow. Cut an 18-inch length of ribbon and tie into bow matching bow on overskirt. Glue 2nd bow to center of bow on overskirt to create multi-lp bow. Trim all ribbon ends to length illustrated. Glue ribbon rose to center of bows. Tie an 8-inch length of ribbon into a bow and glue to front center of neckline, trim ends.

Hat

CROWN
Note: Do not join rnds unless otherwise indicated.

RND 1: With sage green, ch 2, 6 sc in 2nd ch from hook. (6 sc)

RND 2: 2 sc in each st around. (12 sc)

RND 3: [Sc in next st, 2 sc in next st] 6 times. (18 sc)

RND 4: [Sc in each of next 2 sts, 2 sc in next st] 6 times. (24 sc)

RND 5: [Sc in each of next 3 sts, 2 sc in next st] 6 times. (30 sc)

RNDS 6–8: Sc in each st around.

RND 9: [Dec 1 sc over next 2 sts] rep around, working in front lp, sl st to join in next sc. (15 sc)

BRIM
RND 10: Working in front lps for this rnd only, ch 3, dc in same st, 2 dc in each rem st around, join in 3rd ch of beg ch-3. (30 dc)

RND 11: Ch 3, dc in same st, 2 dc in each rem st around, join in 3rd ch of beg ch-3. (60 dc)

RND 12: Ch 3, dc in each of next 2 sts, 2 dc in next st, [dc in each of next 3 sts, 2 dc in next st] rep around, join in 3rd ch of beg ch-3, fasten off. (75 dc)

Sew ecru lace ruffle around top edge of brim. Sew ecru lace pearl trim over top edge of lace ruffle. Glue 3 or 4 craft feathers to left side of hat at base of brim. Cut 2 lengths of ribbon each 15 inches long, hold evenly tog and tie in a bow, separate into 4 lps. Glue bow to base of brim over bottom ends of feathers. Glue ribbon rose across center of bow. Trim ribbon streamers evenly.

Place hat on top side of doll's head, positioned as illustrated. Secure in place with map pins pushed through hat into doll's head.

FEATHER FAN
Arrange rem craft feathers tog into a fan shape, glue tog at bottom ends. Trim bottom ends evenly. Tie small ribbon bow around bottom of feather fan, trim streamers to length shown. Glue fan to inside of doll's right hand. ❖

Chapter Six

Timeless Wearables

Capture the glamorous look displayed in fashion of the pre-1950s with this collection of unique garments. From elegant collars and sweet sweaters for women, to delicate baby booties and darling little girl dresses, this chapter brings you many old-time treasures to recreate today!

Twinkletoes Dress

How cute and adorable can a little girl be? You'll find out as soon as she puts on this dress. Fun and frilly, lavender and lacy, this dress has all the "sugar and spice" that little girls are made of. Originally designed as a minidress in 1936, we've lengthened it for extra sweetness.

SKILL LEVEL: INTERMEDIATE

SIZE
3T–4T

MATERIALS
➤ DMC Cebelia size 10 crochet cotton (50 grams per ball): 7 balls lavender #210 and 1 ball white
➤ Size 6 steel crochet hook or size needed to obtain gauge
➤ 2 small pearl buttons

GAUGE
{Sc row and dc row} twice = 1 inch
Check gauge to save time.

PATTERN NOTES
Weave in loose ends as work progresses.

Join rnds with a sl st unless otherwise stated.

Skirt

FIRST RUFFLE
RND 1: Beg at waist, with lavender, ch 240 loosely to prevent pulling, sl st to join in beg ch to form a ring, ch 3 (counts as first dc throughout), dc in each ch around, join in top of beg ch-3. (240 dc)

RND 2: Ch 5, sk 2 dc, [sc in next dc, ch 5, sk 2 dc] rep around, join in beg sc. (80 ch-5 lps)

RND 3: Sl st to center of first ch lp, ch 1, sc in same ch lp, ch 5, [sc in next ch lp, ch 5] rep around, join in beg sc.

RNDS 4–8: Rep Rnd 3.

At the end of Rnd 8, fasten off.

RND 9: Attach white in center of ch-5 lp, ch 1, sc in same ch lp, ch 5, sc in 4th ch of ch-5, ch 1, [sc in next ch lp, ch 5, sc in 4th ch of ch-5, ch 1] rep around, join in beg sc, fasten off.

SECOND RUFFLE
RND 1: With lavender, ch 250, sl st to join to form a ring, ch 3, dc in each ch around, join in top of beg ch-3. (250 dc)

RNDS 2–4: Ch 3, dc in each dc around, join in top of beg ch-3.

RND 5: Ch 3, dc around, inc 8 dc evenly sp around, join in top of beg ch-3. (258 dc)

RND 6: Rep Rnd 2 of first ruffle. (86 ch-5 lps)

RNDS 7–13: Rep Rnds 3–9 of first ruffle.

Make 6 more ruffles the same as 2nd ruffle, but with 9 more sts in the starting ch of each new ruffle, so that each lower ruffle is 9 sts larger than the previous. Join ruffles in correct position (smallest one first at top and largest at bottom). To join, starting with bottom ruffle, sew the chain edge (opposite side of foundation ch) to the last dc rnd of previous ruffle. The chain edge of the first ruffle will rem free.

BACK YOKE
ROW 1 (RS): Attach lavender to joining of foundation ch of first ruffle, working across opposite side of foundation ch, [ch 5, sk 2 sts, sc in next st] rep until a total of 40 lps (half of skirt top of first ruffle), turn.

ROW 2: Sl st to center of first lp, [ch 2, sc in next ch lp] rep across, turn.

ROW 3: Ch 3, dc in each ch and each sc across, turn.

ROW 4: Ch 1, sc in each dc across, turn.

ROW 5: Ch 3, dc in each sc across, turn.

ROWS 6 & 7: Rep Rows 4 and 5.

ROW 8: Rep Row 4.

ROW 9: Ch 1, sc in first sc, [ch 5, sk 2 sts, sc in next st] rep across, turn.

ROW 10: Rep Row 2. (38 ch-2 sps)

ARMHOLE SHAPING & BACK OPENING
ROW 1: Sl st over first 2 sps, ch 3, 1 dc in each st across to center of row, turn. (52 dc)

ROW 2: Ch 1, sc in each dc across, turn.

ROW 3: Ch 3, dc in each sc across, turn.

Rep Rows 2 and 3 until shaping measures 3¾ inches from underarm, ending with Row 3 of pattern.

Continued on page 137

Butterfly Mesh Blouse & Scarf

The socialite in you will be eager to stitch this dainty fitted blouse and matching scarf for any number of occasions. From weddings and dinner parties to garden shows and sailing trips, this set will be the perfect complement to your lifestyle.

SKILL LEVEL: ADVANCED

SIZE
Approximately size 6; 35 inch chest

MATERIALS
➤ Crochet cotton size 10 (50 grams per ball): 5 balls white (W), 2 balls cornflower blue (B)
➤ Size 3 steel crochet hook or size needed to obtain gauge
➤ Size 5 steel crochet hook
➤ 4 coordinating blue 10mm shank buttons
➤ Tapestry needle

GAUGE
6 sc and ch l = 1 inch; and 11 rows = inch on waistband; Rows 1–8 of back = 2 inches
Check gauge to save time.

PATTERN NOTES
Weave in loose ends as work progresses.

Ch 3 counts as first dc throughout.

Blouse

BACK WAISTBAND
ROW 1: With B and hook size 5, ch 131, sc in 3rd ch from hook, [ch 1, sk 1 st, sc in next st] rep across, turn.

ROW 2: Ch 1, sc under ch-1 sp, [ch 1, sc under next ch-1 sp] rep across, turn.

Rep Row 2 until waistband measures 3 inches.

BACK
ROW 1: With W and hook size 3, ch 3, sk first ch-1, *under next ch-1 make [1 dc, ch 3, sl st under same ch-1, ch 3, 1 dc] under same ch-1 (1 butterfly mesh), sk next ch-1, rep from * across, ending with dc of last butterfly mesh, turn. (32 butterfly mesh)

ROW 2: Ch 3, 1 dc in joining tip of first and 2nd butterfly mesh and complete butterfly mesh as before, continue making mesh to end of row, turn.

Rep Row 2 until there are 40 rows, which will be the beg of armhole. The length should now measure 10½ inches from top of waistband.

ARMHOLE SHAPING
Note: Dec at the beg and end of the next 8 rows.

ROW 1: To dec at the beg of the first row, ch 3, 1 sc in center of first 2 mesh of previous row, then ch 3, beg regular butterfly mesh between next 2 mesh. At the end, after last butterfly mesh, sc in ast dc of last mesh of previous row, turn.

ROW 2: Ch 3, work pattern between first and 2nd mesh ending row with sc in last dc of last mesh of previous row, turn.

ROWS 3–8: Rep Row 2. (23 mesh left on Row 8)

Work even for 15 rows to equal 4¼ inches.

Dec one butterfly mesh at armhole side for 6 rows, fasten off.

FRONT
With B and size 5 hook, ch 139 and make the same as for back including the dec for armhole, but having 34 butterfly mesh over waistband.

NECKLINE SHAPING
On the next row, turn at the neck after the 7th mesh has been completed about 3½ inches from the armhole. Complete one side making the neck edge straight and dec for the shoulder as in the back 5 rows, fasten off. Finish other side the same way.

SLEEVE (*make 2*)
With B and size 5 hook, make a ch 10 inches long, then work 8 rows as for back waistband. Change to W and size 3 hook and work 22 butterfly mesh across, work in pattern for 12 rows. Continue for 16 rows, dec ½ pattern at the beg and end of each row. The last row will be 2 inches long with 6 butterfly mesh.

JOINING
With white, sew front and back tog at shoulders, sew sleeve into armhole opening.

Sew left side seam from underarm to top of waistband, with

Continued on page 129

Wraparound Turban

Ingeniously designed not to disturb your hair, this 1914 pattern still looks contemporary today. Enjoy crocheting its unusual shape, then have fun wrapping, crossing and buttoning it into turban form.

SKILL LEVEL: INTERMEDIATE

SIZE
11 inches in diameter

MATERIALS
➤ Worsted weight yarn (3.5 oz per skein): 3 skeins off-white
➤ Size F/5 crochet hook or size needed to obtain gauge
➤ Size E/4 crochet hook
➤ 5 large wooden buttons
➤ 2 elastic hair bands
➤ Tapestry needle

GAUGE
2 roll sts and 2 rows = 1 inch
Check gauge to save time.

PATTERN NOTES
Weave in loose ends as work progresses.

Join rnds with a sl st unless otherwise stated.

Turban

CROWN
ROW 1: Using larger hook, ch 85 loosely, sk first ch, draw up a lp through each of next 4 sts, yo and draw through all 5 lps on hook, ch 1 (first star), *draw up a lp through eye of star just made, draw up a lp through back of last lp of star and 1 through each of next 2 sts of ch, yo, draw through all 5 lps on hook, ch 1, rep from * across, turn. (41 stars)

Note: At the end of Row 1, piece should measure 15 inches; if it does not, inc or dec number of stars.

ROW 2: Ch 3, draw up a lp in 2nd ch from hook, draw up a lp in 3rd ch, draw up a lp in eye of star below, draw up 1 lp in back of upper lp of star below, yo, draw through all 5 lps on hook, ch 1, *draw up 1 lp through eye of star, draw up 1 lp through back of last lp of star, draw up 1 lp through eye of next star below, draw up 1 lp through back of upper lp of same star, yo, draw through all 5 lps on hook, ch 1, rep from * across, turn.

Rep Row 2 until piece measures 9 inches deep. On next row work 20 stars, ch 45, turn. Work 21 stars on ch and continue to end of row. Continue until this 2nd half measures 9 inches wide, fasten off.

FRONT BAND

ROW 1: With smaller hook, ch 58, sc in 2nd ch from hook, sc in each rem ch across, turn. (57 sc)

ROW 2: Ch 1, [working in front lp only, sc in next st, working in back lp only, sc in next st] rep across, turn.

Rep Row 2 until piece measures 4 inches.

ROW 3: Ch 1, maintaining pattern of working in front and back lps of sts, sc across next 47 sts, leaving rem sts unworked, turn. (47 sc)

ROW 4: Ch 1, maintaining pattern of working in front and back lps of sts, sc across 37 sts, leaving rem sts unworked, turn. (37 sc)

ROW 5: Ch 1, maintaining pattern of working in front and back lps, sc across 47 sts, turn.

ROW 6: Ch 1, maintaining pattern of working in front and back lps of sts, sc in each of next 57 sts, turn.

ROW 7: *Ch 3, [yo, insert hook in first ch of ch-3, yo, draw up a lp]

twice, sk 2 sts on edge, insert hook in next st, yo, draw lp through st and 5 sts on hook, rep from * across edge, fasten off.

FINISHING

ROW 1: With smaller hook, working across 18-inch end of crown, sc across skipping sts on edge sufficiently to gather edge to 10½ inches.

ROW 2: Holding gathered edge of crown to straight edge of front band, ch 1, sc across, leaving a length of yarn, fasten off.

Fold opposite edge of front band to Row 2 and with rem length of yarn sew edge of band in place.

Working across 9-inch end of crown, fold into pleats to measure about 2 inches, with smaller hook, attach yarn and work 2 rows of tight sc across edge, fasten off. Rep in same manner on other 9-inch section of crown.

ELASTIC HAIR BAND COVER (*make 2*)

With smaller hook, attach yarn to

elastic hair band, ch 1, cover band with sc sts, join in beg sc, leaving a length of yarn, fasten off.

With rem length of yarn, sew elastic hair band to center of gathered 9-inch end of crown.

BUTTONS (*make 5*)

RND 1: With smaller hook, ch 4, join to form a ring, ch 1, 8 sc in ring, do not join. (8 sc)

RND 2: [Sc in next sc, 2 sc in next sc] 4 times. (12 sc)

RND 3: [Sc in each of next 2 sc, 2 sc in next sc] 4 times. (16 sc)

Continue to sc around, inc 4 sc evenly sp around until crocheted piece is same size a button.

RND 4: Ch 1, sc in each sc around.

RND 5: Holding button onto crocheted piece, [sc in next st, sk 1 st] rep around until button is secure, sl st in next st, leaving a length of yarn, fasten off.

Sew opening of button closed. Sew buttons evenly sp across front band. ✦

Butterfly Mesh Blouse & Scarf continued from page 126

blue, sew waistband closed. On right edge, sew from underarm to within waistband. Do not sew across right edge of waistband.

NECK OPENING

RND 1: With size 5 hook, attach B at shoulder seam, ch 1, sc evenly sp around neckline opening, join in beg sc.

RNDS 2–4: Ch 1, sc in each sc around, join in beg sc. At the end of Rnd 4, fasten off.

BUTTONHOLE LOOPS

With hook size 5, attach B at top edge of front waistband, ch 1, sc in same st, sc across side edge of waistband making four ch-9 lps evenly sp across. Sew buttons opposite button lps on edge of back waistband.

Scarf

ROW 1: With W and size 3 hook, ch 80, sl st in 6th ch from hook, ch 3, dc in same st, *sk 6 ch, 1 dc in next st, ch 3, sl st in same st as last dc, ch 3, 1 dc in same st, rep from * across, turn.

ROWS 2–6: Ch 3, *1 dc in center of 2 mesh of previous row, ch 3, sl st in same st as last dc was worked, ch 3, 1 dc in same st, rep from * across, turn. At the end of Row 6, fasten off, attach B, turn.

ROWS 7–11: Ch 1, keeping work flat, sc into every lp of mesh with ch 1 between each sc, turn. At the end of Row 11, fasten off, attach W, turn.

ROWS 12–17: Continue in butterfly mesh, making a butterfly mesh in every 2nd ch-1.

ROWS 18–22: With B, rep Rows 7–11.

ROWS 23–65: With W, continue in butterfly mesh for about 17 inches. Then make a slit by working in butterfly mesh to center of scarf only, instead of to the end of row for 6 rows, fasten off.

Attach cotton to center of row at base of split and work on rem half for 6 row (6 rows split in center of scarf), continue working across entire piece for 5 rows.

[Rep Rows 7–17] twice, changing color to maintain pattern. On last Row 17 rep, work a ch 3 sl st in first ch for p between each butterfly mesh.

Attach W at the beg of scarf to last butterfly mesh, ch 3, *ch 3, sl st in first ch for p, 1 sc under ch lp, ch 3, 1 sc at bottom of butterfly mesh, ch 3, 1 sc under next ch lp, rep from * across, fasten off. ✦

Sparkling Scarf

Put on a sparkling personality with this elegant scarf. Floral and leaf motifs grace the body and borders, while the long, lush fringe adds just the right amount of old-fashioned decorum.

SKILL LEVEL: INTERMEDIATE

SIZE
63 x 21 inches

MATERIALS
➤ Honeysuckle Yarns cotto metallic size 10 (100 yds per ball): 24 balls light aqua #8332

➤ Size 8 steel crochet hook or size needed to obtain gauge

➤ Tapestry needle

GAUGE
9 dc and 3 dc rows = 1 inch
Check gauge to save time.

PATTERN NOTE
Weave in loose ends as work progresses.

PATTERN STITCHES
BLOCK (BL): Dc in each of next 3 dc.

SPACE (SP): Ch 2, sk 2 sts, dc in next st.

INC 2 SPS AT BEG OF ROW: Ch 10, dc in 8th ch from hook, ch 2, sk 2 ch, dc in next dc.

2 SP DEC AT BEG OF ROW: Sl st across to dc of first sp.

2 SP DEC AT END OF ROW: Work across row to within last sp indicated on graph, turn.

Scarf

LACE EDGE (make 2)
Note: Lace edge is crocheted vertically.

ROW 1: Ch 101, dc in 8th ch from hook, [ch 2, sk 2 ch, dc in next ch] 27 times, dc in each of next 3 dc, [ch 2, sk 2 ch, dc in next ch] 3 times, turn. (28 sps: 1 bl; 3 sps)

ROW 2: Ch 5 (counts as first dc, ch 2), dc in next dc, [ch 2, sk 2 sts, dc in next st] twice (3 sps), dc in each of next 3 sts (1 bl), [ch 2, sk 2 sts, dc in next st] 6 times (6 sps), dc in each of next 3 sts (1 bl), [ch 2, sk 2 sts, dc in next st] 21 times (21 sps), turn.

ROW 3: Ch 10, dc in 8th ch from hook, ch 2, sk 2 ch, dc in next dc (2 sp inc at beg of row), work 20 sps, 1 bl, 7 sps, 1 bl, 3 sps, turn.

Follow Chart A (page 132) for rem of lace edge, inc and dec as indicated on bottom edge of lace. At the end of last rep, fasten off.

BODY
Note: Body is crocheted horizontally.

ROW 1: Ch 228, dc in 4th ch from hook, dc in each rem ch across, turn. (226 dc)

Note: If desired, Row 1 of body

can be worked across the top straight edge of lace edge, work evenly sp across until a total of 226 dc.

ROW 2: Ch 5 (counts as first dc, ch 2), dc in next dc, [ch 2, sk 2 sts, dc in next st] 74 times, turn. (75 sps)

ROW 3: Ch 5, dc in next dc, [ch 2, sk 2 sts, dc in next dc] 6 times (7 sps), * [dc in each of next 3 sts] 3 times (3 bls), [ch 2, sk 2 sts, dc in next st] 17 times (17 sps), rep from * twice, [dc in each of next 3 sts] 3 times (3 bls), [ch 2, sk 2 sts, dc in next st] 5 times (5 sps), turn.

Follow Chart B (page 132), ch 5 to beg each row for first dc, ch 2, turn at the end of each row. Rep body Rows 12–31 to desired for length minus the lace edges, ending with a row of dc in each st across, fasten off.

With tapestry needle, sew lace edge to body.

Knot a heavy fringe in each end of scarf. Trim ends to length desired. ✧

Chart A: Lace Edge

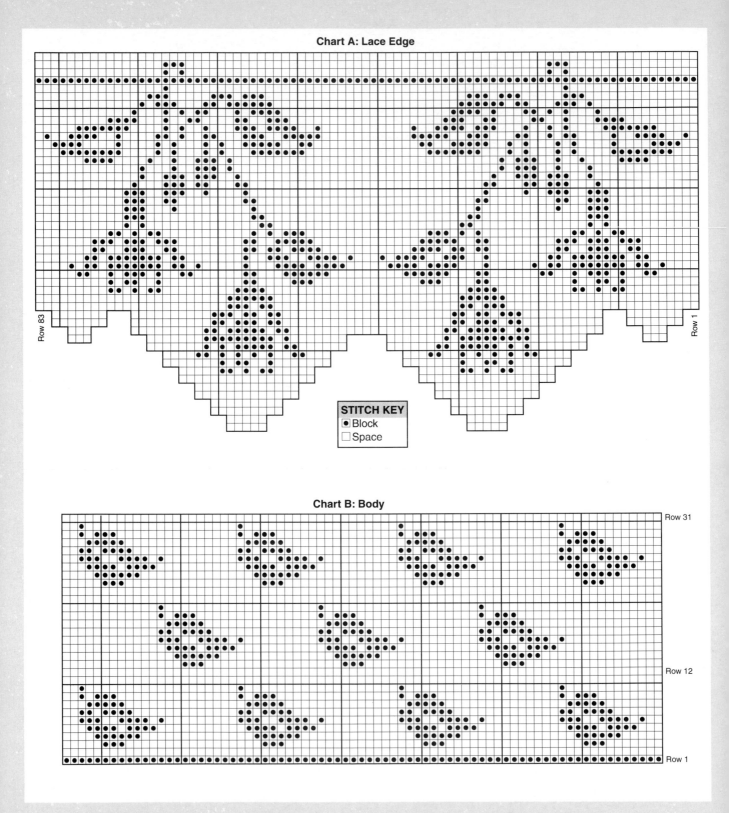

STITCH KEY
- ● Block
- □ Space

Chart B: Body

Tam-o'-Shanter

Hats are enjoying a new popularity, especially hand-crafted beauties like this tam-o'-shanter from 1916. Let its blousy Irish appeal accompany you on the golf course or in the garden.

SKILL LEVEL: BEGINNER

SIZE
Young adult

MATERIALS
➢ Brown Sheep Handpaint Originals 70 percent mohair/ 30 percent wool worsted weight yarn (88 yds per skein): 5 skeins mineral green #HP-10
➢ Size G/6 crochet hook or size needed to obtain gauge

GAUGE
4 sc and 4 rows = 1 inch
Check gauge to save time.

PATTERN NOTES
Weave in loose ends as work progresses.

Join rnds with a sl st unless otherwise stated.

Tam

RND 1 (RS): Ch 4, sl st to join to form a ring, ch 1, work 6 sc in each ch of ring, join in beg sc. (18 sc)

RND 2: Ch 1, [sc in each of next 2 sts, 2 sc in next st] rep around, join in beg sc. (24 sc)

RND 3: Ch 1, [sc in each of next 3 sc, 2 sc in next sc] rep around, join in beg sc. (30 sc)

RND 4: Ch 1, [sc in each of next 4 sc, 2 sc in next sc] rep around, join in beg sc. (36 sc)

Continue in sc working one more sc each rnd between inc sts (2 sc in same st), 6 sc will be inc each rnd. Continue until piece measures 8 inches from center to outer edge.

RND 5: Ch 1, sc around, sk 1 st at

each widening point and 1 sc in the center of each section. (12 skipped sc)

RND 6: Rep Rnd 5.

RND 7: Ch 1, [sc in each of next 3 sc, sk 1 sc] rep around, join in beg sc.

RND 8: Ch 1, [sc in each of next 2 sc, sk 1 sc] rep around, join in beg sc.

Rep in this way until tam measures 22 inches, or the size desired to within the hatband.

HATBAND
RNDS 1–10: Ch 1, sc in each st

around, join in beg sc.

RND 11: Sl st in each sc around, fasten off.

Make a pompom the size desired and attach to center top of tam over Rnd 1. ✧

Shoulderette

This pattern from 1945 is the forerunner of what we would now call a "shrug." With its gathered cuffs and fold-back collar, the shoulderette will keep you warm and make you feel pretty all through the evening.

SIZE
One size fits most

MATERIALS
➤ Caron Dazzlaire worsted weight yarn (3 oz per skein) 9 skeins celestial blue

➤ Size G/6 crochet hook or size needed to obtain gauge

➤ 2 yds 1-inch-wide satin ribbon

➤ Yarn needle

GAUGE
3 puff sts and ch sps = 2 inches; 6 rows = 2 inches

Check gauge to save time.

PATTERN NOTE
Weave in loose ends as work progresses.

PATTERN STITCHES
½ KNOT ST: Draw up ch on hook for ½ inch lp, draw yarn through lp and work 1 sc in back strand of lp.

PUFF ST: [Yo, insert hook in st, yo, draw up a lp] 3 times in same st, yo, draw through all 7 lps on hook.

PATTERN STITCH: *Note: Pattern st is multiple of 6 sts plus 4.*

ROW 1: Make ch, 1 dc in 4th ch from hook, *work ½ knot st, sk 2 ch, 1 sc in next ch, work ½ knot st as before, sk 2 ch, 1 puff st in next st, ch 1, rep from * across, ch 1, turn.

ROW 2: Work 1 sc in last puff st, *½ knot st, 1 puff st in next sc, ½ knot st, 1 sc in next puff st, rep from * across, ending with 1 sc in last st, ch 3, turn.

ROW 3: Work 1 puff st in last sc, *½ knot st, 1 sc in puff st, ½ knot st, 1 puff st in next sc, rep from * across, ch 1, turn.

Rep Rows 2 and 3 for pattern.

Shoulderette
Ch 94, work in pattern st for 50 inches, ending with Row 3 of pattern st, ch 1, then work border at side as follows.

BORDER
ROW 1: [1 sc in puff st, 1 sc in each of next 2 lps] rep across side edge, turn.

ROWS 2 & 3: Ch 1, sc in each st across, turn.

ROW 4: Ch 3, work 1 tr in each st across, turn.

ROWS 5 & 6: Ch 1, sc in each st across, turn.

ROW 7 (KNOT ST EDGE): Ch 1, work 1 sc in first st, *draw up a 1-inch lp, draw yarn through lp, 1 sc through back strand of lp st, draw up a 1-inch lp, draw yarn through lp, work 1 sc through back strand of lp, sk 1 st, 1 sc in next sc, rep from * across row, fasten off.

Rep Rows 1–7 on opposite side of shoulderette.

CUFF (make 2)
ROW 1: Attach yarn in side edge of border, ch 1, work 5 sc evenly sp across edge of border, [1 sc in puff st, 1 sc in next sc between puff st] rep across, ending with 5 sc evenly sp across opposite edge of border. (about 40 sc across row)

ROWS 2–7: Rep Rows 2–7 of border.

Sew cuff seam.

FINISHING
Weave ribbon through the tr sts of Row 4 of cuff, tie ends in a bow.

Find and mark center 22 inches of Row 4 of border worked on one side edge, weave ribbon through tr sts, tie ends in a bow. Turn border across ribbon weave back for collar as shown in photo. ✦

Cascade Collar

Fun and fanciful, light and fluffy, this pretty collar from 1936 will delight you as you make it and wear it. Attach it around any neckline for a multitude of fashionable possibilities!

SKILL LEVEL: BEGINNER

SIZE
11 inches in diameter

MATERIALS
- ➤ Crochet cotton size 30 (50 grams per ball): 5 balls white
- ➤ Size 10 steel crochet hook
- ➤ Snap fasteners
- ➤ Sewing needle

GAUGE
Work evenly and consistently.

PATTERN NOTES
Weave in loose ends as work progresses.
Collar may be worn two ways:

With opening at back (ends fastened together) and collar cascading down front (see old-time photo); or as shown in modern photo with opening in front and sides clasped together with a brooch.

Collar

ROW 1: Beg at neckline, make a ch about 1 yard long, dc in 4th ch from hook, dc in each ch of foundation until piece measures 31 inches of dc, turn.

ROW 2: [Ch 4, sc in next dc] rep across, turn.

ROWS 3–5: Ch 6, sc in next ch sp, [ch 4, sc in next ch sp] rep across, turn.

ROWS 6–9: Ch 7, sc in next ch sp, [ch 5, sc in next ch sp] rep across, turn.

ROWS 10–13: Ch 8, sc in next ch sp, [ch 6, sc in next ch sp] rep across, turn.

ROWS 14–17: Ch 9, sc in next ch sp, [ch 7, sc in next ch sp] rep across, turn.

ROWS 18–21: Ch 10, sc in next ch sp, [ch 8, sc in next ch sp] rep across, turn.

ROWS 22–32: Ch 11, sc in next ch sp, [ch 9, sc in next ch sp] rep across, turn. At the end of Row 32, fasten off.

Starch lightly and press. ✧

Twinkletoes Dress continued from page 124

SHOULDER SHAPING
ROW 1: From shoulder edge, ch 1, sc in each st across to last 6 sts, turn.

ROW 2: Sl st in first 6 sts, ch 3, dc in each rem sc across, turn.

ROW 3: Sl st over 18 sts, ch 1, sc in each st to last 6 sts from shoulder edge, turn.

ROW 4: Sl st over first 6 sts, ch 3, dc in each rem sc across, fasten off.

Rep armhole shaping, back opening and shoulder shaping the same on opposite side of back yoke reversing shaping.

FRONT YOKE
Work the same as back, omitting the center opening. When work measures 3 inches from armhole, last row being a sc row and ending at armhole edge, start neckline shaping. (104 sc)

ROW 1: Ch 3, dc in each of next 43 sts, turn. (44 dc)

ROW 2: Ch 1, sk 2 sts, sc in each dc across, turn.

ROW 3: Ch 3, dc across to last dc from neck edge, turn.
Rep Rows 2 and 3.

Then shape shoulder same as for back, continuing to shape neck as for the last 2 rows.

Sk 16 sc, attach thread to next sc and work the other shoulder to correspond.

Sew side and shoulder seams.

SLEEVE (*make 2*)
RND 1: Attach lavender at underarm, work 34 ch-5 lps around armhole opening (1 lp to each sc row and enough to keep work from pulling along armhole shaping).

RNDS 2–19: Sl st into ch-5 sp, ch 1, sc in same ch-5 sp, ch 5, [sc in next ch-5 sp, ch 5] rep around, join in beg sc.

Cuff
Note: Work Rnds 20–24 loosely.

RND 20: Sl st into ch-5 sp, ch 1, 2 sc in same ch sp, work 2 sc in each ch-5 sp around, join in beg sc.

RND 21: Ch 3, dc in each sc around, join in top of beg ch-3.

RND 22: Ch 1, sc in each dc around, join in beg sc.

RNDS 23 & 24: Rep Rnds 21 and 22. At the end of Rnd 22, fasten off.

COLLAR
ROW 1: Attach lavender at back neck opening, ch 1, sc in same st, [ch 5, sc in next st] 44 times evenly sp around neckline opening, turn.

ROWS 2–9: Sl st into ch-5 lp, ch 1, sc in same ch lp, ch 5, [sc in next ch-5 lp, ch 5] rep across, turn.

ROW 10: With white, rep Rnd 9 of first ruffle for p edge, do not join, fasten off.

FINISHING
Attach lavender at top of right back opening, ch 1, sc evenly sp down back opening making two buttonhole lps, one at top opening and another at the middle, fasten off. Sew buttons opposite buttonholes. ✧

Filet Collar

Take a touch of romance with you, wherever you go, when you wear this pretty collar. The rectangular sailor-style back tapers into a pearl-studded rosette at the front neckline. Feminine and delicate, it gives any modern blouse a vintage look.

Design revised by Agnes Russell

SKILL LEVEL: INTERMEDIATE

SIZE
12½ x 15 inches

MATERIALS
➤ Crochet cotton size 40: 500 yds white
➤ Size 13 steel crochet hook or size needed to obtain gauge
➤ 8mm pearl bead
➤ V-neck jersey
➤ Sewing needle

GAUGE
7 sps = 1 inch; 8 rows = 1 inch
Check gauge to save time.

PATTERN NOTES
Weave in loose ends as work progresses.

Row 1 establishes the RS, work chart (page 140) right to left including sp or bl marked as center, then sk center sp or bl and work graph left to right across the same row.

When Rows 1–103 are completed, return to opposite side of foundation ch and work Rows 104 and 105.

Sl st to join each rnd in beg st unless otherwise indicated.

PATTERN STITCHES
DEC SP AT BEG OF ROW: Ch 1, sl st in 3 sts across for each sp dec, sl st in next dc, ch 5 (counts as first dc, ch 2).

DEC A SP AT END OF ROW: Leave 3 sts of each sp unworked.

INC SP AT END OF ROW: Yo hook 4 times, insert hook in same st as last dc, yo, draw up a lp, [yo, draw through 2 lps on hook] 5 times.

INC SP AT BEG OF ROW: Ch 7, dc in next dc.

Collar

ROW 1 (RS): Ch 268, dc in 8th ch from hook, [ch 2, sk 2 ch, dc in next ch] 20 times, dc in each of next 3 ch, [ch 2, sk 2 ch, dc in next ch] 43 times, dc in each of next 3 chs, [ch 2, sk 2 ch, dc in next ch] 21 times, turn. (21 sps; 1 bl; 43 sps; 1 bl; 21 sps)

ROW 2 (WS): Ch 7, dc in next dc (1 bl inc at beg of row), [ch 2, sk 2 sts, dc in next st] twice, dc in each of next 3 sts, [ch 2, sk 2 sts, dc in next st] 19 times, dc in each of next 3 sts, [ch 2, sk 2 sts, dc in next st] 41 times, dc in each of next 3 sts, [ch 2, sk 2 sts, dc in next st] 19 times, dc in each of next 3 sts, [ch 2, sk 2 sts, dc in next st] twice, ch 2, inc 1 sp at end of row, turn. (3 sps; 1 bl; 19 sps; 1 bl; 41 sps; 1 bl; 19 sps; 1 bl; 3 sps)

ROW 3: Ch 5 (counts as first dc, ch 2 throughout), dc in next dc, [ch 2, sk 2 sts, dc in next st] 5 times, dc in each of next 15 sts (5 bls), [ch 2, sk 2 sts, dc in next st] 9 times, dc in each of next 18 sts (6 bls), [ch 2, sk 2 sts, dc in next st] 10 times, dc in each of next 18 sts (6 bls), [ch 2, sk 2 sts, dc in next st] 5 times, dc in each of next 18 sts (6 bls), [ch 2, sk 2 sts, dc in next st] 10 times, dc in each of next 18 sts (6 bls), [ch 2, sk 2 sts, dc in next st] 9 times, dc in each of next 15 sts 95 bls), [ch 2, sk 2 sts, dc in next st] 6 times, turn. (6 sps; 5 bls; 9 sps; 6 bls; 10 sps; 6 bls; 5 sps; 6 bls; 10 sps; 6 bls; 9 sps; 5 bls; 6 sps)

ROWS 4–37: Follow chart (page 140) as indicated, inc or dec sps at beg and end of row as indicated by graph, turn each row.

ROW 38: Work across 34 bls and sps of graph, turn.

ROWS 39–103: Follow chart as indicated. At the end of Row 103, fasten off.

Sk center 21 ch-2 sps for back neck, attach cotton in next dc, ch 5, work across rem bls and sps of

Continued on next page

Filet Collar continued from previous page

graph. Rep Rows 39–103 of graph.

Extended Edging

ROW 104 (RS): Attach cotton in opposite side of foundation ch, ch 5, sk 2 ch, dc in next ch, [ch 2, sk 2 ch, dc in next ch] 10 times, turn. (11 sps)

ROW 105: Sl st across to 4th dc, ch 5, dc in next dc, [ch 2, sk 2 sts, dc in next st] 6 times, fasten off, turn. (7 sps)

With RS facing and finished section to the right, sk next 3 ch-2 sps, attach cotton in next dc, follow graph to complete rem extended rows of edging.

TRIM

RND 1 (RS): Attach cotton in any dc at back neck (Row 37), ch 1, sc evenly sp around entire outer edge of collar, join in beg sc.

RND 2: Ch 1, [sc, ch 3, sc] in same st as beg ch-1, [sk next 2 sts, {sc, ch 3, sc} in next st] rep around entire outer edge, skipping 1 sc at outer corners as needed to keep piece flat, join in beg sc, fasten off.

Lightly starch and press collar.

IRISH ROSE

RND 1: (RS) Ch 5, sl st to join to form a ring, ch 1, 14 sc in ring, join in beg sc. (14 sc)

RND 2: Ch 1, beg in same sc, [sc in next sc, ch 3, sk 1 sc] rep around, join in beg sc. (7 ch-3 lps)

RND 3: Ch 1, [sc, 3 dc, sc] in each ch-3 sp around, join in beg sc. (7 petals)

RND 4: Sl st in next skipped sc if Rnd 1, ch 1, sc in same sc as beg ch-1, ch 5, [sc in next skipped sc of Rnd 1, ch 5] rep around, join in beg sc. (7 ch-5 lps)

RND 5: Ch 1, [sc, 6 dc, sc] in each ch-5 lp around, join in beg sc. (7 petals)

RND 6: Working behind petals of Rnd 5, ch 1, [sc around post of sc of Rnd 4, ch 7] rep around, join in beg sc. (7 ch-7 lps)

RND 7: Ch 1, [sc, 3 dc, 3 tr, 3 dc, sc] in each ch-7 lp around, join in beg sc. (7 petals)

RND 8: Working behind petals of Rnd 7, ch 1, [sc around post of sc of Rnd 6, ch 9] rep around, join in beg sc. (7 ch-9 lps)

RND 9: Ch 1, [sc, 3 dc, 6 tr, 3 dc, sc] in each ch-9 lp around, join in beg sc, fasten off.

Sew pearl bead to center of Irish rose.

FINISHING

Using straight pins, pin collar to V-neck jersey. Base collar invisibly to neckline. Tack Irish rose to center front of V-neck.

Use care to launder and do not place collar in dryer. If desired, use snap fasteners to secure collar and Irish rose to V-neck and remove to launder. ✧

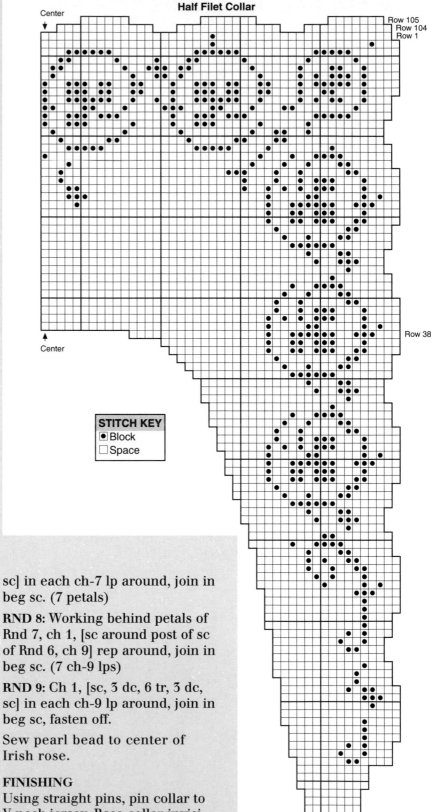

Half Filet Collar

Center
Row 105
Row 104
Row 1
Center
Row 38
Row 103

STITCH KEY
● Block
☐ Space

Embroidered Booties

Almost like little sandals, these charming booties from 1920 will look adorable on baby and bring smiles to mom. The front-button closure and delicate floral embroidery make them even more special.

PATTERN NOTES
Weave in loose ends as work progresses.

Join rnds with a sl st unless otherwise stated.

Bootie

INSTEP
ROW 1: Ch 92, sl st to join in beg ch to form a ring, beg in 2nd ch from hook, draw up a lp in each of next 14 chs, yo, draw through first lp on hook, [yo, draw through 2 lps on hook] rep across until 1 lp rem.

ROW 2: Sk first vertical bar, [draw up a lp around next vertical bar] rep across retaining all lps on hook, yo, draw through first lp, [yo, draw through 2 lps on hook] rep across until 1 lp rem on hook.

Rep Row 2 until 11 rows of afghan st for instep. Fasten off.

SIDES
RND 1: From center front instep, attach cotton in ch at center back, ch 1, sc in each ch to instep, sc evenly sp across side edge of instep, 2 sc in corner, sc across instep front, 2 sc in corner, sc evenly sp across opposite side of instep, sc in each rem ch, join in beg sc.

RNDS 2–16: Ch 1, sc in each sc around, join in beg sc. At the end of last rep, fasten off.

STRAP
ROW 1: Count sts on sides from each side of instep around, find center 24 sc of back, attach cotton, ch 1, sc in each of next 24 sc, turn.

ROW 2: Ch 1, sc in each of next 24 sc, turn.

ROW 3: Ch 24, sc in 2nd ch from hook, sc in each rem ch across, sc

in each of next 24 sc, turn. (47 sc)

ROW 4: Ch 24, sc in 2nd ch from hook, sc in each rem ch across, sc in each of next 47 sc, turn. (70 sc)

ROWS 5–7: Ch 1, sc in each sc across, turn.

RND 8: Working around entire strap and top of bootie, ch 1, [sc in each of next 3 sts, ch 3, sl st in last sc for p] rep around, working a ch 3 at center front of right strap for buttonhole, join, fasten off.

SOLE
ROW 1: Ch 12, sc in 2nd ch from hook, sc in each rem ch across, turn. (11 sc)

ROW 2: Ch 1, sc in each sc across, turn.

ROW 3: Ch 1, 2 sc in first sc, sc in each sc across to last sc, 2 sc in last sc, turn. (13 sc)

ROWS 4–6: Rep Row 3. (19 sc)

Work 1 sc in each st for next 36 rows.

ROWS 7–10: Dec 1 sc over next 2 sc, sc in each sc across to last 2 sc, dec 1 sc over next 2 sc, turn. (11 sc)

JOINING
Holding sole to side of bootie, sc evenly sp around, join in beg sc, fasten off.

EMBROIDERY
The bootie may be finished with a group of 3 flowers in French knots in light and dark blue, consisting of 5 French knots, made with 1 ply twice around needle. The centers are French knots in gold made in the same way. There are short stems from each flower in green, using three plies. ✧

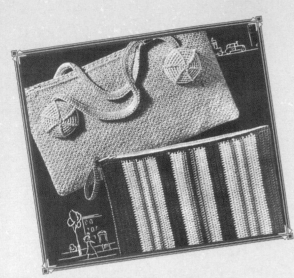

Envelope Purses

For a truly timeless handbag, try these classically shaped envelope purses. Whimsical "knobs" that are attached to the straps give one purse a modern sensibility, while the tweedy stitch pattern keeps it demure. The other purse features eye-catching stripes, a fashion statement in any generation.

Tweed Envelope Purse

SKILL LEVEL: BEGINNER

SIZE
12 x 7¾ inches

MATERIALS
➤ Crochet cotton size 10: 500 yds cornflower blue
➤ Crochet cotton size 30: 500 yds white
➤ Size 3 steel crochet hook or size needed to obtain gauge
➤ 4 (2-inch) buttons
➤ 9-inch zipper
➤ Sewing needle and thread

GAUGE
6 sts and 5 rows = 1 inch
Check gauge to save time.

PATTERN NOTES
Weave in loose ends as work progresses.

Join rnds with a sl st unless otherwise stated.

Work with 1 strand each ecru and white held tog throughout.

FRONT/BACK
RND 1 (RS): Ch 79, [sc and dc] in 2nd ch from hook, [sc in next ch, dc in next ch] rep across to last ch, [sc, dc] twice in last ch, working on opposite side of foundation ch, [sc in next ch, dc in next ch] rep across, ending with [sc and dc] in same ch

as beg, join in beg sc. (160 sts)

RND 2: Ch 2 (counts as first dc), sc in next dc, [dc in next sc, sc in next dc] rep around, join in top of beg ch-2.

RND 3: Ch 1, sc in same st as joining, dc in next sc, [sc in next dc, dc in next sc] rep around, join in beg sc.

Rep Rnds 2 and 3 until purse is desired depth, fasten off.

HANDLE *(make 2)*
ROW 1: Ch 125, sc in 2nd ch from hook, sc in each rem ch across, turn. (124 sc)

ROW 2: Ch 1, working in front lps for this row only, sc in each st across, turn.

ROW 3: Ch 1, working in back lps for this row only, sc in each st across, turn.

ROW 4: Rep Row 2.

ROW 5: Fold piece in half lengthwise, working through both thickness in back lps only of Row 4 and in opposite side of foundation ch, sl st in each st across, fasten off.

BUTTON COVER *(make 4)*
RND 1: Ch 3, sl st to join to form a ring, ch 1, 6 sc in ring, join in beg sc. (6 sc)

RND 2: Ch 1, [sc and dc] in each sc around, join in beg sc. (12 sts)

RND 3: Ch 1, [sc in next sc, sc in next dc, fpdc around same dc] rep around, join in beg sc. (18 sts)

RND 4: Ch 1, [sc in each sc, sc in next dc, fpdc around same dc] rep around, join in beg sc. (24 sts)

Rep Rnd 4 until large enough to cover front of button. Each additional rnd will add 6 sts to button cover.

RND 5: Holding button on WS of cover, ch 1, [sc in next st, sk 1 sc] rep around until opening is closed, fasten off.

FINISHING
Attach each end of handle 3¼ inches out from center of bag and 1¼ inch down from top. Sew a button over each end of handle. Rep with 2nd handle and buttons on opposite side of purse.

Sew zipper into top opening of purse. Line purse if desired.

Striped Envelope Purse

SKILL LEVEL: BEGINNER

SIZE
8¾ inches x 7 inches

MATERIALS
➤ Crochet cotton size 10 (150 yds per ball): 4 balls each mocha and ecru, 1 ball taupe
➤ Size 6 steel crochet hook or size needed to obtain gauge
➤ 9-inch zipper
➤ Sewing needle and thread

GAUGE
7 sc and 8 rows = 1 inch
Check gauge to save time

PATTERN NOTES

Weave in loose ends as work progresses.

Work with two strands of cotton held tog throughout.

FRONT/BACK

ROW 1: With 2 strands of mocha, ch 92, sc in 2nd ch from hook, sc in each rem ch across, turn. (91 sc)

ROW 2: Ch 1, sc in each sc across, turn.

ROWS 3–9: Rep Row 2. At the end of Row 9, fasten off.

ROWS 10–13: With ecru, rep Row 2. At the end of Row 13, fasten off.

ROWS 14 & 15: With taupe, rep Row 2. At the end of Row 15, fasten off.

ROWS 16 & 17: With ecru, rep Row 2. At the end of Row 17, fasten off.

ROWS 18 & 19: Rep Rows 14 and 15.

ROWS 20–23: Rep Rows 10–13.

ROWS 24–29: With mocha, rep Row 2. At the end of Row 29, fasten off.

ROWS 30–33: Rep Rows 10–13.

ROWS 34 & 35: Rep Rows 14 and 15.

ROWS 36 & 37: With mocha, rep Row 2. At the end of Row 37, fasten off.

ROWS 38 & 39: Rep Rows 14 and 15.

ROWS 40–43: Rep Rows 10–13.

ROWS 44–49: With mocha, rep Row 2. At the end of Row 49, fasten off.

ROWS 50–53: Rep Rows 10–13.

ROWS 54 & 55: Rep Rows 14 and 15.

ROWS 56 & 57: Rep Rows 16 and 17.

ROWS 58 & 59: Rep Rows 14 and 15.

ROWS 60–63: Rep Rows 10–13.

ROWS 64–72: With mocha, rep Row 2. At the end of Row 72, fasten off.

ASSEMBLY

With stripes running vertically, fold piece in half. Working through both thickness, attach navy blue at fold, ch 1, sc evenly sp across edge. Rep in same manner on opposite end.

TOP OPENING TRIM

RND 1: Attach mocha in side seam, ch 1, sc evenly sp around opening, join in beg sc.

RND 2: Ch 1, sc in each sc around, join in beg sc, fasten off.

Sew zipper into top opening. ✧

Raised Shell Bag

This elegant purse is the perfect accessory for those evenings on the town. Wear it over the shoulder for a dinner date, or omit the straps for a more formal clutch purse.

SKILL LEVEL: INTERMEDIATE

SIZE
15 x 7¼ inches

MATERIALS
➤ Crochet cotton size 10 (150 yards per ball): 2 balls ecru and metallic gold blend
➤ Size 6 steel crochet hook or size needed to obtain gauge
➤ 9-inch zipper
➤ Lining material
➤ Sewing needle and thread
➤ ⅝-inch button
➤ Snap fastener

GAUGE
1 shell = 1 inch; 3 rows = 2 inches

Check gauge to save time.

PATTERN NOTE
Weave in loose ends as work progresses.

BAG SIDE (*make 2*)
ROW 1 (WS): Ch 57, [3 tr, ch 1, 4 tr] in 5th ch from hook, [sk 1 st, sl st in next st, sk 1 st, shell of {4 tr, ch 1, 4 tr} in next st] 12 times, sk 1 st, sl st in next st, sk 1 st, half shell of 4 tr in next st, turn. (13 shells; 1 half shell)

ROW 2 (RS): Ch 1, sl st in first tr, [working in back lp of sl st only, shell of {4 tr, ch 1, 4 tr} in next sl st, sl st in ch-1 sp of shell] rep across, ending with half shell of 4 tr in last tr of shell, turn.

Continued on page 147

Women of France Shawl

*This quick-and-easy shawl was originally created as a pattern for charity.
American women crocheted these shawls for the women of France whose lives
had been devastated by World War I. Now you can make this beautiful piece
for any number of happier reasons, while keeping its history in mind.*

SKILL LEVEL: INTERMEDIATE

SIZE
45 inches in diameter

MATERIALS
➤ Brown Sheep Top o' the Lamb worsted weight 100 percent wool yarn (4 oz/190 yds per skein): 7 skeins russet #200

➤ Size G/6 crochet hook or size needed to obtain gauge

GAUGE
Rnds 1–3 = 4 inches in diameter; 4 shells rnds = 3 inches

Check gauge to save time.

PATTERN NOTES
Weave in loose ends as work progresses.

Join rnds with a sl st unless otherwise stated.

Ch 3 counts as first dc throughout.

PATTERN STITCHES
SHELL: [2 dc, ch 1, 2 dc] in indicated sp.

BEG SHELL: Sl st into ch-1 sp, ch 3, 1 dc, ch 1, 2 dc in same sp.

V-ST: Yo, draw up a lp in next ch-1 sp, yo, draw through 2 lps on hook, yo, draw up a lp in next ch-1 sp, yo, draw through 2 lps on hook, yo, draw through all 3 lps on hook.

Shawl

CENTER
RND 1 (RS): Ch 6, sl st to join in first ch to from a ring, ch 1, 12 sc in ring, join. (12 sc)

RND 2: Ch 3, dc in same sc as beg ch, 2 dc in each sc around, join in top of beg ch-3. (24 dc)

RND 3: Ch 4 (counts as first dc, ch 1), [dc in next dc, ch 1] rep around, join in 3rd ch of beg ch-4.

RND 4: Sl st into next ch-1 sp, ch 4, dc in same ch-1 sp (beg inc point), ch 1, dc in next ch-1 sp, ch 1, [{dc, ch 1, dc} in next ch-1 sp (inc point), ch 1, dc in next ch-1 sp, ch 1] rep around, join in 3rd ch of beg ch-4. (12 inc points; 1 dc between each inc points)

RND 5: Sl st into next ch-1 sp, ch 4, dc in same ch-1 sp, ch 1, [dc in next ch-1 sp, ch 1] twice, [{dc, ch 1, dc} in next ch-1 sp, ch 1, {dc in next ch-1 sp, ch 1} twice] rep around, join in 3rd ch of beg ch-4. (12 inc points; 2 dc between each inc point)

RND 6: Sl st into next ch-1 sp, ch 4, dc in same ch-1 sp, ch 1, [dc in next ch-1 sp, ch 1] rep across to inc point, [{dc, ch 1, dc} in next ch-1 sp at inc point, ch 1, {dc in next ch-1 sp, ch 1} rep across to inc point] rep around, join in 3rd ch of beg ch-4. (12 inc points; 3 dc between each inc point)

RNDS 7–16: Rep Rnd 6, having one more dc between each inc point each rnd. At the end of Rnd 16, a total of 13 dc between each inc point.

BORDER
RND 17: Sl st into ch-1 sp, ch 3, *yo, draw up a lp in same ch-1 sp, yo, draw through 2 lps on hook, yo, draw up a lp in next ch-1 sp, yo, draw through 2 lps on hook, yo, draw through all 3 lps on hook, ch 1, rep from * around, join in top of beg ch-3.

RND 18: Beg shell in ch-1 sp, ch 1, sk next ch-1 sp, V-st, ch 1, sk next ch-1 sp, [shell in next ch-1 sp, ch 1, sk next ch-1 sp, V-st, ch 1, sk next ch-1 sp] rep around, join in top of beg ch-3.

RND 19: Beg shell in ch-1 sp of beg shell, *ch 1, dc between next 2 dc (last 2 dc of shell of previous rnd), ch 1, V-st over V-st of previous rnd, ch 1, dc between first 2 dc of next shell, ch 1 **, shell in next ch-1 sp of shell, rep from * around, ending at ** on last rep, join in top of beg ch-3. (1 dc between shell and V-st)

RNDS 20 & 21: Beg shell in ch-1 sp of beg shell, *ch 1, dc between next 2 dc (last 2 dc of shell of previous rnd), ch 1, sk next ch-1 sp, V-st over V-st, ch 1, sk next ch-1 sp, dc between first 2 dc of next shell, ch 1 **, shell in next ch-1 sp of shell, rep from * around, ending at ** on last rep, join in top of beg ch-3. (1 dc between shell and V-st)

RND 22: Beg shell in ch-1 sp of beg shell, *ch 1, dc between next 2 dc, ch 1, dc in next ch-1 sp, ch 1, V-st over V-st, ch 1, dc in next ch-1 sp, ch 1, dc between first 2 dc of next shell, ch 1 **, shell in next ch-1 sp of shell, rep from * around, ending at ** on last rep, join in top of beg ch-3. (2 dc between shell and V-st)

RNDS 23 & 24: Beg shell in ch-1 sp of beg shell, *ch 1, dc between next 2 dc, ch 1, dc in next ch-1 sp, ch 1, sk next ch-1 sp, V-st over V-st, ch 1, sk next ch-1 sp, dc in next ch-1 sp, ch 1, dc between first 2 dc of next shell, ch 1 **, shell in next ch-1 sp of shell, rep from * around, ending at ** on last rep, join in 3rd ch of beg ch-3. (2 dc between shell and V-st)

RND 25: Beg shell in ch-1 sp of beg shell, *ch 1, dc between next 2 dc, [ch 1, dc in next ch-1 sp] twice, ch 1, V-st over V-st, ch 1, [dc in next ch-1 sp, ch 1] twice, dc between first 2 dc of next shell, ch 1 **, shell in next ch-1 sp of shell, rep from * around, ending at ** on last rep, join in top of beg ch-3. (3 dc between shell and V-st)

RNDS 26 & 27: Beg shell in ch-1 sp of beg shell, *ch 1, dc between next 2 dc, [ch 1, dc in next ch-1 sp] twice, ch 1, sk next ch-1 sp, V-st over V-st, ch 1, sk next ch-1 sp, [dc in next ch-1 sp, ch 1] twice, dc between first 2 dc of next shell, ch 1 **, shell in next ch-1 sp of shell, rep from * around, ending at ** on last rep, join in top of beg ch-3. (3 dc between shell and V-st)

RND 28: Beg shell in ch-1 sp of beg shell, *ch 1, dc between next 2 dc, [ch 1, dc in next ch-1 sp] 3 times, ch 1, V-st over V-st, ch 1, [dc in next ch-1 sp, ch 1] 3 times, dc between first 2 dc of next shell, ch 1 **, shell in next ch-1 sp of shell, rep from * around, ending at ** on last rep, join in top of beg ch-3. (4 dc between shell and V-st)

RNDS 29 & 30: Beg shell in ch-1 sp of beg shell, *ch 1, dc between next 2 dc, [ch 1, dc in next ch-1 sp] 3 times, ch 1, sk next ch-1 sp, V-st over V-st, ch 1, sk next ch-1 sp, [dc in next ch-1 sp, ch 1] 3 times, dc between first 2 dc of next shell, ch 1 **, shell in next ch-1 sp of shell, rep from * around, ending at ** on last rep, join in top of beg ch-3. (4 dc between shell and V-st)

RND 31: Sl st into ch-1 sp of shell, ch 6, sl st in 3rd ch from hook, [ch 1, dc in same ch-1 sp of shell, ch 3, sl st in top of last dc made] twice, *[ch 1, dc in next ch-1 sp, ch 3, sl st in top of dc] 3 times, ch 1, dc in next ch-1 sp, ch 1, V-st over V-st, ch 1, dc in next ch-1 sp, [ch 1,dc in next ch-1 sp, ch 3, sl st in top of dc] 3 times, ch 1 **, dc in next ch-1 sp of shell, ch 3, sl st in top of dc, [ch 1, dc in same ch-1 sp of shell, ch 3, sl st in top of dc] twice, rep from * around, ending at ** on last rep, join in 3rd ch of beg ch-6. ✧

Raised Shell Bag continued from page 144

ROW 3: Rep Row 2.

ROW 4: Ch 1, sl st in first tr, [working in back lp of sl st only, shell of {5 tr, ch 1, 5 tr} in next sl st, sl st in next ch-1 sp of shell] rep across, ending with half shell of 5 tr in last tr of shell, turn.

Rep Row 4 until there are a total of 11 rows of raised shells, fasten off.

TOP TRIM

ROW 1: Working across opposite side of foundation ch of Row 1 of bag side, attach cotton, ch 1, sc in each ch across, turn. (56 sc)

ROW 2: Ch 1, sc in each sc across, fasten off.

Rep for other side.

LINING
Use one side as pattern, cut two pieces lining allowing seam allowance.

Sew bag sides tog, leaving 1½ inch openings at each side at top. Line bag and sew handle to top opening of bag.

FASTENER

ROW 1: Ch 10, sc in 2nd ch from hook, sc in each rem ch across, turn. (9 sc)

ROW 2: Ch 1, sc in each sc across, turn.

Rep Row 2 until piece when placed at Row 1 of trim, passes over top of handles to Row 1 at opposite edge of top trim.

ROW 3: Ch 1, dec 1 sc over next 2 sc, sc in each sc across to last 2 sc, dec 1 sc over next 2 sc, turn. (7 sc)

ROWS 4 & 5: Rep Row 3. (3 sc)

ROW 5: Ch 1, draw up a lp in each of next 3 sc, yo, draw through all 4 lps on hook. (1 sc)

RND 6: Ch 1, sc evenly sp around entire outer edge, join in beg sc, fasten off.

Sew Row 1 of fastener to center of Row 1 of top trim.

BUTTON

RND 1: Ch 2, 6 sc in 2nd ch from hook, join. (6 sc)

RND 2: Ch 1, 2 sc in each sc around, join. (12 sc)

RND 3: Ch 1, [sc in next sc, 2 sc in next sc] rep around, join. (18 sc)

RND 4: Ch 1, sc in each sc around, join, leaving a length of cotton, fasten off.

Place button in center of crocheted piece, weave rem length through sts of Rnd 4, pull to close around button and secure.

Sew button centered to dec end of fastener. Sew snap fastener on opposite side of fastener and to bag.

HANDLE
Make a ch about a yard long, sl st in 2nd ch from hook, sl st in each rem ch across, fasten off. Find center and pin to bottom of opening at one side. Whipstitch along opening. Draw ends through holes in handle from inside out. On other side draw ends through from inside out. Join ends at bottom of opening and whipstitch along opening as before. ✧

Stylish Stole

Keep warm the old-fashioned way with this graceful wrap. Thick cluster stitches and a knit-like trim give it texture, while the neatly pointed edges add to its vintage charm.

Design revised by Agnes Russell

SKILL LEVEL: BEGINNER

SIZE
Back neck to front bottom point: 35 inches; 14½ inches wide

MATERIALS
➤ Knitting worsted yarn: 20 oz country rose
➤ Size G/6 crochet hook or size needed to obtain gauge
➤ Yarn needle

GAUGE
Tr shell = 2 inches; 3 shell rows = 2 inches
Check gauge to save time.

PATTERN NOTES
Weave in loose ends as work progresses.

Stole can be made wider by simply repeating Row 5 to the width desired; and longer by repeating Rows 15 and 16 until length desired before front point decreases. Allow sufficient yarn for larger stole.

PATTERN STITCH
TR SHELL: 7 tr in indicated st.

Stole

RIGHT SECTION
ROW 1: Ch 6, 6 tr in 5th ch from hook, turn. (1 tr shell)

ROW 2: Ch 4 (counts as first tr throughout), 6 tr in first tr, sk next 2 tr, sc in next tr, sk next 2 tr, tr shell in last tr, turn. (2 tr shells)

ROW 3: Ch 4, 6 tr in first tr, sk next 2 tr, sc in next tr, sk next 3 tr, tr shell in next sc, sk next 3 tr, sc in next tr, sk next 2 tr, tr shell in last tr, turn. (3 tr shells)

ROW 4: Ch 4, 6 tr in first tr, sk next 2 tr, sc in next tr, *sk next 3 tr, tr shell in next sc, sk 3 tr, sc in next tr, rep from *, sk 2 tr, tr shell in last tr, turn.

ROW 5: Ch 4, 6 tr in first tr, sk next 2 tr, sc in next tr, *sk next 3 tr, tr shell in next sc, sk next 3 tr, sc in next tr, rep from * across row, ending with sk 2 tr, tr shell in last tr, turn.

ROWS 6–14: Rep Row 5. (14 tr shells)

ROW 15: Ch 4, 6 tr in first tr, sk next 2 tr, sc in next tr, *sk next 3 tr, tr shell in next sc, sk next 3 tr, sc in next tr, rep from * across, ending with 1 sc in center tr of end tr shell (do not work over rem sts of end tr shell), turn. (14 tr shells)

ROW 16: Ch 1, sk first sc, sl st in each of next 4 tr, *sk next 3 tr, tr shell in next sc, sk next 3 tr, sc in next tr, rep from * across, ending with sk next 2 tr, tr shell in last tr (this will dec on one side only), turn.

ROWS 17–30: Rep Rows 15 and 16. (14 tr shells)

ROW 31: Ch 1, sl st in each of first 4 tr, *sk next 3 tr, tr shell in next sc, sk next 3 tr, sc in next tr, rep from * across, ending with 1 sc in center tr of end tr shell (do not work over rem sts of tr shell); this will dec at each end of row.

ROWS 32–43: Rep Row 31. (1 tr shell)

LEFT SECTION
ROWS 1–43: Rep Rows 1-43 of right section.

JOINING
Thread yarn needle with a length of yarn, place Rows 1–14 of each section tog, matching sts, sew Rows 1–14 tog.

EDGING
Note: This is a rolled edge created by working in front lps of sl st, edging will curl around itself and form a corded edging.

RND 1: Attach yarn at center inner point at back neckline, sl st evenly sp around entire outer edge of stole, do not join.

RNDS 2–5: Working in front lps of sl sts only, sl st in each st around, use care that sts do not become tight or stole will begin to pucker; if this occurs, remove the puckered section and use a looser tension. At the end of last rnd, fasten off.

Steam press stole under a damp cloth. Remove when dry. ✧

Chapter Seven

Antique Novelties & Gifts

*D*o you remember walking through your grandmother's house looking at all her knick-knacks? Some were allowed to be touched, while others were not! Keep those memories alive by crocheting your own collection of unique items for your children and grandchildren to enjoy!

Glove Purse

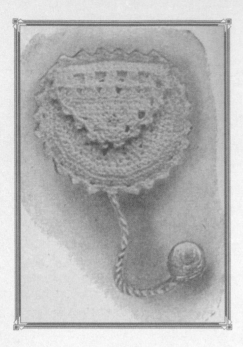

The original instructions for this purse called for a size 50 thread, which made a very tiny purse that could be tucked into one's glove to hold a little "mad money" lest your date prove himself a cad and force you to seek an alternate means of transportation home! Worked in a size 10 crochet cotton, we get a sweet little purse, just the size to hold "milk money" for your daughter. Note the interesting way in which this purse closes to keep your coins or other treasures safe and sound.

Design revised by Maggie Petsch Chasalow

SKILL LEVEL: INTERMEDIATE

SIZE
2¾ inches in diameter

MATERIALS
➤ Crochet cotton size 10: small amount variegated pastels
➤ Size 7 steel crochet hook or size needed to obtain gauge
➤ 24-inch length gold chain (optional)
➤ Scrap of fiberfill
➤ Tapestry needle

GAUGE
Rnds 1–3 = ⅞ inch in diameter
Check gauge to save time.

PATTERN NOTES
Weave in loose ends as work progresses.

Join rnds with a sl st unless otherwise indicated.

PATTERN STITCHES
DC 2 TOG: Holding back on hook last lp of each st, dc in each of next 2 sts, yo, draw through all 3 lps on hook.

BEG DC 2 TOG: Ch 2, dc in next st.

P: Ch 4, sl st in 4th ch from hook.

TRTR: Yo hook 4 times, insert hook in indicated st, yo, draw up a lp, [yo, draw through 2 lps on hook] 5 times.

Purse

BACK
RND 1 (RS): Ch 6, sl st to join to form a ring, ch 1, 8 sc in ring, join in beg sc. (8 sc)

RND 2: Ch 1, 2 sc in each sc around, join in beg sc. (16 sc)

RND 3: Ch 1, sc in same st as beg ch-1, 2 sc in next st, [sc in next st, 2 sc in next st] rep around, join in beg sc. (24 sc)

RND 4: Beg dc 2 tog, ch 3, [dc 2 tog, ch 3] rep around, join in top of beg dc 2 tog. (12 sts)

RND 5: Ch 3 (counts as first dc throughout), 3 dc in same st as joining, [4 dc in top of rem dc 2 tog] rep around, join in 3rd ch of beg ch-3. (48 dc)

RND 6: Ch 1, sc in same st as joining, sc in each of next 2 dc, 2 sc in next dc, [sc in each of next 3 dc, 2 sc in next dc] rep around, join in beg sc. (60 sc)

ROW 7: Ch 1, sc in same st as joining, sc in each of next 3 sc, 2 sc in next sc, [sc in each of next 4 sc, 2 sc in next sc] 7 times, leaving rem 20 sc unworked, turn. (48 sc)

ROW 8: Ch 1, sc in each of next 48 sc, turn.

ROW 9: Ch 1, [sc in each of next 5 sc, 2 sc in next sc] rep across, fasten off. (56 sc)

FRONT
RNDS 1–6: Rep Rnds 1–6 of back.

ROWS 7–9: Rep Rows 7–9 of back. At the end of Row 9, do not fasten off.

JOINING
With WS of back and front tog and front facing, working through back lps only of both thicknesses, sc in each of first 2 sts, [p, sk next st, sc in each of next 2 sts] rep across, do not fasten off.

FLAP
ROW 1 (WS): Working on back only, sl st over end of Row 9, ch 4 (counts as first tr), 2 dtr over end st of next row, trtr over end st of next row, trtr in first unworked sc of Rnd 6, dtr in next sc, tr in next sc, dc in next sc, hdc in next sc, sc in each of next 10 sc, hdc in next sc, dc in next sc, tr in next sc, dtr in next sc, trtr in next sc, trtr over end st of next row, 2 dtr over end st of next row, tr over end st of last row, turn. (28 sts)

ROW 2: Working in front lps for this row only, ch 1, sc in each st across, turn. (28 sc)

ROWS 3 & 4: Ch 1, sc dec, sc in each st across to last 2 sts, sc dec over next 2 sts, turn. (24 sts)

ROW 5: Beg dc 2 tog, ch 3, sk next 3 sts, dc 2 tog, [ch 3, sk next 2 sts, dc 2 tog] 3 times, ch 3, sk next 3 sts, dc 2 tog, turn. (6 dc tog)

ROW 6: Ch 3, dc in first st, 3 dc in each of next 4 dc 2 tog, 2 dc in last dc 2 tog, turn. (16 dc)

ROWS 7–13: Ch 1, sc dec, sc in each st across to last 2 sts, sc dec over last 2 sts, turn. (2 sts)

ROW 14: Ch 1, sc dec over next 2 sts, do not fasten off, do not turn.

FLAP EDGING

P, [sc over end st of each of next 2 rows, p, sk next row] twice, sc over end st of each of next 2 rows, p, 2 sc over end st of next row, p, sk next row, sc over end st of each of next 2 rows, p, working in rem lps across Row 1, sc in each of first 2 sts, p, [sk next st, sc in each of next 2 sts, p] 8 times, sk next st, sc in last st, sc over end st of Row 2, p, sk next row, sc over end st of each of next 2 rows, p, 2 sc over end st of next row, p, [sk next row, sc over end st of each of next 2 rows, p] twice, sc over end st of next row, join at base of beg p, fasten off.

BALL

Note: Do not join rnds unless otherwise indicated; use a scrap of CC yarn to mark rnds.

RND 1: Ch 2, 6 sc in 2nd ch from hook. (6 sc)

RND 2: 2 sc in each sc around. (12 sc)

RND 3: [Sc in next sc, 2 sc in next sc] rep around. (18 sc)

RND 4: [2 sc in next sc, sc in each of next 2 sc] rep around. (24 sc)

RND 5: Sc in each sc around.

RND 6: [Sc in each of next 2 sc, sc dec over next 2 sc] rep around. (18 sts)

RND 7: [Sc in next sc, sc dec over next 2 sc] rep around. (12 sts)

Stuff ball tightly with fiberfill.

RND 8: [Sc dec over next 2 sts] rep around, sl st to join in next sc,

leaving a length of cotton, fasten off. (6 sc)

Weave rem length through rem 6 sts, pull tightly to close opening, secure, fasten off.

CORD

Attach 2 strands of crochet cotton held tog at top center of ball, make a ch approximately 3½ inches long, leaving a short length for finishing, fasten off.

FINISHING

With tapestry needle, weave free end of cord through bottom center of purse from outside to inside and through sp at center of Rnd 1 of purse front from inside to outside. Tack top of cord to WS of section of flap that closes. Pull ball down to close purse. Sew ends of gold chain to top of purse at each side. ✧

Kewpie Hair Pin Holder

Kewpies were all the rage in the very early 1900s, and clever crocheters found all sorts of ways to utilize these adorable little dolls. They used dolls like the one featured to hold their hair pins, but you can make one to hold your bobby pins or safety pins, or just hang on the wall for a lovely decoration and interesting conversation piece.

Design revised by Maggie Petsch Chasalow

SKILL LEVEL: BEGINNER

SIZE
Fits a 5-inch-tall kewpie doll

MATERIALS
➤ Crochet cotton size 10 (300 yards per ball): 1 ball shaded pastels (MC), small amount pink (CC)
➤ Size 7 steel crochet hook or size needed to obtain gauge
➤ 5-inch-tall kewpie doll
➤ 48 inches ¼-inch-wide pink satin ribbon
➤ Sewing needle and thread
➤ Tapestry needle

GAUGE
10 dc = 1 inch
Check gauge to save time.

PATTERN NOTES
Weave in loose ends as work progresses.

Sl st to join each rnd unless otherwise indicated.

Dress

BODICE
ROW 1 (RS): Beg at neck, with MC, ch 56, dc in 4th ch from hook, dc in each rem ch across, turn. (54 dc)

ROW 2: Ch 3 (counts as first dc throughout), dc in each of next 7 dc, ch 12, sk next 12 dc (armhole), [dc in each of next 4 dc, 2 dc in next dc] twice, dc in each of next 4 dc, ch 12, sk next 12 sts (armhole), dc in each of next 8 dc, turn.

ROWS 3 & 4: Ch 3, dc in each st across, turn. (56 dc)

SKIRT
ROW 1: Sl st in each of next 5 sts, ch 3, dc in same st, 2 dc in each st across to last 4 sts, leaving last 4 sts unworked, turn. (96 dc)

ROW 2: Ch 3, dc in each st across, turn.

ROW 3: Ch 3, 2 dc in next st, [dc in next st, 2 dc in next st] rep across, turn. (144 dc)

RND 4: Ch 3, dc in each st around, join in 3rd ch of beg ch-3, turn. (144 dc)

RND 5: Ch 3, dc in next st, 2 dc in next st, [dc in each of next 2 sts, 2 dc in next st] rep around, join in 3rd ch of beg ch-3. (192 dc)

RND 6: Ch 3, dc in each st around, join in 3rd ch of beg ch-3.

RND 7: Ch 3, dc in same st as beg ch, dc in each of next 3 sts, [2 dc in next st, dc in each of next 3 sts] rep around, join in 3rd ch of beg ch-3. (240 dc)

RND 8: Rep Rnd 6.

RND 9: Ch 3, dc in each of next 3 sts, 2 dc in next st, [dc in each of next 4 sts, 2 dc in next st] rep around, join in 3rd ch of beg ch-3. (288 dc)

RND 10: Rep Rnd 6.

RND 11: Ch 3, dc in same st as joining, dc in each of next 5 sts, [2 dc in next st, dc in each of next 5 sts] rep around, join in 3rd ch of beg ch-3. (336 dc)

RND 12: Rep Rnd 6, fasten off.

RND 13 (RS): Attach CC with a sl st in same st as joining, ch 5, sk next st, [sl st in next st, ch 5, sk next st] rep around, join in st at base of beg ch-5, fasten off.

CAP
RND 1 (RS): With MC, ch 4, sl st to join to form a ring, ch 3 (counts as first dc throughout), 11 dc in ring, join in 3rd ch of beg ch-3. (12 dc)

RNDS 2–4: Ch 3, dc in same st as joining, 2 dc in each st around, join in 3rd ch of beg ch-3. (96 dc)

RND 5: Ch 3, 2 dc in next st, [dc in next st, 2 dc in next st] rep around, join in 3rd ch of beg ch-3. (144 dc)

RND 6: Ch 3, dec 1 dc over next 2 sts, [dc in next st, dec 1 dc over next 2 sts] rep around, join in 3rd ch of beg ch-3. (96 sts)

RND 7: Rep Rnd 6. (64 sts)

RND 8: Ch 3, dc in each st around, join in 3rd ch of beg ch-3.

RND 9: Ch 6 (counts as first tr, ch 2), [sk next 2 sts, tr in next st, ch 2] rep around, join in 4th ch of beg ch-6, fasten off.

FINISHING
Cut 2 (8-inch) lengths of ribbon. Tie each into a bow. Tack 1 bow on each sleeve. Trim ends to desired length. Slip dress on doll; overlap bodice opening and sew opening closed.

Weave 14-inch length of ribbon through ch-2 sps of Rnd 9 of cap. Place cap on doll's head, adjust last rnd of cap to fit doll's head by pulling ribbon to desired tightness. Tie ribbon in bow at front on either side. Trim ends to desired length.

Using photo as a guide, weave 1 end of an 18-inch length of ribbon between 2 dc on next-to-last rnd of skirt from back to front to back again, knot securely on WS. Weave other end through approximately 3½ inches from first end. Adjust to desired length for hanging lp and knot 2nd end on WS.

Tack center back of cap to skirt. Tack cap to skirt approximately 1¼ inches from center on each side. ✧

Design revised by Maggie Petsch Chasalow

SKILL LEVEL: INTERMEDIATE

SIZE
Fits 3½-inch-tall lampshade

MATERIALS
➤ Crochet cotton size 30 (500 yds per ball): 1 ball ecru
➤ Size 11 steel crochet hook or size needed to obtain gauge
➤ Lampshade 3¾-inch-tall x 3-inch-diameter top x 5-inch-diameter bottom
➤ 5 (¾-inch-diameter) satin roses with leaves
➤ Sewing needle and thread

GAUGE
Rnd 1 block = ½ inch square
Check gauge to save time.

PATTERN NOTES
Weave in loose ends as work progresses.

Join rnds with a sl st unless otherwise indicated.

PATTERN STITCHES
QUADRUPLE TR (QUADTR): Yo hook 5 times, insert hook in indicated st, yo, draw up a lp, [yo, draw through 2 lps on hook] 6 times.

CH-4 P: Ch 4, sl st in last sc made.

CH-5 P: Ch 5, sl st in 5th ch from hook.

Little Lampshade

This delicate little candle shade is typical of the Victorian era and looks just as lovely on your electric lamp as it did on a candle! The lampshade pictured here was worked with antique Clark's O.N.T. crochet thread and a crochet hook from a set of crochet hooks with interchangeable tips manufactured by Boye in the early 1920s.

Lampshade

RND 1: *Ch 8, sc in 2nd ch from hook, sc in each rem ch across, ch 1, turn, [sc in each of next 7 sc, ch 1, turn] 6 times, sl st in each of next 7 sc (1 block made), rep from * 14 times; taking care not to twist, join in corresponding corner of first block. (15 blocks)

RND 2: Sl st over end st of each of last 7 rows of last block made, ch 1, sc in same st as last sl st made, *ch 5, dtr in st between same block and next block, ch 5 **, sc in upper corner of next block, rep

from * around, ending last rep at **, join in beg sc.

RND 3: Sl st into first ch-5 sp, ch 1, beg in same sp, 6 sc in each sp around, join in beg sc. (180 sc)

RND 4: Ch 3 (counts as first dc throughout), dc in each rem sc around, join in 3rd ch of beg ch-3. (180 dc)

RND 5: Ch 1, beg in same st as joining, sc in each st around, join in beg sc. (180 sc)

RND 6: Ch 1, sc in same st as joining, *ch 3, sk next 4 sc, dc in next sc, ch 4, sk next sc, tr in next sc, ch 4, sk next 4 sc, dtr in next sc, ch 4, sk next 2 sc, [{quadtr, ch 4} twice, quadtr] in next sc, ch 4, sk next 2 sc, dtr in next sc, ch 4, sk next 4 sc, tr in next sc, ch 4, sk next 4 sc, dc in next sc, ch 3, sk next 4 sc **, sc in next sc, rep

from * around, ending last rep at **, join in beg sc. (5 scallops)

RND 7: Sl st in first ch-3 sp, ch 1, 3 sc in same sp, *[3 sc, ch-4 p, 2 sc] in each of next 8 ch-4 sps **, 3 sc in each of next 2 ch-3 sps, rep from * around, ending last rep at **, 3 sc in next ch-3 sp, join in beg sc.

RND 8: Sl st in each of next 2 sc, [sl st, ch 1, sc] in next sc, *ch 3, dc in center sc between next 2 ch-4 p, ch 4, tr in center sc between next 2 ch-4 p, ch 4, dtr in center sc between next 2 ch-4 p, ch 4, [{quadtr, ch 4} twice, quadtr] in center sc between next 2 ch-4 p, ch 4, dtr in center sc between next 2 ch-4 p, ch 4, tr in center sc between next 2 ch-4 p, ch 4, dc in center sc between next 2 ch-4 p, ch 3, sc in 3rd sc after next ch-4 p, ch 1 **, sk next 5 sc, sc in next sc, rep from * around, ending last rep at **, join in beg sc.

RND 9: Sl st in next ch-3 sp, ch 1, 3 sc in same sp, *[3 sc, ch-4 p, 2 sc] in each of next 8 ch-4 sps, 3 sc in next ch-3 sp, sc in next ch-1 sp **, 3 sc in next ch-3 sp, rep from * around, ending last rep at **, join in beg sc.

RND 10: Sl st in each of next 2 sc, [sl st, ch 1, sc] in next sc, *ch 4, dc in center sc between next 2 ch-4 p, ch 5, tr in center sc between next 2 ch-4 p, ch 5, dtr in center sc between next 2 ch-4 p, ch 5, [[quadtr, ch 5] twice, quadtr] in center sc between next 2 ch-4 p, ch 5, dtr in center sc between next 2 ch-4 p, ch 5, tr in center sc between next 2 ch-4 p, ch 5, dc in center sc between next 2 ch-4 p, ch 4, sc in 3rd sc after next ch-4 p, ch 1 **, sk next 5 sc, sc in next sc, rep from * around, ending last rep at **, join in beg sc.

RND 11: Sl st in first ch-4 sp, ch 1, beg in same sp, *5 sc in ch-4 sp, 6 sc in each of next 8 ch-5 sps, 5 sc in next ch-4 sp, sc in next ch-1 sp, rep from * around, join in beg sc. (295 sc)

RND 12: Sl st in each of next 2 sts, ch 3, *dc in each of next 21 sts, [2 dc in next st, dc in next st] 5 times, 2 dc in next st, dc in each of next 21 sts, sk next 5 sts **, dc in next st, rep from * around, ending last rep at **, join in 3rd ch of beg ch-3. (5 groups 60 dc)

RND 13: [Sl st, ch 1, sc] in next st, sc in each of next 57 sts, [sk next 2 sts, sc in each of next 58 sts] rep around, ending with sk last 2 sts, join in beg sc. (5 groups 58 sc)

RND 14: Working in back lps for this rnd only, [sl st, ch 1, sc] in next st, sc in each of next 55 sts, [sk next 2 sts, sc in each of next 56 sts] rep around, ending with sk last 2 sts, join in beg sc. (5 groups 56 sc)

RND 15: Sl st in each of next 4 sts, ch 3, turn, sk last 4 sts on previous scallop, *sl st in each of next 4 sts, ch 3, turn, dc in next ch-3 sp, ch 3, sk next 4 sts on scallop, sl st in each of next 4 sts, ch 3, turn, dc in next ch-3 sp, ch 4, dc

in next ch-3 sp, ch 3, sk next 4 sts on scallop, sl st in each of next 4 sts, ch 4, turn, dc in next ch-3 sp, ch 5, dc in next ch-4 sp, ch 5, dc in next ch-3 sp, ch 4, sk next 4 sts on scallop, sl st in each of next 4 sts, ch 5, turn, dc in next ch-4 sp, ch 5, [dc in next ch-5 sp, ch 5] twice, dc in next ch-4 sp, ch 5, sk next 4 sts on scallop **, sl st in each of next 32 sts on scallop to last 4 sts on same scallop, ch 3, sk next 8 sts, rep from * around, ending

last rep at **, sl st in next st on scallop, turn.

RND 16: Ch 1, 5 sc in first sp, *6 sc in each of next 3 sps, 5 sc in next sp, sc in each of next 14 sts across top of scallop **, 5 sc in next sp, rep from * around, ending last rep at **, join in beg sc. (210 sc)

RND 17: Ch 1, sc in same st as joining, sc in each of next 3 sts, ch-5 p, [sk next st, sc in each of next 4 sts, ch-5 p] rep around,

Continued on page 159

Pin Set & Barrette

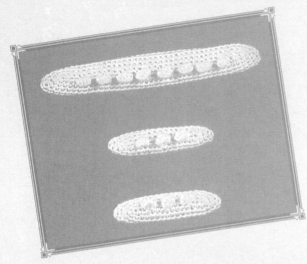

"Crocheted jewelry sounds rather bewildering, and we wonder 'what's next'? Yet this is the latest fad, and very much in keeping with summer toilets, so I advise you to make yourself a set of these pins at once." So reads the copy that accompanies the instructions for these pins when they first appeared in 1910. You can use the same instructions to make a very pretty barrette for yourself or a friend.

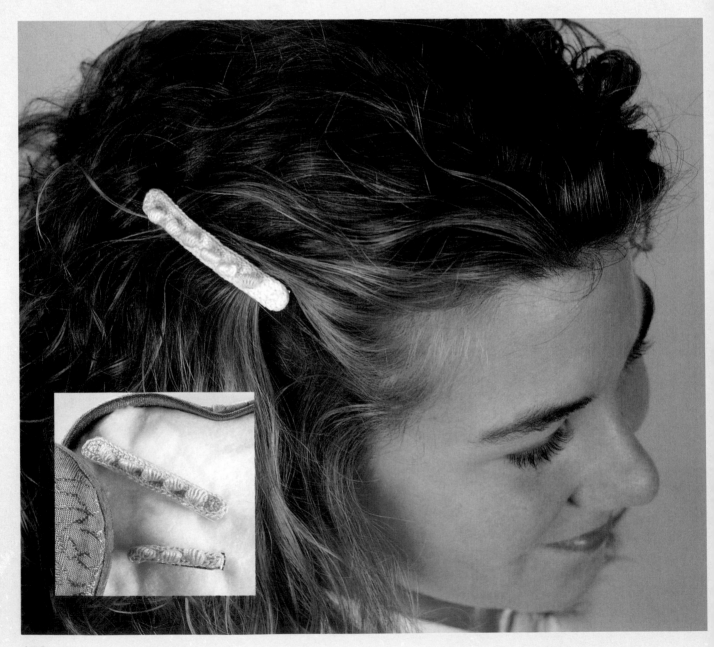

Design revised by
Maggie Petsch Chasalow

SKILL LEVEL:INTERMEDIATE

SIZE:
LARGE PIN: 1½ inches
SMALL PIN: 1 inch
BARRETTE: 2¾ inches

MATERIALS
➤ PINS: crochet cotton size 30: small amount light blue
➤ BARRETTE: crochet cotton size 10: small amount shaded pastels
➤ Size 10 steel crochet hook or size needed to obtain gauge for pins
➤ Size 7 steel crochet hook or size needed to obtain gauge for barrette
➤ 70mm metal hair barrette
➤ 1½-inch pin back
➤ 1-inch pin back
➤ Craft glue

GAUGE
11 sc = 1 inch with size 10 cotton and larger hook
27 sc = 2 inches with size 30 cotton and smaller hook
Check gauge to save time.

PATTERN NOTES
Weave in loose ends as work progresses.

Join rnds with a sl st unless otherwise indicated.

PATTERN STITCH
CLONES KNOT: Ch 7, [yo hook, insert hook under ch-7, yo, draw up a lp] 7 times, yo, draw through all 15 lps on hook, ch 1 tightly to secure.

Small Pin

RND 1: [Clones knot, sl st in 4th ch of last ch-7 made] 3 times, ch 4, 2 sc in 2nd ch from hook, sc in each of next 2 chs, *[sc at base of next clones knot, sc in each of next 3 chs] twice, sc at base of last clones knot, sc in each of next 2 chs *, 3 sc in last ch, working in rem lps across opposite side, sc in each of next 2 chs, rep from * to *, sc in same ch as beg sc, join in beg sc.

RND 2: Sl st in each st around, join in beg sl st, fasten off.

FINISHING
With craft glue, glue crocheted pin covering to top of 1-inch pin back.

Large Pin

RND 1: [Clones knot, sl st in 4th ch from last ch-7 made] 5 times, ch 4, 2 sc in 2nd ch from hook, sc in each of next 2 chs, *[sc at base of next clones knot, sc in each of next 3 chs] 4 times, sc at base of last clones knot, sc in each of next 2 chs *, 3 sc in last ch, working in rem lps across opposite side, sc in each of next 2 chs, rep from * to *, sc in same ch as beg sc, join in beg sc.

RND 2: Ch 1, 2 sc in same st as joining, 2 sc in next sc, *sc in each of next 21 sts *, 2 sc in each of next 3 sts, rep from * to *, 2 sc in next sc, join in beg sc, fasten off.

FINISHING
With craft glue, glue crocheted pin covering to top of 1½-inch pin back.

Barrette

RND 1: [Clones knot, sl st in 4th ch of last ch-7 made] 6 times, ch 4, 2 sc in 2nd ch from hook, 2 sc in each of next 2 chs, *[sc at base of next clones knot, sc in each of next 3 chs] 5 times, sc at base of last clones knot, sc in each of next 2 chs *, 3 sc in last ch, working in rem lps across opposite side, sc in each of next 2 chs, rep from * to *, sc in same ch as beg sc, join in beg sc.

RND 2: Ch 2 (counts as first hdc), hdc in same st as joining, *[hdc, sc] in next st, sc in each of next 25 sts, [sc, hdc] in next st *, 2 hdc in next st, rep from * to *, join in 2nd ch of beg ch-2, fasten off.

FINISHING
With craft glue, glue crocheted barrette covering to top of metal hair barrette. ✧

Little Lampshade continued from page 157

ending with sk last st, join in beg sc, fasten off.

TOP BORDER
RND 1: With RS facing, attach thread with a sl st at the tip of any block of Rnd 1, ch 1, sc in same st, *ch 5, dtr in st between same block and next block, ch 5 **, sc in upper corner of next block, rep from * around, ending last rep at **, join in beg sc. (30 ch-5 sps)

RND 2: Ch 1, 5 sc in each sp around, join in beg sc. (150 sc)

RND 3: Ch 3, dc in each rem sc around, working 10 dc dec evenly sp around, join in 3rd ch of beg ch-3. (140 sts)

RND 4: Rep Rnd 17.

RUFFLE
RND 1: With RS facing and bottom of lampshade pointing down, working in rem free lps of Rnd 13, attach thread with a sl st in 2nd sc of any 58-sc group, ch 1, sc in same st, *sc in each rem st across to last sc of same 58-sc group, sk last sc of same group and first sc of next group, sc in next st, rep from * around, join in beg sc. (5 groups 56 sc)

RND 2: [Sl st, ch 1, sc] in next sc, *[ch 5, sk next sc, sc in next sc] 26 times, ch 1, sk next 3 sc **, sc in next sc of next 56-sc group, rep from * around, ending last rep at **, join in beg sc.

RND 3: Sl st in first ch-5 sp, ch 1, [sc, ch-5 p, sc] in same sp, [sc, ch-5 p, sc] in each of next 25 sps, sc in next ch-1 sp **, [sc, ch-5 p, sc] in next sp, rep from * around, ending last rep at **, join in beg sc, fasten off.

FINISHING
Steam-press lampshade lightly. With sewing needle and thread, tack 1 rose between each pair of scallops. ✧

Irish Crochet Picture Frame

Irish crochet, as most crocheters know, became extremely popular during the mid-1800s potato famine in Ireland. It became the saving grace of many an Irishman and woman who needed a means of support. The Victorians enthusiastically adopted this beautiful form of crochet that replicates nature's own designs and used it to adorn everything from clothing to picture frames. Make this beautiful frame to show off one of your special photos.

Design revised by Maggie Petsch Chasalow

SKILL LEVEL: INTERMEDIATE

SIZE
Fits an 8 x 10-inch picture frame with 1½-inch-wide border

MATERIALS
➤ Crochet cotton size 10 (225 yds per ball): 1 ball white
➤ Size 7 steel crochet hook or size needed to obtain gauge
➤ 8 x 10-inch picture frame with 5 x 7-inch opening
➤ 4 (7mm) pearls
➤ 8 (5mm) pearls
➤ Sewing needle and thread
➤ Craft glue

GAUGE
Corner flower = 1½ inches in diameter
Check gauge to save time.

PATTERN NOTES
Weave in loose ends as work progresses.

Sl st to join rnds unless otherwise indicated.

PATTERN STITCHES
P: Ch 4, sl st in 4th ch from hook.
P SHELL: [2 dc, p, 2 dc] in indicated sp.

CORNER FLOWER *(make 4)*
RND 1 (RS): Ch 6, sl st to join to form a ring, ch 1, [sc in ring, ch 2] 5 times, join in beg sc. (5 ch-2 sps)
RND 2: Sl st in first sp, ch 1, beg in same sp, [sc, 3 dc, sc] in each ch-2 sp around, do not join. (5 petals)
RND 3: Working behind petals of previous rnd, sc in first sc of Rnd 1, ch 3, [sc in next sc of Rnd 1, ch 3] rep around, join in beg sc. (5 ch-3 sps)
RND 4: Sl st in first sp, ch 1, beg in same sp, [sc, 2 dc, tr, 2 dc, sc] in each ch-3 sp around, do not join. (5 petals)
RND 5: Working behind petals of previous rnd, sc in first sc of Rnd 3, ch 4, [sc in next sc of Rnd 3, ch 4] rep around, join in beg sc. (5 ch-4 sps)
RND 6: Sl st in first sp, ch 1, beg in same sp, [sc, 2 dc, 2 tr, 2 dc, sc] in each sp around, do not join. (5 petals)
RND 7: Working behind petals of previous rnd, sc in first sc of Rnd 5,

ch 5, [sc in next sc of Rnd 5, ch 5] rep around, join in beg sc. (6 ch-5 sps)
RND 8: Sl st in first sp, ch 1, beg in same sp, [sc, 2 dc, 3 tr, 2 dc, sc] in each sp around, join in beg sc, fasten off.

SIDE BORDER *(make 2)*
ROW 1 (RS): Ch 14, dc in 6th ch from hook, [ch 1, sk next ch, dc in next ch] rep across, turn. (5 ch-1 sps)
ROW 2: Ch 4 (counts as first dc, ch 1 throughout), [dc in next dc, ch 1] 4 times, sk next ch, dc in next ch of turning ch, turn. (5 ch-1 sps)
ROWS 3–27: Rep Row 2. At the end of Row 27, do not turn.

SIDE EDGING
RND 28: Sc in last sp worked, p shell over post of dc of same sp, working over end of row sps across long edge of side border, [sc in next sp, {p shell in next sp, sc in next sp} rep across to next corner sp *, {p shell, sc, p shell} in corner sp] rep around, ending at * on last rep, p shell in same sp as beg sc, join in beg sc, fasten off.

TOP BORDER
ROWS 1 & 2: Rep Rows 1 and 2 of side border.

ROWS 3–19: Rep Row 2. At the end of Row 19, do not turn.

RND 20: Rep Rnd 28 of edging.

BOTTOM BORDER
ROWS 1–19: Rep Rows 1–19 of top border.

TOP & BOTTOM EDGING
RND 20: Rep Rnd 28 of side edging.

BORDER FLOWER *(make 8)*
RND 1: Ch 2, 6 sc in 2nd ch from hook, join in front lp only of beg sc. (6 sc)

RND 2: Working in front lps for this rnd only, ch 3, [sl st in next st, ch 3] rep around, join at base of beg ch-3. (6 ch-3 sps)

RND 3: Working in rem back lps of Rnd 1, [sl st, ch 2, 2 dc, ch 2, sl st] in each rem free lp of Rnd 1, join in same st as beg sl st, fasten off.

CENTER LEAF
ROW 1: Ch 8, sc in 2nd ch from hook, sc in each of next 5 chs, [sc, ch 3, sc] in last ch, working on opposite side of foundation ch, sc in each of next 5 chs, leaving last ch unworked, turn.

ROW 2: Working in back lps only, ch 2, sk first sc, sc in each sc across to ch-3 sp, [sc, ch 3, sc] in ch-3 sp, sc in each rem st across to last sc, leaving last sc unworked, turn.

ROWS 3 & 4: Rep Row 2. At the end of Row 4, fasten off.

FIRST OUTER LEAF
ROWS 1–3: Rep Rows 1–3 of center leaf.

ROW 4: Working in back lps only, ch 2, sk first sc, sc in next sc on working leaf; sl st in first sc on Row 4 of center leaf, [sc in next sc on working leaf, sl st in next sc on center leaf] 4 times, sc in next sp on working leaf, sl st in next sc on center leaf, ch 1, sl st in next sp on center leaf, ch 1, sc in same sp on working leaf as last sc made, continue across as for Row 4 of center leaf.

SECOND OUTER LEAF
ROWS 1–3: Rep Rows 1–3 of center leaf.

ROW 4: Working in back lps

only, ch 2, sk first sc, sc in each sc across to ch-3 sp, [sc, ch 1] in ch-3 sp, sl st in ch-3 sp on center leaf, ch 1, sc in ch-3 sp on working leaf, sl st in next sc on center leaf, [sc in next sp on working leaf, sl st in next sc on center leaf] 6 times, fasten off.

FINISHING
With sewing needle and thread, sew a 7mm pearl at center of each corner flower. Sew a 5mm pearl to the center of each border flower.

Sew one border flower over center sp of Row 14 of either side border. Sew one border flower over center sp of 7th row from each end of same side border. Rep on opposite side border. Sew one border flower over center sp of Row 10 of bottom border. Rep on top border. Sew leaves to top center of top border.

Using photo as a guide, glue corner flowers and side, top and bottom borders in place. ✧

The Victorians were not only creative in the application of their crocheting skills, they were also apparently frugal as evidenced by this thimble holder made from the wishbone left over from Sunday dinner!

Design revised by Maggie Petsch Chasalow

SKILL LEVEL: INTERMEDIATE

SIZE

LARGE HOLDER: 4 x 4½ inches

SMALL HOLDER: 2½ x 2¾ inches

MATERIALS

➤ **Large Holder:** crochet cotton size 10: small amount each aqua (MC) and cream (CC)

➤ **Small Holder:** crochet cotton size 30: small amount each jade (MC) and white (CC)

➤ Size 7 steel crochet hook or size needed to obtain gauge for large holder

➤ Size 10 steel crochet hook or size needed to obtain gauge for small holder

➤ 28 inches ⅜-inch-wide cream satin ribbon for large wishbone cover

➤ 28 inches ¼-inch-wide white satin ribbon for small wishbone cover

➤ 3-inch-long x 2½-inch-wide turkey wishbone for large thimble holder

➤ 2½-inch-long x 1¼-inch-wide chicken wishbone for small thimble holder

➤ Thimble

➤ Sewing needle

GAUGE

Rnds 1–4 of thimble cover bottom for small thimble holder = ⅝ inch in diameter

Rnds 1 and 2 of thimble cover bottom for large thimble holder = ⅝ inch in diameter

Check gauge to save time.

PATTERN NOTES

Weave in loose ends as work progresses.

Join rnds with sl st unless otherwise indicated.

Instruction are given for small thimble holder; directions for large thimble holder follow in parentheses. If only one number is given, it applies to both sizes.

PATTERN STITCHES

V-ST: [Dc, ch 3, dc] in indicated st or sp.

BEG V-ST: [Ch 6, dc] in indicated st or sp.

P: Ch 3, sl st in 3rd ch from hook.

3-P SHELL: [{Dc, p} 3 times, dc] in indicated st or sp.

5-P SHELL: [{Sc, p} 5 times, dc] in indicated st or sp.

Wishbone Cover

ROW 1 (RS): Attach MC with a sl st approximately ¼ inch in from end of wishbone, ch 1, 34 (42) sc across to bottom of wishbone, ch 2, 34 (42) sc across to top of opposite edge of wishbone, turn.

ROW 2: Ch 3 (counts as first dc throughout), dc in next dc, *[ch 2, sk next 2 sts, dc in each of next 2 sts] 8 (10) times *, ch 2, sk ch-2 sp, dc in each of first 2 dc on next side, rep from * to *, turn. (17 (21) ch-2 sps)

ROW 3: Ch 3, dc in next dc, *[2 dc in next sp, dc in each of next 2 dc] 7 (9) times *, [3 dc in next sp, dc in each of next 2 dc] 3 times, rep from * to *, turn.

ROW 4: Beg V-st in first st, [sk next 3 sts, V-st in next st] rep across, fasten off, turn. (19 (23) V-sts)

ROW 5: With RS facing, attach CC with a sl st in first V-st, ch 1, sc in same sp, *[3-p shell in next sp, sc in next sp] 4 (5) times *, ch 2, 5-p shell in next sp, ch 2, sc in next sp, rep from * to *, fasten off.

HANGING CHAIN

With 2 strands of CC held tog, make a ch approximately 20 (27) inches long or desired length; do not fasten off.

Weave free end of ch through ch-2 sps on Row 2, sl st ends tog, fasten off.

Thimble Holder for Small Wishbone

BOTTOM

Note: Do not join rnds unless otherwise indicated; use a scrap of thread to mark rnds.

RND 1: With MC, ch 5, sl st to join to form a ring, ch 1, 10 sc in ring. (10 sc)

RND 2: [Sc in next sc, 2 sc in next sc] rep around. (15 sc)

RND 3: [2 sc in next sc, sc in each of next 2 sc] rep around. (20 sc)

RND 4: [Sc in each of next 3 sc, 2 sc in next sc] rep around. (25 sc)

SIDES

RND 1: Working in back lps for

top of wishbone. Trim ends on all bows to desired length.

Thimble Holder for Large Wishbone

BOTTOM
RNDS 1 & 2: Rep Rnds 1 and 2 of bottom for thimble holder for small wishbone. (15 sc)

SIDES
RND 1: Working in back lps only for this rnd, sc in each sc around, join in beg sc. (15 sc)

RNDS 2 & 3: Ch 1, sc in same st as joining, sc in each rem sc around, join in beg sc. (15 sc)

RND 4: Ch 1, sc in same st as joining, sc in next sc, 2 sc in next sc, [sc in each of next 2 sc, 2 sc in next sc] rep around, join in beg sc. (20 sc)

RNDS 5 & 6: Rep Rnds 2 and 3. (20 sc)

RND 7: Ch 1, sc in same st as joining, ch 4, sk next 3 sc, sc in next sc, [ch 4, sk next 2 sc, sc in next sc] twice, ch 4, sk next 3 sc, sc in next sc, ch 4, sk next 2 sc, sc in next sc, ch 4, sk next 2 sc, join in beg sc. (6 ch-4 sps)

RND 8: Sl st in first sp, ch 1, sc in same sp, ch 4, [sc in next sp, ch 4] rep around, join in beg sc. (6 ch-4 sps)

RND 9: Rep Rnd 11 of sides for thimble holder for small wishbone; do not fasten off at end of rnd; sl st in each of next 2 chs, sl st in border p.

FINISHING
Holding thimble cover to top center of wishbone, make a ch long enough to reach end st of first row of wishbone cover on either side, leaving a length of thread, fasten off. Attach MC with a sl st in border p directly opposite last border p, make a ch long enough to reach end st of first row on opposite side of wishbone cover, leaving a length of thread, fasten off. Tack ch at each side of thimble cover to end st at each side of wishbone cover.

Rep instructions for bows for finishing of small wishbone cover. ✧

this rnd only, sc in each st around, join in beg sc. (25 sc)

RND 2: Ch 1, sc in same st as joining, sc in each rem st around, join in beg sc.

RNDS 3 & 4: Rep Rnd 2.

RND 5: Ch 1, 2 sc in same st as joining, sc in each of next 4 sts, [2 sc in next st, sc in each of next 4 sts] rep around, join in beg sc. (30 sc)

RNDS 6–8: Rep Rnd 2.

RND 9: Ch 1, sc in same st as joining, ch 3, [sk next 2 sts, sc in next st, ch 3] rep around, join in beg sc. (10 ch-3 sps)

RND 10: Sl st in first sp, ch 1, sc in same sp, ch 3, [sc in next sp, ch 3] rep around, join in beg sc. (10 ch-3 sps)

RND 11: Sl st in first sp, ch 1, sc in same sp, *ch 6, sl st in 5th ch from hook for border p, ch 2 **, sc in next sp, rep from * around, ending last rep at **, join in beg sc, fasten off.

FINISHING
Tack border p to end st at either side of Row 1 of wishbone cover. Tack border p directly opposite to end st at opposite side of Row 1 of wishbone cover.

Cut a 12-inch length of ribbon. Tie into bow at top of hanging ch. Cut 2 (8-inch) lengths of ribbon. Tie each into bow at each side of

Table Decorations

This nut basket, candle holder and bonbon basket won first prize in the Class 8, Novelties division of a September 1914 crochet competition. They will still make lovely party favors for your baby shower or wedding reception table today.

Design revised by Maggie Petsch Chasalow

SKILL LEVEL: INTERMEDIATE

SIZE
CANDLEHOLDER: 4 inches wide x 1 inch high
BONBON BASKET: 3¼ inches wide x 3 inches high
NUT BASKET: 2¼ inches wide x 1¼ inches high

MATERIALS
➤ Crochet cotton size 50 (284 yds per ball): 1 ball ecru
➤ Size 13 steel crochet hook or size needed to obtain gauge
➤ 1 yard ¼-inch-wide red satin ribbon
➤ Fabric stiffener
➤ 3¹⁄₁₆ x 2¹⁵⁄₁₆-inch plastic foam egg
➤ 6-inch square cardboard
➤ Plastic wrap
➤ Straight pins
➤ Sewing needle

GAUGE
Rnd 1 of upper portion of candleholder = ⁹⁄₁₆ inch in diameter
Check gauge to save time.

PATTERN NOTES
Weave in loose ends as work progresses.

Join rnds with sl st unless otherwise indicated.

PATTERN STITCHES
DTR 3 TOG: Holding back on hook last lp of each st, dtr in each of next 3 sts, yo, draw through all 4 lps on hook.

BEG DTR 3 TOG: Ch 4, holding back on hook last lp of each st, dtr in each of next 2 sts, yo, draw through all 3 lps on hook.

P: Ch 6, sc in 6th ch from hook.

P CH: P, [ch 6, sc in last sc made] 5 times.

CL: Holding back on hook last lp of each st, 3 dtr in indicated sp, yo, draw through all 4 lps on hook.

BEG CL: Ch 4, holding back on hook last lp of each st, 2 dtr in same sp as ch-4, yo, draw through all 3 lps on hook.

SHELL: [{Dtr, ch 6, sl st in top of dtr just made, ch 1} 5 times, dtr, ch 6, sl st in top of dtr just made] in indicated st or sp.

Candle Holder

UPPER PORTION
RND 1 (RS): Ch 10, sl st to join to form a ring, ch 5 (counts as first tr, ch 1), [tr in ring, ch 1] 19 times, join in 4th ch of beg ch-5. (20 ch-1 sps)

RND 2: Ch 4 (counts as first tr), tr in next sp, [tr in next tr, tr in next sp] rep around, join in 4th ch of beg ch-4. (40 tr)

RND 3: Ch 6 (counts as first dtr, ch 1), sk next tr, [dtr in next st, ch 1, sk next tr] rep around, join in 5th ch of beg ch-6. (20 dtr)

RND 4: Ch 5 (counts as first dtr), dtr in each sp and in each dtr around, join in 5th ch of beg ch-5. (40 dtr)

RND 5: Beg dtr 3 tog, ch 4, sk next st, [dtr 3 tog, ch 4, sk next st] rep around, join in top of beg dtr 3 tog. (10 dtr 3 tog)

RND 6: Ch 8 (counts as first tr, ch 4), [tr in top of next dtr 3 tog, ch 4] rep around, join in 4th ch of beg ch-8.

RND 7: *Ch 5, p **, ch 5, sl st in top of next tr, rep from * around, ending last rep at **, dtr in st at base of beg ch-5 to form last ch-5 sp, turn.

RND 8: Ch 1, beg in last p made, [sl st, p ch, sl st, ch 3] in each p around, join in same st as beg sl st, fasten off.

SAUCER

RND 1: Attach thread with a sl st over post of any tr of upper portion Rnd 1, ch 7 (counts as first dtr, ch 2), working over rem posts, [dtr over next st, ch 2] rep around, join in 5th ch of beg ch-7, turn. (20 dtr)

RND 2: Ch 4 (counts as first tr), 3 tr in next sp, [tr in next dtr, 3 tr in next sp] rep around, join in 4th ch of beg ch-4. (80 tr)

RND 3: Beg dtr 3 tog, ch 6, sk next st, [dtr 3 tog, ch 6, sk next st] rep around, join in top of beg dtr 3 tog. (20 dtr 3 tog)

RND 4: Ch 7 (counts as first tr, ch 3), *tr in next sp, ch 3 **, tr in top of next dtr 3 tog, ch 3, rep from * around, ending last rep at **, join in 4th ch of beg ch-7.

RND 5: Ch 8 (counts as first tr, ch 4), *sc in next tr, ch 4 **, tr in next tr, ch 4, rep from * around, ending last rep at **, join in 4th ch of beg ch-8.

RND 6: Ch 1, sc in same st as joining, *ch 5, p **, ch 5, sc in next tr, rep from * around, ending last rep at **, dtr in beg sc to form last ch-5 sp, ch 1, turn, sl st in last p made, turn.

RND 7: [P ch, sl st] in same p as last sl st made, ch 7, [sl st, p ch, sl st] in next p, rep from around, ending with ch 7, join in st at base of beg ch-7, fasten off.

HANDLE

ROW 1: Leaving a short length at beg, ch 11, dc in 4th ch from hook, ch 3, sk next 2 chs, sl st in next ch, ch 3, sk next 2 chs, dc in each of next 2 chs, turn.

ROW 2: Ch 3 (counts as first dc throughout), dc in next dc, ch 5, dc in each of next 2 dc, turn.

ROW 3: Ch 3, dc in next dc, ch 3, sk next 2 chs, sl st in next ch, ch 3, dc in each of next 2 dc, turn.

ROWS 4–15: Rep Rows 2 and 3.

ROW 16: Rep Row 2, leaving a short length of thread, fasten off.

FINISHING

With needle, sew rem lps of foundation ch of handle to any 9 sts on Rnd 4 of saucer. Sew top of Row 16 of handle to Rnd 5 of upper portion directly above bottom of handle. Apply fabric stiffener to candleholder. Pin last rnd of saucer out on plastic wrap covered cardboard. Shape upper portion of candleholder and handle and continue to shape as candleholder dries. Cut a 12-inch length of ribbon. Tie in a bow through sps on handle. Trim ends to desired length.

Bonbon Basket

UPPER PORTION

RND 1 (RS): Rep Rnd 1 of upper portion of candleholder.

RND 2: Ch 8 (counts as first dtr, ch 3), [dtr in next tr, ch 3] rep around, join in 5th ch of beg ch-8. (20 ch-3 sps)

RND 3: Sl st in first sp, beg cl in same sp, [ch 7, cl in next sp] rep around, ending with ch 3, tr in top of beg cl to form last ch-7 sp. (20 cl)

RND 4: Ch 1, sc in sp just formed, [ch 7, sc in next sp] rep around, ending with ch 3, tr in beg sc to form last ch-7 sp. (20 ch-7 sps)

RND 5: Ch 3, 2 dc in sp just formed, [ch 3, 3 dc in next sp] rep around, ending with ch 1, hdc in 3rd ch of beg ch-3 to form last ch-3 sp.

RNDS 6 & 7: Rep Rnd 4.

RND 8: Rep Rnd 5.

RNDS 9–11: Rep Rnds 6–8.

RNDS 12 & 13: Rep Rnds 6 and 7.

RND 14: Ch 1, sc in sp just formed, *ch 3, shell in center ch of next ch-7, ch 3 **, sc in next sp, rep from * around, ending last rep at **, join in beg sc, fasten off.

SAUCER

RND 1: With RS facing, attach thread with sl st at top of any cl on Rnd 3 of upper portion, [ch 7, sl st in top of next cl] rep around, ending with ch 3, tr in st at base of beg ch-7 to form last ch-7 sp, turn. (20 ch-7 sps)

RND 2: Beg cl in top of tr just made, [ch 9, cl in center ch of next ch-7] rep around, ending with ch 4, dtr in top of beg cl to form last ch-9 sp.

RND 3: Ch 1, sc in sp just formed, *ch 3, shell in next sp, ch 3 **, sc in next sp, rep from * around, ending last rep at **, join in beg sc, fasten off.

HANDLE

ROW 1: Leaving a short length at beg, ch 7, tr in 5th ch from hook, tr in next 2 chs, turn. (4 tr)

ROWS 2–28: Ch 4 (counts as first tr throughout), tr in each of next 3 tr, turn. (4 tr)

At the end of Row 28, leaving a length of thread, fasten off.

FINISHING

With needle, sew ends of handle to top of basket between shells of Rnd 14. Apply fabric stiffener to basket. Pin saucer out on plastic wrap covered cardboard. Place plastic wrap covered plastic foam egg inside basket. Pin top of basket and handle to egg. Let dry completely. Cut a 12-inch length of ribbon. Tie in a bow around top of handle. Trim ends to desired length.

Nut Basket

RNDS 1–10: Rep Rnds 1–10 of upper portion of bonbon basket.

RND 11: Beg cl over sp just formed, ch 7, [cl in next sp, ch 7] rep around, join in top of beg cl.

RND 12: Ch 1, sc in same st as joining, ch 7, [sc in top of next cl, ch 7] rep around, join in beg sc.

Continued on page 169

Powder Jar

This beautiful little jar can be used to hold powder, potpourri or anything your heart desires! It introduces a different kind of popcorn stitch which a 1915 publication described as a "raised shell."

Design revised by Maggie Petsch Chasalow

SKILL LEVEL: INTERMEDIATE

SIZE
Fits 5½-inch high glass bowl

MATERIALS
➤ Crochet cotton size 10 (225 yrds per ball): 1 ball white
➤ Size 7 steel crochet hook or size needed to obtain gauge
➤ 6-strand embroidery floss (8.75 yds per skein): 2 skeins turquoise, 1 skein yellow
➤ Glass fish bowl: 5½ inches high, 3⅛ inches in diameter at top
➤ 3½-inch-diameter plastic canvas circle
➤ 12 inches ⅛-inch-wide elastic
➤ 24 inches ¼-inch-wide yellow satin ribbon
➤ Small amount fiberfill
➤ Embroidery needle

GAUGE
Rnds 1–3 = 1½ inches in diameter
Check gauge to save time.

PATTERN NOTES
Weave in loose ends as work progresses.

Join rnds with sl st unless otherwise indicated.

PATTERN STITCHES
SHELL: 5 dc in indicated st or sp.

BEG SHELL: [Ch 3, 4 dc] in indicated st or sp.

OPEN SHELL: [3 dc, ch 2, 3 dc] in indicated st or sp.

RAISED SHELL: [Sc, hdc, 3 dc, hdc, sc] in indicated st, turn; pushing shell to RS, sc in first sc made, turn.

P: Ch 4, sl st in 4th ch from hook.

Jar

BOTTOM

RND 1 (RS): Ch 7, sl st to join to form a ring, ch 3 (counts as first dc throughout), 15 dc in ring, join in 3rd ch of beg ch-3. (16 dc)

RND 2: Ch 3, dc in same st as joining, 2 dc in each rem st around, join in 3rd ch of beg ch-3. (32 dc)

RND 3: Ch 3, 2 dc in next st, [dc in next st, 2 dc in next st] rep around, join in 3rd ch of beg ch-3. (48 dc)

RND 4: Ch 3, dc in same st as joining, dc in each of next 2 sts, [2 dc in next st, dc in each of next 2 sts] rep around, join in 3rd ch of beg ch-3. (64 dc)

RND 5: Ch 3, dc in each of next 2 sts, 2 dc in next st, [dc in each of next 3 sts, 2 dc in next st] rep around, join in 3rd ch of beg ch-3. (80 dc)

SIDE

RND 6: Ch 1, sc in same st as joining, ch 5, sk next dc, sc in next dc, [ch 5, sk next 2 dc, sc in next dc] rep around, ending with ch 2, sk last 2 dc, dc in beg sc to form last ch-5 sp. (27 ch-5 sps)

RND 7: Ch 1, sc in sp just formed, *[ch 5, sc in center ch of next ch-5 sp] 4 times, [shell in next sc, sc in center ch of next ch-5, ch 5, sc in center of next ch-5] twice, shell in next sc **, sc in center ch of next ch-5, rep from * around, ending last rep at **, join in beg sc. (9 shells; 18 ch-5 sps)

RND 8: Sl st in each of first 2 chs of first ch-5, ch 1, sc in next ch, *[ch 5, sc in center ch of next ch-5] 3 times **, [ch 5, sc in center dc of next shell, ch 5, sc in center ch of next ch-5] 3 times, rep from * around, ending last rep at **, [ch 5, sc in center dc of next shell, ch 5, sc in center ch of next ch-5] twice, ch 5, sc in center dc of next shell, ch 2, dc in beg sc to form last ch-5 sp. (27 ch-5 sps)

RND 9: Ch 1, sc in sp just formed, shell in next sc, *sc in center ch of next ch-5, ch 5, 3 dc in center ch of next ch-5, ch 5, sc in center ch of next ch-5 **, [shell in next sc, sc in center ch of next ch-5, ch 5, sc in center ch of next ch-5] 3 times, shell in next sc, rep from * around, ending last rep at **, [shell in next sc, sc in center ch of next ch-5, ch 5, sc in center ch of next ch-5] twice, shell in next sc, sc in center ch of next ch-5, ch 2, dc in beg sc to form last ch-5 sp. (12 shells)

RND 10: Ch 1, sc in sp just formed, ch 5, sc in center dc of next shell, ch 5, sc in center ch of

next ch-5, *ch 3, 2 dc in next dc, dc in next dc, 2 dc in next dc, ch 3, sc in center ch of next ch-5 **, [ch 5, sc in center dc of next shell, ch 5, sc in center ch of next ch-5] 4 times **, rep from * around, ending last rep at **, [ch 5, sc in center dc of next shell, ch 5, sc in center of next ch-5] twice, ch 5, sc in center dc of next shell, ch 2, dc in beg sc to form last ch-5 sp. (24 ch-5 sps)

RND 11: Ch 1, sc in sp just formed, shell in next sc, [sc in center ch of next ch-5, ch 5] twice, *2 dc in next dc, dc in each

of next 3 dc, 2 dc in next dc, [ch 5, sc in center ch of next ch-5] twice **, [shell in next sc, sc in center ch of next ch-5, ch 5, sc in center ch of next ch-5] 3 times, ch 5, rep from * around, ending last rep at **, shell in next sc, sc in center ch of next ch-5, ch 5, sc in center ch of next ch-5, shell in next sc, sc in center ch of next ch-5, ch 2, dc in beg sc to form last ch-5 sp. (9 shells; 3 groups of 7-dc)

RND 12: Ch 1, sc in sp just formed, ch 5, sc in center dc of next shell, *[ch 5, sc in center ch

of next ch-5] twice, ch 3, 2 dc in next dc, dc in each of next 5 dc, 2 dc in next dc, ch 3, sc in center ch of next ch-5 **, [ch 5, sc in center ch of next ch-5, ch 5, sc in center dc of next shell] 3 times, rep from * around, ending last rep at **, [ch 5, sc in center ch of next ch-5, ch 5, sc in center dc of next shell] twice, ch 2, dc in beg sc to form last ch-5 sp. (24 ch-5 sps, 3 groups 9-dc)

RND 13: Ch 1, sc in sp just formed, shell in next sc, sc in center ch of next ch-5, ch 5, sc in center ch of next ch-5, *shell in next sc, sc in center ch of next ch-5, ch 5, 2 dc in first dc of 9-dc group, dc in each of next 7 dc, 2 dc in next dc, ch 5, sc in center ch of next ch-5 **, [shell in next sc, sc in center ch of next ch-5, ch 5, sc in center ch of next ch-5] 3 times, rep from * around, ending last rep at **, shell in next sc, sc in center ch of next ch-5, ch 5, sc in center ch of next ch-5, shell in next sc, sc in center ch of next ch-5, ch 2, dc in beg sc to form last ch-5 sp.

RND 14: Ch 1, sc in same sp as joining, [ch 5, sc in center dc of next shell, ch 5, sc in center ch of next ch-5] twice, *ch 3, 2 dc in next dc, dc in each of next 9 dc, 2 dc in next dc, ch 3, sc in center ch of next ch-5 **, [ch 5, sc in center dc of next shell, ch 5, sc in center ch of next ch-5] 4 times, rep from * around, ending last rep at **, ch 5, sc in center dc of next shell, ch 5, sc in center ch of next ch-5, ch 5, sc in center dc of next shell, ch 2, dc in beg sc to form last ch-5 sp.

RND 15: Ch 1, sc in same st as joining, [shell in next sc, sc in center ch of next ch-5, ch 5, sc in center ch of next ch-5] twice, *ch 5, 2 dc in next dc, dc in each of next 11 dc, 2 dc in next dc, [ch 5, sc in center ch of next ch-5] twice **, [shell in next sc, sc in center ch of next ch-5, ch 5, sc in center ch of next ch-5] 3 times, rep from * around, ending last rep at **, shell in next sc, sc in center ch of next ch-5, ch 2, dc in beg sc to from last ch-5 sp.

RND 16: Ch 1, sc in same st as joining, [ch 5, sc in center dc of next shell, ch 5, sc in center ch of next ch-5] twice, ch 5, sc in center ch of next ch-5, *ch 3, dc in each of next 15 dc, ch 3, sc in center ch of next ch-5 **, [ch 5, sc in center ch of next ch-5, ch 5, sc in center dc of next shell] 3 times, [ch 5, sc in center ch of next ch-5] twice, rep from * around, ending last rep at **, ch 5, sc in center ch of next ch-5, ch 5, sc in center dc of next shell, ch 2, dc in beg sc to form last ch-5 sp.

RND 17: Ch 1, sc in sp just

formed, [shell in next sc, sc in center ch of next ch-5, ch 5, sc in center ch of next ch-5] twice, shell in next sc, sc in center ch of next ch-5, *ch 5, dc in each of next 15 dc **, [ch 5, sc in center ch of next ch-5, shell in next sc, sc in center ch of next ch-4] 4 times, rep from * around, ending last rep at **, ch 5, sc in center ch of next ch-5, shell in next sc, sc in center of next ch-5, ch 2, dc in beg sc to form last ch-5 sp.

RND 18: Ch 1, sc in sp just formed, *[ch 5, sc in center dc of next shell, ch 5, sc in center of next ch-5] 3 times, ch 3, dc in each of next 15 dc, ch 3, sc in center ch of next ch-5, ch 5, sc in center dc of next shell **, ch 5, sc in center ch of next ch-5, rep from * around, ending last rep at **, ch 2, dc in beg sc to form last ch-5 sp.

RND 19: Ch 1, sc in sp just formed, *[shell in next sc, sc in center ch of next ch-5, ch 5, sc in center ch of next ch-5] 3 times, ch 5, dc in each of next 15 dc **, [ch 5, sc in center ch of next ch-5] twice, rep from * around, ending last rep at **, ch 5, sc in center ch of next ch-5, ch 2, dc in beg sc to form last ch-5 sp.

RND 20: Ch 1, sc in sp just formed, *[ch 5, sc in center dc of next shell, ch 5, sc in center ch of next ch-5] 3 times, ch 5, sk next sp, dc in each of next 15 dc, ch 5, sk next sp **, sc in center ch of next ch-5, rep from * around, ending last rep at **, join in beg sc.

RND 21: Sl st in each of next 2 chs of first ch-5 sp, ch 1, sc in next ch, *ch 5, sc in center of next ch-5, [shell in next sc, sc in center ch of next ch-5, ch 5, sc in center ch of next ch-5] twice, ch 5, sk next ch-5 sp, dc in each of next 15 dc, ch 5, sk next ch-5 sp **, sc in center of next ch-5, rep from * around, ending last rep at **, join in beg sc.

RND 22: Sl st into first ch of next ch-5, ch 3, dc in next ch, *[ch 3, dc in each of first 2 dc of next shell, ch 3, dc in each of first 2 chs of next ch-5] twice, ch 3, dc in each of first 2 chs of next ch-5, ch

3, dc in each of next 2 dc, [ch 3, sk next 3 dc, dc in each of next 2 dc] twice **, [ch 3, dc in each of first 2 chs of next ch-5] twice, rep from * around, ending last rep at **, ch 3, dc in each of first 2 chs of next ch-5, ch 3, join in 3rd ch of beg ch-3.

RND 23: Sl st in next dc and in first sp, ch 1, sc in same sp, open shell in next sp, [sc in next sp, open shell in next sp] rep around, join in beg sc.

RND 24: Beg shell in same st as joining, 3 sc in next shell sp, [shell in next sc, 3 sc in next shell sp] rep around, join in 3rd ch of beg ch-3.

RND 25: Ch 1, sc in same st as joining, sc in each of next 4 sts, p, [sc in each of next 5 sts, p] rep around, join in beg sc, fasten off.

Lid

TOP

RND 1 (RS): Ch 7, sl st to join to form a ring, ch 3, 14 dc in ring, join in 3rd ch of beg ch-3. (15 dc)

RND 2: Ch 3, dc in same st as joining, 2 dc in each rem st around, join in 3rd ch of beg ch-3. (30 dc)

RND 3: Ch 3, 2 dc in next st, [dc in next st, 2 dc in next st] rep around, join in 3rd ch of beg ch-3. (45 dc)

RNDS 4–6: Ch 3, dc in each st around, inc 15 sts evenly sp each rnd and staggering incs so they do not fall directly over incs of previous rnd, join in 3rd ch of beg ch-3. (90 dc)

RND 7: Ch 1, sc in same st as joining, sc in each of next 4 sts, raised shell in next st, [sc in each of next 5 sts, raised shell in next st] rep around, join in beg sc. (15 raised shells)

RND 8: Ch 3, dc in each of next 4 sts, 2 dc in sc behind raised shell, [dc in each of next 5 sts, 2 dc in sc behind raised shell] rep around, join in 3rd ch of beg ch-3. (105 dc)

RND 9: Ch 1, sc in same st as joining, sc in each rem st around, join in beg sc, fasten off. (105 sc)

BOTTOM

RNDS 1–6: Rep Rnds 1–6 of top.

RND 7: Ch 1, sc in same st as joining, sc in each rem st around, join in beg sc.

RND 8: Rep Rnd 4 of top. (105 dc)

RND 9: Rep Rnd 9 of top.

KNOB

Note: Do not join rnds unless otherwise indicated; use scrap of CC to mark rnds.

RND 1: Ch 5, sl st to join to form a ring, ch 1, 8 sc in ring. (8 sc)

RND 2: 2 sc in each sc around. (16 sc)

RND 3: [Sc in next sc, 2 sc in next sc] rep around. (24 sc)

RNDS 4–7: Sc in each sc around. Stuff knob with fiberfill.

RND 8: [Sk next sc, sc in next sc] rep around until 8 sc rem, stuffing with fiberfill as work pro-gresses, leaving an 18-inch length of cotton, fasten off. Weave rem length through sts of last rnd, pull tightly to close opening.

FINISHING

With embroidery needle and turquoise, embroider 15 (8-petalled) flowers around lid top with straight st between raised shells. With yellow, embroider one French knot at center of each flower. With turquoise, embroider one 8-petalled flower over top of knob. With yellow, embroider a French knot in the center of flower. Sew knob to center of lid top.

JOINING TOP & BOTTOM LID

RND 1: With lid top facing, holding WS of top and bottom tog with plastic canvas circle sandwiched between and working through both thicknesses of lid bottom and top, attach thread with a sl st in any sc of Rnd 9, ch 1, sc in same st, sc in each of next 5 sts, 2 sc in next st, [sc in each of next 6 sts, 2 sc in next st] rep around, join in beg sc. (120 sc)

RND 2: Ch 1, sc in same st as joining, sc in each of next 4 sc, p, [sc in each of next 5 sc, p] rep around, join in beg sc, fasten off.

With embroidery needle and turquoise, using photo as a guide, embroider 13 (8-petalled) flowers with straight st on each of 3 solid dc sections of sides. With yellow, embroider 1 French knot in center of each flower.

Cut length of elastic to fit snugly around top of bowl. Weave elastic through ch-3 sps of Rnd 22 of sides and tack ends tog. Beg at center of any openwork section, weave yellow ribbon through ch-3 sps over elastic. Slip cover over bowl, pulling tautly to reach top of bowl. Tie ribbon into a bow. Trim ends of ribbon to desired length. ✧

Table Decorations continued from page 165

RND 13: Sl st in first sp, ch 1, [4 sc, ch 5, 4 sc] in same sp, [4 sc, ch 5, 4 sc] in each of next 2 sps, *ch 20 for handle, turn, sk last 2 ch-5 sps and next 3 sc, sl st in next sc, ch 1, turn, 20 sc over ch-20 sp *, [4 sc, ch 5, 4 sc] in each of next 10 sps, rep from * to *, [4 sc, ch 5, 4 sc] in each rem sp around, join in beg sc, fasten off.

FINISHING

Apply fabric stiffener to basket. Place plastic-wrap-covered plastic foam egg inside basket. Pin top of basket to egg. Allow to dry completely. Cut a 12-inch length of ribbon. Tie ribbon in a bow around handle. Trim ends to desired length. ✧

Chapter Eight

Collectible Afghans

Perfect for keeping loved ones snug and cozy on a cold night, afghans have long since brought comfort and warmth to those who enjoy them. Revive this collection of cozy and colorful old-time afghans by working them in today's colors and yarns.

Victoriana Rose Wreath

Stitch this simple openwork afghan, originally created in 1947, then embellish it with delicate crocheted flowers and leaves. You'll love its outdoor freshness and old-fashioned charm!

SKILL LEVEL: BEGINNER

SIZE
53 x 69 inches

MATERIALS
➤ Caron Wintuk worsted weight yarn: 55 oz off-white #3002, 19 oz strawberry #3057, and 3 oz each jonquil #3256, tea rose #3257, deep periwinkle #3255 and woodsy green #3008
➤ Size H #/8 crochet hook or size needed to obtain gauge
➤ Tapestry needle

GAUGE
5 rows in main pattern = 2 inches; [dc, sc, ch 2] = 1 inch
Check gauge to save time.

PATTERN NOTES
Weave in loose ends as work progresses.

Join rnds with a sl st unless otherwise stated.

PATTERN STITCH
PUFF ST: Yo hook, insert hook in st, yo, draw up a lp the length of a dc, [yo, insert hook in same st, yo, draw up a lp the length of a dc] twice, yo, draw through 6 lps on hook, yo, draw through 2 lps on hook.

AFGHAN
ROW 1: With off-white, ch 200, sc in 2nd ch from hook, sc in each rem ch across, turn. (199 sc)

ROW 2: Ch 2, dc in same st as beg ch-2, sk next 2 sc, *[sc, ch 2, dc] in next sc, sk next 2 sc, rep from * across, ending with sc in last sc, turn.

ROW 3: Ch 2, dc in same sc as beg ch-2, sc in next ch-2 sp, *ch 2, dc in same ch-2 sp, sc in next ch-2 sp, rep from * across, turn.

Rep Row 3 until afghan measures 60 inches from beg.

EDGING
RND 1: Ch 1, **sc in next sc, *2 sc in next ch-2 sp, sc in next sc, rep from * across to corner, work 3 sc in corner st, rep from ** across long edge, work 3 sc in corner, work 1 sc in each st across opposite side of foundation ch, 3 sc in corner st, rep from ** across 2nd long edge, ending with 3 sc in corner st, join in beg sc.

RND 2: Ch 1, sc in each sc around, working 3 sc in each center corner sc, join in beg sc, fasten off.

RND 3: Attach strawberry in 3rd sc from corner, ch 3 puff st in same st, [ch 1, sk next sc, puff st in next sc] rep around, working [puff st, ch 1] 3 times in each center corner st, join in top of beg puff st, fasten off.

RND 4: Attach off-white in any puff st, ch 1, sc in top of same puff st, [sc in next ch-1 sp, sc in top of next puff st] rep around, working 3 sc in each center corner puff st, join in beg sc, fasten off.

RND 5: Attach strawberry in any sc above a puff st, puff st in same sc above a puff st, ch 1, sk 1 sc, [puff st in next sc above a puff st, ch 1, sk 1 sc] rep around, working [puff st, ch 1] 3 times in center sc of each corner, join in top of beg puff st, fasten off.

RNDS 6–11: Rep Rnds 4 and 5.

RND 12: With off-white, rep Rnd 4, do not fasten off.

RND 13: Ch 1, sc in each sc around, working 3 sc in each center corner sc, join in beg sc.

RND 14: Ch 1, sc, ch 3, dc in same sc, sk 2 sc, [sc in next sc, ch 3, dc in same sc, sk 2 sc] rep around, join in beg sc, fasten off.

FLOWERS
RND 1: With strawberry, ch 6, dc in first ch of ch-6, [ch 2, dc in same first ch of ch-6] 3 times, ch 2, join in 4th ch of beg ch-6. (5 ch-2 sps)

RND 2: Ch 1, [sc, 3 dc, sc] in each ch-2 sp, join in beg sc. (5 petals)

RND 3: [Ch 4, sc in back of work between next 2 petals] rep around, join.

RND 4: Ch 1, [sc, 5 dc, sc] in each ch-4 sp around, join in beg sc.

RND 5: [Ch 5, sc in back of work between next 2 petals] rep around, join.

RND 6: Ch 1, [sc, 7 dc, sc] in each ch-5 sp around, join in beg sc.

RND 7: [Ch 6, sc in back of work between next 2 petals] rep around, join.

RND 8: Ch 1, [sc, 9 dc, sc] in each ch-6 sp around, join in beg sc, fasten off.

Note: *Rep flower rnds as follows for various size and colors of flowers.*

With strawberry, rep Rnds 1–8 for 3 more flowers.

Work 2 flowers working Rnds 1–4 with jonquil.

Work 2 flowers working Rnds 1–4 with strawberry and Rnds 5–8 with tea rose.

Work 4 flowers Rnds 1–6 with strawberry.

Work 1 flower Rnds 1–4 with strawberry.

Work 2 flowers working Rnds 1 and 2 with strawberry and Rnds 3 and 4 with tea rose.

Work 3 flowers Rnds 1–4 with tea rose.

Work 3 flowers Rnds 1–6 with tea rose.

Work 1 flower Rnds 1–4 with jonquil, Rnds 5 and 6 with tea rose and Rnds 7 and 8 with strawberry.

Work 1 flower Rnds 1–4 with jonquil and Rnds 5–8 with tea rose.

Work 8 flowers Rnds 1–4 with deep periwinkle.

Work 1 flower Rnds 1 and 2 with jonquil and Rnds 4–6 with deep periwinkle.

LEAVES *(make 30)*
ROW 1: With woodsey green, ch 7, sc in 2nd ch from hook, sc in each of next 4 chs, 3 sc in next ch, working on opposite side of foundation ch, sc in each of next 3 chs, turn.

ROW 2: Ch 3, working in back lps only, sc in each of next 4 sts, 3 sc in next st, sc in each of next 3 sts, turn.

ROWS 3–5: Rep Row 2. At the end of Row 5, turn, sl st in each of next 2 sts, fasten off.

FINISHING
Using photo as a guide, appliqué flowers and leaves as illustrates, arranging colors as desired. ✧

Mosaic Tiles Afghan

Long stitches and strategic placement of colors give this 1947 afghan texture while creating a wonderful 3-D effect. We've stitched it in minty hues, but you can experiment with shades of any color to suit your home and family members.

SIZE

58 x 51 inches

MATERIALS

➤ Coats & Clark Red Heart Classic worsted weight yarn: 27 oz mist green #681, 16 oz light seafoam #683, 14 oz seafoam #684 and 11 oz teal #48

➤ Size H/8 crochet hook or size needed to obtain gauge

➤ Tapestry needle

GAUGE

Each square measures 7 inches

Check gauge to save time.

PATTERN NOTES

Weave in loose ends as work progresses.

Join rnds with a sl st unless otherwise stated.

PATTERN STITCH

TRTR: Yo hook 4 times, insert hook front to back to front again around indicated sc st, yo, draw up a lp, [yo, draw through 2 lps on hook] 4 times.

SQUARE

(Make 70)

RND 1: With light seafoam, ch 2, work 8 sc in 2nd ch from hook, join in beg sc. (8 sc)

RND 2: Ch 1, [{sc, ch 3, sc} in same sc for corner, sc in next sc] 4 times, join in beg sc. (12 sc)

RND 3: Sl st into corner ch-3 sp, ch 1, *[sc, ch 3, sc] in corner sp, sc in each sc to next corner ch-3 sp, rep from * around, join in beg sc. (20 sc)

RNDS 4–7: Rep Rnd 3. At the end of Rnd 7, fasten off. (13 sc between each corner ch-3 sp)

RND 8: Attach teal in any corner ch-3 sp, ch 1, *[sc, ch 3, sc] in corner ch-3 sp, sc in each of next 6 sc, trtr around next deep sage green sc in Rnd 3 directly below (3rd sc of Rnd 3), sk sc directly behind trtr, sc in each of next 6 sc, rep from * around, join in beg sc.

RND 9: Sl st into corner ch-3 sp, ch 1, *[sc, ch 3, sc] in corner ch-3 sp, sc in each of next 6 sc, trtr around 3rd sc of Rnd 4 directly below, sk sc directly behind trtr, sc in next trtr, trtr around 5th sc of Rnd 4 directly below, sk sc directly behind trtr, sc in each of

next 6 sc, rep from * around, join in beg sc, fasten off.

RND 10: Attach seafoam in corner ch-3 sp, ch 1, *[sc, ch 3, sc] in corner ch-3 sp, sc in each of next 6 sc, trtr around 3rd sc of Rnd 5 directly below, sk sc directly behind trtr, 1 sc in each of next 3 sts, trtr around 7th sc of Rnd 5 directly below, sk sc directly behind trtr, sc in each of next 6 sc, rep from * around, join in beg sc.

RND 11: Sl st into corner ch-3 sp, ch 1, *[sc, ch 3, sc] in corner ch-3 sp, sc in each of next 6 sc, trtr around 3rd sc of Rnd 6 directly below, sk sc directly behind trtr, sc in each of next 5 sts, trtr around 9th sc of Rnd 6 directly below, sk sc directly behind trtr, sc in each of next 6 sc, join in beg sc, fasten off.

RND 12: Attach mist green in corner ch-3 sp, ch 1, *[sc, ch 3, sc] in corner ch-3 sp, sc in each of next 6 sc, trtr around 3rd sc of Rnd 7 directly below, sk sc directly behind trtr, sc in each of next 7 sts, trtr around 11th sc of Rnd 7 directly below, sk sc directly behind trtr, sc in each of next 6 sc, rep from * around, join in beg sc.

RND 13: Sl st into corner ch-3 sp,

ch 1, *[sc, ch 3, sc] in corner ch-3 sp, sc in each of next 6 sc, trtr around 2nd sc of Rnd 7 directly below, sk sc directly behind trtr, sc in each of next 9 sts, trtr around 13th sc of Rnd 7 directly below, sk sc directly behind trtr, sc in each of next 6 sts, rep from * around, join in beg sc.

RND 14: Sl st into corner ch-3 sp, ch 1, *[sc, ch 3, sc] in corner ch-3 sp, sc in each st across edge, rep from * around, join in beg sc, fasten off.

JOINING
Matching sts, sew squares tog 10 rows of 7 squares.

EDGING
RND 1: Attach mist green in any corner ch-3 sp, ch 1, [3 sc in corner ch-3 sp, sc evenly sp across edge, working 2 sc in each corner lp of joining of squares across edge] rep around, join in beg sc.

RNDS 2 & 3: Ch 1, sc in each sc around, working 3 sc in each center corner sc, join in beg sc.

RND 4: Sl st into center corner sc, ch 1, sc in corner sc, ch 4, 2 tr in same sc, sk 3 sc, [sc in next sc, ch 4, 2 tr in same sc, sk 3 sc] rep around, join in beg sc, fasten off. ✧

Baby Afghan in Star & Afghan Stitch

Wrap Baby up in the peaceful elegance of days gone by. This vintage baby blanket brings the look of antique lace and fine embroidery to the modern nursery.

SKILL LEVEL: INTERMEDIATE

SIZE
38 x 36½ inches

MATERIALS
➤ Coats & Clark Baby Sport pompadour yarn (6 oz per skein): 10 oz white #1001, 11 oz light pink #1722 and 1 oz pastel green #1680
➤ Afghan hook size E/4
➤ Size E/4 crochet hook or size needed to obtain gauge
➤ Yarn needle

GAUGE
5 sts and 4 rows = 1 inch in afghan stitch

Check gauge to save time.

PATTERN NOTES
Weave in loose ends as work progresses.

Sl st to join each rnd in beg st.

PATTERN STITCH
P: Ch 3, sl st in top of last sc.

AFGHAN STITCH PANEL *(make 3)*
ROW 1: With white, ch 25, draw up a lp in 2nd ch from hook, retaining all lps on hook, draw up a lp in each rem ch across, yo, draw through first lp on hook, [yo, draw through 2 lps on hook] rep across. (24 sts)

ROW 2: Draw up a lp under each vertical bar across retaining all lps on hook, yo, draw through first lp on hook, [yo, draw through 2 lps on hook] rep across until 1 lp rems.

Rep Row 2 for a total of 125 rows, ending with sl st in each st across row, fasten off.

Following graph, embroider cross-stitch design on each panel, working one cross-stitch over one afghan stitch.

BORDER
ROW 1: Attach light pink, working in side of strip, work 1 sc in each of the first 3 sts, *dc next st picking up the entire st in the 2nd row, tr next st picking up the entire st in 3rd row, sk 3 sts worked, work 1 sc in each of the next 3 sc, rep from * for entire row.

ROW 2: Ch 3, draw lp through 2nd and 3rd st of ch, draw lp through next 3 sts, yo, draw through all lps on hook, yo and draw through lp, this last st forms the eye of the star st and is referred to as the eye, *draw a lp through eye, lp through lp of star st, lp through the last worked st of previous row, lp through the next 2 sts, yo and draw through all sts on hook, yo and draw through lp, rep from * to end of row, turn.

ROW 3: Ch 3, draw a lp through eye of last star st, lp through star st, lp through eye of next star st in previous row, yo and draw through all lps, yo and draw through lp, *draw lp through eye of star st just made, lp through star st, lp through eye of star st

directly below star st just made, lp through next star st, lp through eye of next star st, yo and draw through all lps on hook, yo and draw through, rep from * to end of row. [Rep Row 3] twice.

Rep border on other side of stripe and work other two stripes to correspond. Sew or crochet stripes tog.

EDGING
RND 1: Beg in corner with light pink, *[ch 3, dc, 6 tr, 2 dc] in corner, working down side, [sk next 3 sts, sc in next sp, sk 3 sts, {2 dc, 3 tr, 2 dc} in next sp] rep to corner, [2 dc, 6 tr, 2 dc] in corner, rep from * around, join, fasten off.

RND 2: Working in back lps only, attach white with sc in same sp as joining, sc in next st, p, [sc in next 2 sts, p] 3 times, *[sk next sc, {sc in each of next 2 sts, p} twice, sc in same st as last, sc in next st, p, sc in each of next 2 sts] rep to corner, [{sc in each of next 2 sts, p} 4 times, sc in each of next 2 sc] in corner, rep from * around, join, fasten off. ✧

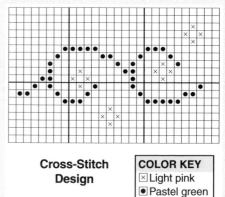

Cross-Stitch Design

COLOR KEY
☒ Light pink
⬤ Pastel green

Columbia Patchwork Afghan

Little baskets tilt and turn amid flowering meadows, lending this afghan a timeless appeal. Enjoy stitching the various pieces and joining them into such a pretty finished piece!

SKILL LEVEL: INTERMEDIATE

SIZE
34 x 40 inches

MATERIALS
➤ Coats & Clark TLC worsted weight yarn (5 oz per skein): 10 oz white #5001, 15 oz spruce #5662, and 3 oz each lavender #5585, light blue #5815, butterscotch #5263, peach #5247, light pink #5718 and coral rose #5730

➤ Size G/6 crochet hook or size needed to obtain gauge

➤ Size F/5 crochet hook

➤ Yarn needle

GAUGE
4 sc and 4 rows = 1 inch
Check gauge to save time.

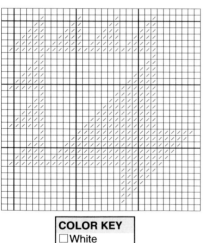

COLOR KEY
☐ White
☑ Basket color

PATTERN NOTES
Weave in loose ends as work progresses.

Alternate all colors except white and spruce for basket patches. Use white as background for all basket patches.

BASKET PATCH
ROW 1: With size G hook and white, ch 33, sc in 2nd ch from hook, sc in each rem ch across, turn. (32 sc)

ROWS 2–32: Following graph, ch 1, sc in each st across working with white and basket color, turn. At the end of last rep, fasten off.

CONNECTING BAND
Attach spruce, ch 1, dec 1 sc over next 2 sc, sc in each rem 30 sc, turn. (31 sc)

ROWS 1–3: Ch 1, sc in each sc across, turn.

ROW 4 (RAISED PATTERN ST): Ch 1, sc in each of next 3 sc, *yo, draw up a lp around 4th sc of Row 2, yo and draw through 2 lps, yo, draw up a lp around 5th sc of Row 1, yo and draw through 2 lps on hook, yo and draw up a lp around 6th sc of Row 2, yo and draw through 2 lps on hook, yo and draw up a lp around 6th sc of Row 2, yo and draw through 2 lps on hook, yo and draw through all lps, sk 1 sc, sc in each of next 7 sc, rep from *, ending with sc in each of next 3 sc, turn.

ROWS 5–7: Ch 1, sc in each st across, turn.

ROW 8: Ch 1, sc in first sc, 1 raised pattern st close to edge, *sc in each of next 6 sc, 1 raised pattern st, sk 1 st, rep from *, ending with sc in next 6 sc, raised pattern st in edge, 1 sc, turn.

ROWS 9–11: Rep Rows 5–7.

ROW 12: Rep Row 4.

ROW 13: Ch 1, sc across, inc 1 sc, fasten off, turn. (32 sc)

With white and basket color, rep basket block, but with the handle of the basket at the left. Throughout the afghan, alternate the direction of the basket handles. Work strip until 4 basket and 3 connecting bands are completed. Alternate basket colors, make 2 more strips of 4 baskets.

JOINING BANDS *(make 2)*
ROW 1: With G hook and spruce, ch 16, sc in 2nd ch from hook, sc in each rem ch across, turn. (15 sc)

ROWS 2 & 3: Ch 1, sc in each sc across, turn.

ROW 4: Ch 1, sc across working 1

raised pattern st at center, turn.

ROWS 5–7: Ch 1, sc in each st across, turn.

ROW 8: Ch 1, sc in 3 sc, work 1 raised pattern st, sc across, ending with 1 raised pattern st and 3 sc, turn.

ROWS 9–11: Ch 1, sc in each st across, turn.

Rep Rows 4–11 until band measures the same length as basket panel. Sew strips tog.

BORDER

RND 1: With hook size F, attach spruce, ch 1, sc evenly sp around, working inc in corner to keep flat, sl st to join in beg sc.

RNDS 2–4: Ch 1, sc around, inc in center corner sc to keep corners flat, sl st to join in beg sc.

RND 5: Ch 1, sc around, working 4 raised pattern sts evenly sp across each edge of each basket patch, 2 raised pattern sts across each band and 1 raised pattern st in each corner, sl st to join in beg sc.

RND 6: Ch 1, sc evenly sp around, working ch 3, sl st in top of last sc for p above each raised st of previous rnd. ✧

Indian Stripe Afghan

For the best in Southwest decorating, look no further than this vintage 1951 afghan pattern. Richly textured afghan and claw stitch combine with fine cross-stitch embroidery for a simply elegant design.

SKILL LEVEL: INTERMEDIATE

SIZE

60 x 60 inches without fringe

MATERIALS

➤ Coats & Clark Classic worsted weight yarn: 48 oz light seafoam #683, 7 oz bronze #286, and 1 oz each eggshell #111 and teal #48

➤ Afghan hook size G/6 or size needed to obtain gauge

➤ Size H/8 crochet hook

➤ 4-inch piece cardboard

➤ Tapestry needle

GAUGE

8 afghan sts and 7 rows = 2 inches

Check gauge to save time.

PATTERN NOTES

Weave in loose ends as work progresses.

Join rnds with a sl st unless otherwise stated.

PATTERN STITCH

AFGHAN STITCH

ROW 1: Ch for desired length, draw up a lp through each st of ch and retaining all lps on hook, yo, draw through 1 lp on hook, [yo, draw through 2 lps on hook] rep across until 1 lp rem.

ROW 2: Insert hook under 2nd post and draw up a lp, [insert hook under next post and draw up a lp] rep across retaining all lps on hook, yo, draw through 1 lp on hook, [yo, draw through 2 lps on hook] rep across until 1 lp rem.

Rep Row 2 for pattern.

AFGHAN STITCH PANELS *(make 3)*

With afghan hook and light seafoam, ch 56, work 55 afghan sts across ch.

Work in afghan st for 219 complete rows. With 1 lp on hook, insert hook under 2nd post and draw a lp through, yo and draw through 2 lps, insert hook under 3rd post, draw through, yo and draw through both lps, continue working in sc across row and down left side only, working 1 sc in each row and inserting hook far enough back to catch 2 strands for strength, fasten off.

NARROW STRIP

ROWS 1–6: With afghan hook and bronze, ch 9, work in afghan st for 6 complete rows.

ROW 7 (CLAW PATTERN): Pick up and draw lp through post 2, 3, 4 and 5 only (5 lps on hook), yo, insert hook under the 4th post of 3rd row and draw lp through (7 lps on hook), yo and draw through 1 lp, yo and draw through 2 lps, yo and draw through 1 lp (6 lps on hook), yo, sk 1 post of 3rd row, insert hook through next post (6th post) and draw through (8 lps on hook), yo and draw through 1 lp, yo and draw through 2 lps, yo and draw through 1 lp (7 lps on hook), yo and draw through 3 lps (5 lps on hook), pick up and draw a lp through post 6, 7, 8 and 9 and work back same as before.

Work 1 complete row of afghan sts. Rep from 7th row until there are 217 complete rows and inserting hook in 4th row below for claw pattern.

Indian Stripe Afghan

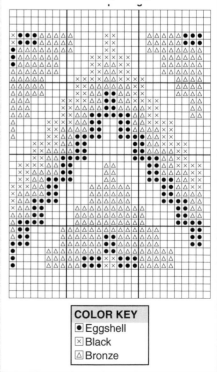

COLOR KEY
- ● Eggshell
- ✕ Black
- △ Bronze

Work 2 complete rows in afghan st. Finish same as large strips.

Work 3 more strips with bronze and 4 strips with light seafoam.

JOINING
Crochet strips tog with sc, working on WS and starting at left side crochet a narrow light seafoam claw strip to large afghan strip picking up back lp of sts of each edge, row for row. Crochet a bronze claw strip to opposite side of large light seafoam afghan strip.

Crochet rem strips tog as follows: narrow light seafoam claw strip, bronze claw strip, large seafoam afghan strip, bronze claw strip, narrow light seafoam claw strip, bronze claw strip, large light seafoam afghan strip and narrow light seafoam claw strip.

FRINGE
Wind yarn over cardboard once and cut one end. Fold one strand in half and with crochet hook pull fold through st, draw cut ends through lp on hook, pull gently to secure. Rep fringe across top and lower edge of each strip having colors to correspond with strip.

EMBROIDERY
Embroider as illustrated following diagram and starting pattern in 15th row from top and lower edge. Embroidery is worked in large afghan strips only using a cross-stitch. Each post represents one st and the cross sts are worked over the post. ✧

Pompom Afghan

A real treat for fun-loving kids, this playful afghan from 1937 is made in pentagon and diamond motifs which are then sewed together. Originally designed in two colors, we've stitched it in child-pleasing circus brights!

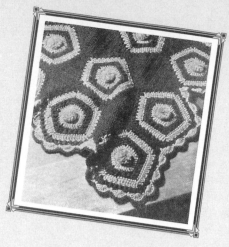

PATTERN NOTES
Weave in loose ends as work progresses.

Join rnds with a sl st unless otherwise stated.

Ch 3 counts as first dc throughout.

PENTAGON MEDALLION *(make 48)*
RND 1: With bright yellow, ch 6, sl st to join to form a ring, ch 3, 19 dc in ring, join in top of beg ch-3. (20 dc)

RND 2: Ch 1, [sc in each of next 3 sts, 2 sc in next st] 5 times, join in beg sc. (25 sc)

RND 3: Ch 3, dc in each of next 3 sts, [dc, ch 2, dc] in next st, *dc in each of next 4 sts, [dc, ch 2, dc] in next st, rep from * around, join in top of beg ch-3, fasten off. (30 dc)
Note: For Rnds 4, 5 and 8, half of

the pentagon medallions are worked with each royal and paddy green.

RND 4: Attach royal (paddy green) in top of ch-3, ch 1, sc in each dc around, working [sc, ch 2, sc] in each ch-2 sp around, join in beg sc. (40 sc)

RND 5: Ch 4, being careful to hold yarn loosely, work a dc around ch-4, *[sk 1 sc, dc in next sc, work a dc around post of last dc (wrapped dc)] rep across edge to next ch-2 sp, [dc in ch-2 sp, work a dc around post of last dc] 3 times in ch-2 sp, rep from * around, join in top of beg ch-4, fasten off. (4 wrapped dc each side; 3 wrapped dc in each ch-2 sp)

RND 6: Attach yellow in top of beg ch of previous rnd, ch 1, sc in each st around entire outer edge, working [sc, ch 2, sc] over center wrapped dc group in each ch-2 sp, join in beg sc. (70 sc)

RND 7: Ch 3, dc in each st around, working [dc, ch 3, dc] in each ch-2 sp around, join in top of beg ch-3, fasten off. (80 dc)

RND 8: Attach royal (paddy green) in top of beg ch of previous rnd, ch 4, wrapped dc around ch, *[sk next dc, dc in next dc, wrapped dc around dc] rep across edge to corner ch sp, [dc, wrapped dc around dc] 3 times in corner ch-3 sp, rep from * around, join in top of beg ch-4, fasten off. (8 wrapped dc each side; 3 wrapped dc in each corner ch-3 sp)

Join pentagon medallions in strips of like color, alternate royal and paddy green strips.

DIAMOND MEDALLIONS
Note: These diamond-shaped medallions fill in between the pentagons tension varies. The number of sts to the row may need to be varies to suit the individual, being careful not to make them larger than the sps they are to fill after the pentagons are connected. There are 2 sizes, which alternate with one another in horizontal rows from top to bottom. No. 1 is placed vertically and fits between the pairs of pentagons which are joined along their straight edges. No. 2 is placed horizontally and fits in between the points.

Diamond No. 1 (make 20)

Note: Finished size is approximately 4¼ x 8½ inches.

ROW 1: With cherry red, ch 4, dc in first ch, turn. (2 dc)

ROW 2: Ch 3, dc in same st as beg ch, 2 dc in next dc, turn. (4 dc)

ROW 3: Ch 3, dc in same st as beg ch, dc in each dc across to last dc, 2 dc in last dc, turn. (6 dc)

Continue to rep Row 3 until widest part of diamond is reached to properly fit between pentagons.

ROW 4: Ch 2, dc in next dc (beg dc dec), dc in each dc across to last 2 dc, dc dec over next 2 dc, turn.

Continue dec one st at the beg and end of each row until point is reached, leaving a length of yarn, fasten off.

Diamond No. 2 (make 15)

Note: Finished size is approximately 6¼ x 8¼ inches.

ROW 1: With cherry red, ch 4, 3 dc in first ch, turn. (4 dc)

ROW 2: Ch 3, dc in same st as beg ch, dc in each dc across to last dc, 2 dc in last dc, turn. (6 dc)

ROW 3: Rep Row 2. (8 dc)

ROW 4: Ch 3, dc in same st as beg ch, 2 dc in next dc, dc in each dc across to last 2 dc, 2 dc in each of next 2 dc, turn. (12 dc)

ROW 5: Rep Row 2. (14 dc)

ROW 6: Rep Row 4. (18 dc)

ROW 7: Rep Row 2. (20 dc)

ROW 8: Rep Row 4. (24 dc)

ROW 9: Ch 2, dc in next dc (beg dc dec), dc dec over next 2 dc, dc across to last 4 sts, [dc dec over next 2 sts] twice, turn. (20 dc)

ROW 10: Ch 2, dc in next dc, dc in each dc across to last 2 dc, dc dec over next 2 dc, turn. (18 dc)

ROW 11: Rep Row 9. (14 dc)

ROW 12: Rep Row 10. (12 dc)

ROW 13: Rep Row 9. (8 dc)

ROW 14: Rep Row 10. (6 dc)

ROW 15: Rep Row 10. (4 dc)

ROW 16: Ch 2, [yo, insert hook in next st, yo, draw through 2 lps on hook] 3 times, yo, draw through all 4 lps on hook, ch 1, fasten off.

EDGING

RND 1: Attach yellow at point where 2 of the pentagon medallions are joined, work loosely, work 8 dc in top of 2nd wrapped dc, sk 1 wrapped dc, dc in next st, continue in this manner, working 3 shells along side of each angle.

When working the first shell on the 2nd side of the point where 2 blocks meet, join it to the last shell worked by removing hook, drawing dropped lp through st of first shell and then continue as before. Because of the nature of the shape of these pentagons and their arrangement, the angles between them differ along side and end edge. When the angle is acute the joining of the adjacent shells is done in the 3rd and 4th st. When shallow, 2nd st is one connected.

RND 2: Attach cherry red, ch 1, working in back lps only, sc in each st around, join in beg sc, fasten off.

POMPOMS

Use royal and paddy green for pompoms to match pentagon medallions.

Wrap respective yarn about 30 times around a 1-inch cardboard; tie securely at top, leaving ends for sewing. Clip opposite ends and shape; pass rem ends through center of pentagon medallion and secure invisibly. ✧

Hop o' My Thumb

This fanciful afghan is named for the speed with which it "hops off your thumb!" Quick-to-stitch and completely reversible, you'll enjoy its puffy charm.

SKILL LEVEL: BEGINNER

SIZE
44 x 62 inches

MATERIALS
➤ Coats & Clark Red Heart Classic 4-ply yarn (3½ oz per skein): 7 skeins teal #48, 4 skeins light seafoam #683, 2 skeins each of cameo rose #759, pale rose #755

➤ Size I/9 crochet hook or size needed to obtain gauge

➤ Tapestry needle

GAUGE
1 shell = 1 inch wide x 1¼ inches high
Check gauge to save time.

PATTERN NOTE
Weave in loose ends as work progresses.

AFGHAN
ROW 1: With teal, ch 194, 4 tr in 4th ch from hook, *sk 5 ch, sc in next ch, ch 2, 4 tr in same st as last sc, rep from * across, fasten off, turn. (28 shells)

ROW 2: Attach light seafoam in first ch-2 sp, ch 1, sc in same sp, *ch 2, 4 tr in same ch-2 sp, sc in next ch-2 sp, rep from * across to last ch-2 sp, sc in next ch-2 sp, ch 2, 4 tr in same ch-2 sp, fasten off, turn.

ROW 3: With teal, rep Row 2.

ROW 4: With pale rose, rep Row 2.

ROW 5: With teal, rep Row 2.

ROW 6: With light seafoam, rep Row 2.

ROW 7: With teal, rep Row 2.

ROW 8: With cameo rose, rep Row 2.

ROW 9: With teal, rep Row 2.

ROW 10: With light seafoam, rep Row 2.

ROW 11: With teal, rep Row 2.

Rep Rows 4–11 into established color sequence until afghan measures 62 inches, ending with Row 11 to correspond with beg color sequence. ✧

Fan Afghan

The fan or half-shell motif is a treasured part of crocheting history. Put it to new use in this perky updated version of a 1951 pattern. Originally designed for three shades of one color, plus white, we've added more color for extra fun!

SKILL LEVEL: INTERMEDIATE

SIZE
65 x 62 inches

MATERIALS
➤ Caron Wintuk worsted weight yarn (3½ oz per skein): 47 oz white #3001, 26 oz tea rose #3257, 22 oz dark Persian #3197 and 11 oz strawberry #3057

➤ Size I/9 crochet hook or size needed to obtain gauge

➤ Yarn needle

GAUGE
Each fan motif measures 15 inches at widest point x 8 inches at center

Check gauge to save time.

PATTERN NOTES
Weave in loose ends as work progresses.

Ch 3 counts as first dc throughout.

PATTERN STITCH
POPCORN (PC): 4 dc in indicated st, draw up a lp, remove hook, insert hook in first dc of 4-dc group, pick up dropped lp, draw through st on hook, ch 1 to lock.

FAN MOTIF *(make 53)*
ROW 1: With white, ch 2, sc in 2nd ch from hook, turn.

ROW 2: Ch 1, 3 sc in the sc, turn.

ROW 3: Ch 1, 2 sc in first sc, sc in next sc, 2 sc in last sc, turn. (5 sc)

ROW 4: Ch 1, 2 sc in first sc, sc in each sc across to last sc, 2 sc in last sc, turn. (7 sc)

ROWS 5–10: Rep Row 4. At the end of Row 10, fasten off. (19 sc)

ROW 11: Attach tea rose, ch 3, [pc in next st, dc in next st] rep across, turn. (9 pc)

ROW 12: Ch 1, 2 sc in first dc, [sc in top of pc, sc in next dc, 2 sc in next pc, sc in next dc] rep across, ending with 2 sc in last dc, fasten off, turn. (25 sc)

ROW 13: Attach white, rep Row 4. (27 sc)

ROW 14: Rep Row 4, fasten off, turn. (29 sc)

ROW 15: Attach dark Persian, rep Row 11. (14 pc)

ROW 16: Ch 1, sc in same st as beg ch, [sc in next pc, 2 sc in next dc] rep across, fasten off, turn. (43 sc)

ROWS 17 & 18: Rep Rows 13 and 14. (47 sc)

ROW 19: Attach strawberry, rep Row 11. (23 pc)

ROW 20: Rep Row 4, fasten off, turn. (49 sc)

ROWS 21 & 22: Rep Rows 13 and 14. (53 sc)

FIRST HALF MOTIF *(make 7)*
ROW 1: With white, ch 2, sc in 2nd ch from hook, turn.

ROW 2: Ch 1, 2 sc in sc, turn. (2 sc)

ROW 3: Ch 1, sc in first sc, 2 sc in next sc, turn. (3 sc)

ROW 4: Ch 1, 2 sc in first sc, sc in each of next 2 sc, turn. (4 sc)

ROW 5: Ch 1, sc in each of next 3 sc, 2 sc in next sc, turn. (5 sc)

ROW 6: Ch 1, 2 sc in first sc, sc in each rem sc across, turn. (6 sc)

ROWS 7–9: Rep Rows 5 and 6. (9 sc)

ROW 10: Ch 1, 2 sc in first sc, sc in each sc across to last sc, 2 sc in last sc, fasten off, turn. (11 sc)

ROW 11: Attach tea rose, rep Row 11 of fan motif. (5 pc)

ROW 12: Rep Row 12 of fan motif, fasten off. (15 sc)

ROW 13: Attach white, ch 1, sc in each sc across to last sc, 2 sc in last sc, turn. (16 sc)

ROW 14: Ch 1, 2 sc in first sc, sc in each rem sc across, fasten off, turn. (17 sc)

ROW 15: Attach dark Persian, rep

Row 15 of fan motif. (8 pc)

ROW 16: Rep Row 16 of fan motif, but working 1 sc in each of the last 2 dc, fasten off, turn. (23 sc)

ROW 17: Attach white, rep Row 13.

ROW 18: Rep Row 14.

ROW 19: Attach strawberry, rep Row 15. (12 pc)

ROW 20: Rep Row 6, fasten off. (26 sc)

ROWS 21 & 22: Rep Rows 17 and 18. At the end of Row 18, fasten off.

SECOND HALF MOTIF
(make 7)
Rep in the same manner as first half-motif, except work inc sts on opposite edge.

ASSEMBLY
Sew motifs tog as follows: Sew half of the last row of first motif to one side of 2nd motif. Sew other half of last row of first motif to side of 3rd motif. Continue across 2 rows having 5 motifs in first row and 4 motifs in 2nd row. Continuing sewing motifs tog in same manner always sewing the side of next row of motifs to the top of motifs of previous row. Sew half motifs in position on each side. Reverse and sew 4 motifs at the bottom of afghan between points and half motifs at each corner.

EDGING
ROW 1 (RS): Attach white, ch 1, work a row of sc on side edge, working 22 sc on each half motif, turn.

ROW 2: Ch 1, sc in each sc across, fasten off.
Rep Rows 1 and 2 on opposite edge of afghan.

FRINGE
Wind white yarn around a 2-inch cardboard; cut lps at 1 end. Using 2 strands, fold in half and knot fringe in every other st at scalloped ends. Trim ends evenly. ✧

Field of Flowers

Poppies, petunias, buttercups—no matter what you call them, the blooming flowers gracing this enchanting afghan will brighten everyone's day. Best of all, these petaled beauties are ideal scrap-users!

SKILL LEVEL: BEGINNER

SIZE

47 x 60 inches plus fringe

MATERIALS

➤ Coats & Clark Super Saver worsted weight yarn: 30 oz spruce #362, 6 oz each cornmeal #320, dark spruce #361 and dark sage #633

➤ Coats & Clark Red Heart Classic worsted weight yarn: 6 oz yellow #230, small amounts of sea coral #246, jockey red #902, cameo rose #759, skipper blue #848, pink #737, tangerine #253, white #1, light lavender #579, peacock green #508 and light plum #531

➤ Size G/6 crochet hook or size needed to obtain gauge

➤ 9-inch piece cardboard

➤ Tapestry needle

GAUGE

4 sc = 1 inch

Motif = 7¼ x 8¼ inches

Check gauge to save time.

PATTERN NOTES

Weave in loose ends as work progresses.

Sl st to join each rnd in beg st unless otherwise indicated.

With the exception of yellow, which is used for all flower centers, Classic yarn colors are flowers.

Use your leftover small amounts of worsted weight yarn for flowers or make flowers to match your decor.

MOTIF *(make 71)*

Center

RND 1 (RS): With yellow, ch 4, sl st to join to form a ring, ch 2 (counts as first hdc throughout), 15 hdc in ring, join in top of beg ch-2, fasten off. (16 hdc)

Flower

RND 2 (RS): Attach any flower color in any hdc with sl st, [ch 2, dc] in same st as joining, *3 tr in next st, [dc, ch 2, sl st] in next st, sl st in next st **, [sl st, ch 2, dc] in next st, rep from * around, ending

last rep at **, sl st in same st as beg sl st, fasten off. (4 petals)

Border

RND 3 (RS): Attach spruce in center tr of any petal, ch 1, *[sc, ch 3, sc] in center tr of petal, ch 4, working over sl st between petals, dc in next hdc of Rnd 1, ch 4, rep from * around, join in beg sc.

RND 4 (RS): Ch 1, sc in same sc as beg ch-1, *3 sc in ch-3 sp, sc in next sc, 3 sc over ch-4 sp, hdc in next dc, [2 hdc, 2 dc] over next ch-4 sp, tr in next sc, 5 tr in next ch-3 sp, tr in next sc, [2 dc, 2 hdc] over next ch-4 sp, hdc in next dc, 3 sc over next ch-4 sp, **, sc in next sc, rep from *, ending at ** on last rep, join in beg sc.

RND 5 (RS): Ch 1, sc in same sc as beg ch-1, sc in next sc, [3 sc in next st, sc in each of next 13 sts] 3 times, 3 sc in next st, sc in each of next 11 sts, join in beg sc, fasten off. (64 sc)

RND 6 (RS): Attach cornmeal in

Fig. 1

Corner straight edge

A

center sc of 3-sc group, ch 1, *[sc, ch 2, sc] in center sc of 3-sc group, [ch 1, sk next sc, sc in next sc] 7 times, ch 1, sk next sc, rep from * around, join in beg sc, fasten off. (4 ch-2 sps; 32 ch-1 sps)

RND 7 (RS): Attach spruce in any ch-2 sp, ch 1, *[sc, ch 2, sc] in ch-2 sp, [ch 1, sc in next ch-1 sp] 8 times, ch 1, rep from * around, join in beg sc, fasten off.

ASSEMBLY
Using diagram as a guide, with RS facing with spruce, whipstitch motifs tog.

BORDER
RND 1 (RS): Attach dark spruce in ch-2 corner point sp at A as indicated on diagram, ch 1, *[sc, ch 2, sc] in ch-2 corner point sp, [ch 1, sc in next ch-1 sp] 9 times, ch 1, [ch 1, sc in next ch-2 sp] twice, [ch 1, sc in next ch-1 sp] 9 times, ch 1, [sc, ch 2, sc] in corner point ch-2 sp *, **[ch 1, sc in next ch-1 sp] 9 times, ch 1, dec 1 sc over next 2 corner ch-2 sps drawing up a lp in each of 2 outer corner ch-2 sps, [ch 1, sc in next ch-1 sp] 9 times, ch 1 [sc, ch 2, sc] in ch-2 sp, **, rep from ** to ** across each edge, rep from * to * across each corner, ending with join in beg sc, turn.

RND 2 (WS): Ch 1, [sc in next ch-1 sp, ch 1] 9 times, *draw up a lp in each of next 2 ch-1 sps, yo, draw through all 3 lps on hook, ch 1, [sc in next ch-1 sp, ch 1] 9 times, [sc, ch 2, sc] in each ch-2 sp, rep from * around entire outer edge, working ch 1, [sc in next ch-1 sp, ch 1] rep across each corner straight edge, join in beg sc, fasten off, turn.

RND 3 (RS): Attach spruce in corner ch-2 sp, rep Rnd 2, fasten off.

RND 4 (RS): Attach dark sage in corner ch-2 sp, ch 3, drop lp from hook, insert hook RS to WS through corner ch-2 sp, pick up dropped lp and draw through ch-2 sp, [ch 3, drop lp from hook, insert hook from RS to WS in next ch sp, pick up dropped lp and draw through ch sp] rep around entire outer edge, working at each ch-2 sp, [ch 3, insert hook in

ch-2 sp form RS to WS, pick up dropped lp and draw through ch-2 sp] twice (you will have a draw through, ch 3 and draw through at each corner ch-2 sp to keep corners from curling), ending rnd with draw through last ch-3 in same ch-2 sp as beg, fasten off.

TASSEL FRINGE
[Working with 1 strand each of spruce, dark spruce and dark sage held tog, wind around cardboard

6 times, cut strands at bottom edge; fold strands in half, insert hook from WS to RS in bottom (top) outer point of afghan in ch-2 sp, draw strands at fold through ch-2 sp to form a lp on hook, draw cut ends to lp on hook, pull gently to secure] rep in each bottom and top edge of afghan in each ch-2 sp of point. (10-tassel fringe) Trim ends as desired.

With WS facing, block lightly. ✦

General Instructions

Please review the following information before working the projects in this book. Important details about the abbreviations and symbols used are included.

HOOKS

Crochet hooks are sized for different weights of yarn and thread. For thread crochet, you will usually use a steel crochet hook. Steel crochet hook sizes range from size 00 to 14. The higher the number of hook, the smaller your stitches will be. For example, a size 1 steel crochet hook will give you much larger stitches than a size 9 steel crochet hook.

Keep in mind that the sizes given with the pattern instructions were obtained by working with the size thread or yarn and hook given in the materials list. If you work with a smaller hook, depending on your gauge, your project size will be smaller; if you work with a larger hook, your finished project's size will be larger.

GAUGE

Gauge is determined by the tightness or looseness of your stitches, and affects the finished size of your project. If you are concerned about the finished

size of the project matching the size given, take time to crochet a small section of the pattern and then check your gauge. For example, if the gauge called for is 10 dc = 1 inch, and your gauge is 12 dc to the inch, you should switch to a larger hook. On the other hand, if your gauge is only 8 dc to the inch, you should switch to a smaller hook.

If the gauge given in the pattern is for an entire motif, work one motif and then check your gauge.

UNDERSTANDING SYMBOLS

As you work through a pattern, you'll quickly notice several symbols in the instructions. These symbols are used to clarify the pattern for you: Brackets [], curlicue brackets {}, asterisks *.

Brackets [] are used to set off a group of instructions worked a number of times. For example, "[ch 3, sc in ch-3 sp] 7 times" means to work the instructions inside the [] seven times. Brackets [] also set off a group of stitches to be worked in one stitch, space or loop. For example, the brackets [] in this set of instructions, "Sk 3 sc, [3 dc, ch 1, 3 dc] in next st" indicate that after skipping 3 sc, you will work 3 dc, ch 1 and 3 more dc all in the next stitch.

Occasionally, a set of instructions inside a set of brackets needs to be repeated too. In this case, the text within the brackets to be repeated will be set off with curlicue brackets {}. For example, "[Ch 9, yo twice, insert hook in 7th ch from hook and pull up a loop, sk next dc, yo, insert hook in next dc and pull up a loop, {yo and draw through 2 lps on hook} 5 times, ch 3] 8 times." In this case, in each of the eight times you work the instructions included in brackets, you will work the section included in curlicue brackets five times.

Asterisks * are also used when a group of instructions is repeated. They may either be used alone or with brackets. For example, "*Sc in each of the next 5 sc, 2 sc in next sc, rep from * around, join with a sl st in beg sc" simply means you will work the instructions from the first * around the entire round.

"*Sk 3 sc, [3 dc, ch 1, 3 dc] in next st, rep from * around" is an example of asterisks working with brackets. In this set of instructions, you will repeat the instructions from the asterisk around, working the instructions inside the brackets together. ✧

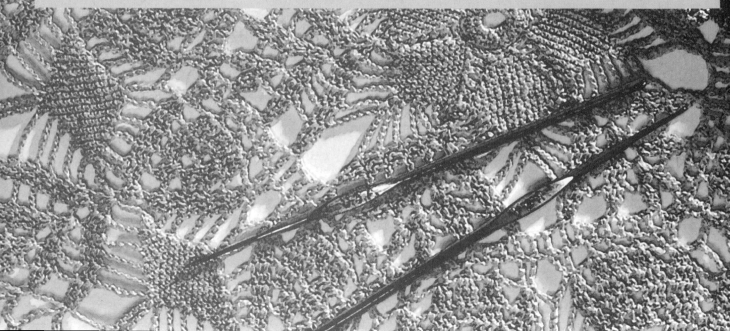

Stitch Guide

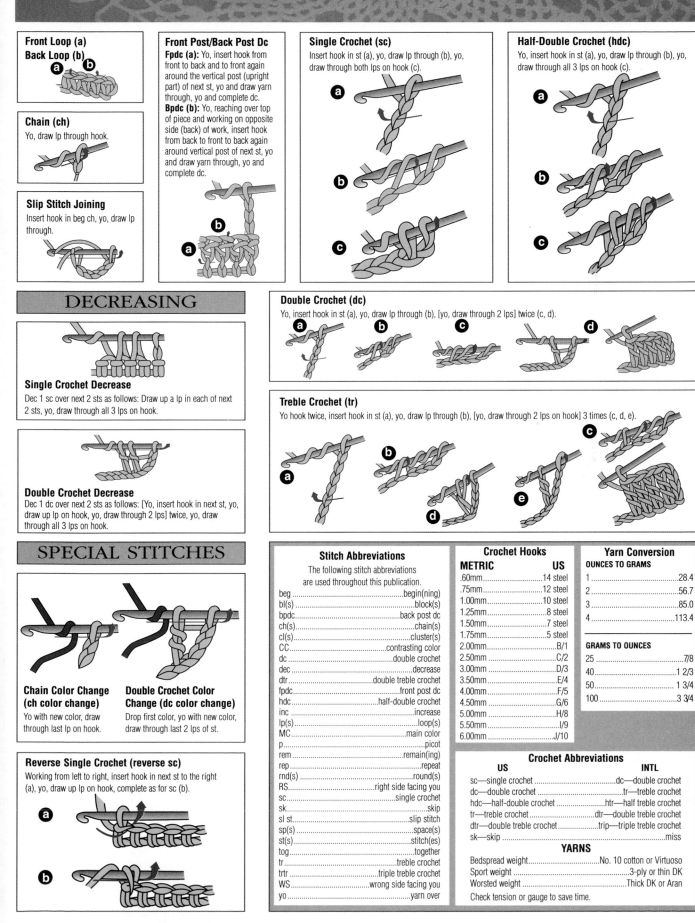

Front Loop (a) Back Loop (b)

Chain (ch)
Yo, draw lp through hook.

Slip Stitch Joining
Insert hook in beg ch, yo, draw lp through.

Front Post/Back Post Dc
Fpdc (a): Yo, insert hook from front to back and to front again around the vertical post (upright part) of next st, yo and draw yarn through, yo and complete dc.
Bpdc (b): Yo, reaching over top of piece and working on opposite side (back) of work, insert hook from back to front to back again around vertical post of next st, yo and draw yarn through, yo and complete dc.

Single Crochet (sc)
Insert hook in st (a), yo, draw lp through (b), yo, draw through both lps on hook (c).

Half-Double Crochet (hdc)
Yo, insert hook in st (a), yo, draw lp through (b), yo, draw through all 3 lps on hook (c).

DECREASING

Single Crochet Decrease
Dec 1 sc over next 2 sts as follows: Draw up a lp in each of next 2 sts, yo, draw through all 3 lps on hook.

Double Crochet Decrease
Dec 1 dc over next 2 sts as follows: [Yo, insert hook in next st, yo, draw up lp on hook, yo, draw through 2 lps] twice, yo, draw through all 3 lps on hook.

Double Crochet (dc)
Yo, insert hook in st (a), yo, draw lp through (b), [yo, draw through 2 lps] twice (c, d).

Treble Crochet (tr)
Yo hook twice, insert hook in st (a), yo, draw lp through (b), [yo, draw through 2 lps on hook] 3 times (c, d, e).

SPECIAL STITCHES

Chain Color Change (ch color change)
Yo with new color, draw through last lp on hook.

Double Crochet Color Change (dc color change)
Drop first color, yo with new color, draw through last 2 lps of st.

Reverse Single Crochet (reverse sc)
Working from left to right, insert hook in next st to the right (a), yo, draw up lp on hook, complete as for sc (b).

Stitch Abbreviations
The following stitch abbreviations are used throughout this publication.

beg	begin(ning)
bl(s)	block(s)
bpdc	back post dc
ch(s)	chain(s)
cl(s)	cluster(s)
CC	contrasting color
dc	double crochet
dec	decrease
dtr	double treble crochet
fpdc	front post dc
hdc	half-double crochet
inc	increase
lp(s)	loop(s)
MC	main color
p	picot
rem	remain(ing)
rep	repeat
rnd(s)	round(s)
RS	right side facing you
sc	single crochet
sk	skip
sl st	slip stitch
sp(s)	space(s)
st(s)	stitch(es)
tog	together
tr	treble crochet
trtr	triple treble crochet
WS	wrong side facing you
yo	yarn over

Crochet Hooks

METRIC	US
.60mm	14 steel
.75mm	12 steel
1.00mm	10 steel
1.25mm	8 steel
1.50mm	7 steel
1.75mm	5 steel
2.00mm	B/1
2.50mm	C/2
3.00mm	D/3
3.50mm	E/4
4.00mm	F/5
4.50mm	G/6
5.00mm	H/8
5.50mm	I/9
6.00mm	J/10

Yarn Conversion

OUNCES TO GRAMS

1	28.4
2	56.7
3	85.0
4	113.4

GRAMS TO OUNCES

25	7/8
40	1 2/3
50	1 3/4
100	3 3/4

Crochet Abbreviations

US	INTL
sc—single crochet	dc—double crochet
dc—double crochet	tr—treble crochet
hdc—half-double crochet	htr—half treble crochet
tr—treble crochet	dtr—double treble crochet
dtr—double treble crochet	trip—triple treble crochet
sk—skip	miss

YARNS

Bedspread weight	No. 10 cotton or Virtuoso
Sport weight	3-ply or thin DK
Worsted weight	Thick DK or Aran

Check tension or gauge to save time.